Benjamin Franklin

An Autobiographical Portrait

Benjamin Franklin, 1762

Benjamin Franklin

An Autobiographical Portrait

Edited by Alfred Tamarin

The Macmillan Company
Collier-Macmillan Ltd., London

The Macmillan Company
Collier-Macmillan Canada, Ltd., Toronto, Ontario

Library of Congress catalog card number: 78–78091

Printed in the United States of America

FIRST PRINTING

Introduction

Benjamin Franklin was the first American to become a world figure. From an ambitious young man with a bent for self-education and self-advertisement he became a world-famous scientist, inventor, legislator, diplomat and statesman. He was the genius of electricity, and the only figure whose name appears on all four of the major documents of the founding of the United States: the Declaration of Independence, the Constitution, the Treaty of Alliance with France and the Treaty of Peace with England.

The latest collection of Franklin's *Papers*, now being compiled by Leonard W. Labaree for the American Philosophical Society and Yale University, will probably fill more than forty volumes. Yet for the past two centuries, the image of Franklin has rested on less than two hundred pages: his *Autobiography* and the long list of Poor Richard's pious maxims, strung together as *A Way to Wealth*. These two hundred pages provide a very limited view of the man. The *Autobiography* ends around the year 1760, before the great events of his lifetime took place. It stops short of the dramatic days of his missions to London and Paris. It reveals only hints of his brilliant spontaneous variety, his playful wit and biting satire.

Franklin started writing the story of his life as a collection of anecdotes for his son. He ended writing it as a preachment to the young, extolling the sober virtues and endless industry which he considered appropriate for a new and rising country. A reading of these pages alone makes it not too difficult to appreciate why some later generations, including Mark Twain, fumed at the example that Franklin was supposed to have set for them: the "water" American, up all night studying the classics.

Franklin's unfinished life story in his *Autobiography* neglects some of his more human aspects: his disappointments and pain. It does not go far enough to include the years of separation from his sick and lonely wife, left behind in Philadelphia. It does not reach the bitter break with his only son, who openly sided with the mortal enemies of his perhaps too indulgent father.

But, in fact, Franklin never stopped writing his life story. Many of his letters, journals, articles, etc., written after 1760, continue his autobiographical narrative. His last known letter was written in 1790, just nine days before he died at eighty-three. This edition of his works has set out to fill in Franklin's autobiographical portrait from these voluminous autobiographical writings.

In presenting another edition of the much-thumbed *Autobiography*, this version avoids making the hard choice between rival texts, preferring to follow the lead of Max Farrand's *Restoration of a "Fair Copy"* (Berkeley, Calif., 1945), which he edited from four basic documents, two in English, two in French. This version goes along with Farrand's about "the perplexity as to what Franklin wished the final wording to be."

The history of Franklin's original manuscript of the *Autobiography*, and the two copies which were sent to England and to France, is a fascinating story in itself, which Farrand reviews, coming to the following conclusion:

"Before Franklin's return to Philadelphia in 1785, the original of Part I was restored to him. He probably had not seen it since it was written at Twyford—certainly not for ten years. He naturally re-read it, and, as was also natural, he made a good many changes. There were some bits of additional information, but most of the changes were in the nature of improvements in style, largely for the purpose of simplifying and clarifying sentences and passages. A few of the changes one regrets. . . . Two fair copies of Parts I, II and III of the Memoirs were made by young [Benjamin] Bache. The original manuscript, with its many corrections was interlined, confused and in places difficult to read. At some stage in the copying further changes were made. Changes were embodied in the fair copies. So much can be stated with reasonable assurance. To what extent they were made or approved by Franklin will never be known. The fair copies embodied changes which, it must be assumed, were made with Franklin's tacit or expressed approval."

Other authorities differ with Farrand's findings. The editors of the *Papers* at Yale give less weight to the evidence that can be read into the printed texts of the missing fair copies. They prefer instead the visual evidence of Franklin's own handwriting in the original manuscript, now carefully preserved in the Huntington Library.

It must be remembered that Franklin was both the intimate familiar writer of Part I, and the formal, consciously moralizing author of Parts II, III and IV. It is easy to visualize him, finally back in Philadelphia, past eighty, making editorial revisions as he reviewed his long life, clarifying a sentence, sharpening a point, and instructing his grandson to carry on his editorial chores. This edition, therefore, does not pretend to guarantee the final Franklin phrasing. It assumes his hand in all versions and thus has chosen the formulation which seemed most vivid and uncomplicated for the modern reader.

With the modern reader also in mind, the older spellings have been updated, except in the very few instances where the language itself had to be demonstrated for its own reasons. The spelling of names has been made uniform in spite of textual variations, and the repetition of Franklin's warm closing phrases and his bold signature—B. FRANKLIN—which ended not only his most formal communications but even his most intimate and endearing correspondence, has been omitted. And to include as much as possible of his graceful, clear and enormous prose output, most of the material has been presented in excerpted form.

For those who want more of this inexhaustible man, there are rich sources besides the ones already cited. Farrand also published a Parallel Text Edition of the *Autobiography* (Berkeley, Calif., 1949), in which the four basic versions have been set side by side for comparison. There are the William Temple Franklin edition (London, 1818), the Jared Sparks collection (10 vols., Philadelphia, 1840), the John Bigelow compilation (Philadelphia, 1868) and the Albert Henry Smyth ten-volume set (New York and London, 1905), all of which contain more complete texts of some of the material in this volume. There are many biographies of Franklin. James Parton's two-volume work (New York, 1865) is still a classic. In more recent years there have been Carl Van Doren's Pulitzer Prize volume (New York, 1938), Verner W. Crane's

Benjamin Franklin and a Rising People (Boston, 1954) and Alfred
Owen Aldridge's *Benjamin Franklin: Philosopher and Man* (Philadelphia, 1965). There is the feminine angle by a Frenchwoman,
Claude-Ann Lopez, in her *Mon Cher Papa* (New Haven, 1965)
and many more letters and documents in Van Doren's *Autobiographical Writings* (New York, 1945).

There is, in addition, a vast library of books and articles by
scholars, historians, bibliographers, editors, and literary figures,
among them Paul Leicester Ford, Vernon Parrington, John William Ward and Charles L. Sanford. Franklin printed material
abounds in the William Smith Mason collection at Yale. Letters and
documents in manuscript can be seen at the American Philosophical
Society and in university libraries at Yale, Princeton, Pennsylvania
and Michigan, as well as in the Library of Congress and the
British Museum.

In his introduction to the American Philosophical Society—Yale
University new collection of the *Papers*, the chairman of the admin-
istrative committee, Roy Franklin Nichols, pointed out that Franklin
and his associates relied almost exclusively on intellect and reason,
which represented the spirit of his times, and linked him directly to
the nineteenth century, but at the same time he discounted "the
forces of human emotion," which might have kept him from a
keener kinship with the twentieth century. In this edition, the
exploration is suggested of some of Franklin's feelings, both expressed and unexpressed. For the man who could write so much and
so expressively, silences become eloquent.

For the historical settings in which Franklin's writings can
become his autobiographical portrait, the assistance and advice are
acknowledged of Ellen Malino James of the American history
faculty of the New School for Social Research in New York; and
for help in solving textual and other problems, the editor's thanks
go to Gertrude Hess of the American Philosophical Society Library
in Philadelphia.

Alfred Tamarin

May 1969

✐ Contents

✐ List of Illustrations

Totuna gay

Chilaga
Avanares
Albardos

Auacal
alicuas

FLORIDA

Sinus
exicanus

NOVA
FRANCIA

Normbega

Virg

Terra
de La
brador

Terra
Cortereals

Terra
Nova

Terra de
Bacalaos
bona vista
d bacalaos
Razo
Banca

C Breton

S. Anna

Sept eter

Frisland
Soriad

Brazil

Anglia

MARE

ATLAN

TICUM

Asores Ins.
Terce al Flandricæ

Canariæ Ins.
el. Fortunata

MAR

DEL

NORT

Spañola

Barnardo

Ins. d C. Verde

Libia
quæ

Guin

AME

RICA
BRASI
LIA

MERI
DIO NA

Caribana

Amazones

Oma
gua

Picora

Ouram

Touvoupina
bauliy

Quito

Cusco

Moxos

La Plata

CHILI

Patagones

Chica Patagonum

Rio de la
Plata
Bancos des Castellones

ÆTHIO

OCE

I S. Matheo

I Tristan

Promontorium terre
Australis

Terra del
Fuego

Fretum le Maire
Statelant

Calanicum

one

Youth

Boston, Philadelphia, London

1706: Ancestry

Visiting his very good friend, Bishop Jonathan Shipley, near London, in the summer of 1771, Franklin began the "next thing" to living his life over again—his recollections of it in his *Autobiography*. Franklin was sixty-five years old when he started writing what he later called "several little family anecdotes." They were addressed to his son, William, who was then the Royal Governor of the Province of New Jersey.

Autobiography, Part I

Twyford, at the Bishop of St. Asaph's, 1771

Dear Son:

I have ever had a pleasure in obtaining any little anecdotes of my ancestors. You may remember the inquiries I made among the remains of my relations when you were with me in England and the journey I undertook for that purpose. Imagining it may be equally agreeable to you to learn the circumstances of *my* life—many of which you are yet unacquainted with—and expecting the enjoyment of a few weeks' uninterrupted leisure, I sit down to write them for you. Besides, there are some other inducements that excite me to this undertaking. From the poverty and obscurity in which I was born and in which I passed my earliest years, I have raised myself to a state of affluence and some degree of celebrity in the world. As constant good fortune has accompanied me even to an advanced period of life, my posterity will perhaps be desirous of learning the means, which I employed, and which, thanks to Providence, so well succeeded with me. They may also deem them fit to be imitated, should any of them find themselves in similar circumstances.

This good fortune, when I reflect on it, which is frequently the case, has induced me sometimes to say that were it left to my choice, I should have no objection to go over the same life from its beginning, only asking the advantage authors have of correcting in a second edition the faults of the first. So I might, besides correcting the faults, change the incidents of it for others more favorable. But though this were denied, I should still accept the offer of recommencing the same life. But as this repetition is not to be expected, the next thing most like living one's life over again, seems to be to recall all the circumstances of it; and, to render this remembrance more durable, to record them in writing.

Some notes one of my uncles (who had the same curiosity in collecting family anecdotes) once put into my hands furnished me with several particulars relative to our ancestors. From these notes I learned that they had lived in the same village, Ecton in Northamptonshire, on a freehold of about thirty acres, for at least three hundred years, and how much longer could not be ascertained.

When I searched the register at Ecton, I found an account of their marriages and burials from the year 1555 only, as the registers did not commence previous thereto. I however learned from it that I was the youngest son of the youngest son for five generations back. My grandfather Thomas, who was born in 1598, had four sons that grew up; viz., Thomas, John, Benjamin, and Josiah.

My father married young and carried his wife with three children to New England about 1682. By the same wife my father had four children more born there, and by a second ten others—in all seventeen, of which I remember to have seen thirteen sitting together at his table, who all grew up to years of maturity and married. I was the youngest son and the youngest of all the children except two daughters. I was born in Boston, in New England.

My mother, the second wife of my father, was Abiah Folger, daughter of Peter Folger, one of the first settlers of New England.

1713: The Whistle

Franklin's earliest recollection of his boyhood appeared in one of his well-known humorous pieces, called a bagatelle, printed in Paris and dated November 10, 1779.

Anecdote for Mme. Brillon in France

When I was a child of seven years old, my friends on a holiday filled my pockets with coppers. I went directly to a shop where they sold toys for children; and being charmed with the sound of a whistle, that I met by the way in the hands of another boy, I voluntarily offered and gave all my money for one. I then came home, whistling all over the house, much pleased with my whistle, but disturbing all the family. My brothers, sisters and cousins, understanding the bargain I had made, put me in mind what good things I might have bought with the rest of the money, and laughed at me so much for my folly that I cried with vexation; and the reflection gave me more chagrin than the whistle gave me pleasure. . . .

✐ 1714: Schooling in Boston

Autobiography, Part I, continued

My elder brothers were all put apprentices to different trades. I was put to the grammar school at eight years of age, my father intending to devote me as the tithe of his sons to the service of the church. My early readiness in learning to read (which must have been very early, as I do not remember when I could not read) and the opinion of all his friends that I should certainly make a good scholar, encouraged him in this purpose of his. I continued, however, at the grammar school rather less than a year, though in that time I had risen gradually from the middle of the class of that year to be at the head of the same class, and was removed into the next class, whence I was to be placed in the third at the end of the year. But my father, burdened with a numerous family, was unable without inconvenience to support the expense of a college education, considering, moreover, as he said to one of his friends in my presence, the little encouragement that line of life afforded to those educated for it. He gave up his first intentions, took me from the grammar school, and sent me to a school for writing and arithmetic. I learned to write a good hand pretty soon, but I failed entirely in the arithmetic. At ten years old, I was taken home to help my father in his business, which was that of a tallow chandler and soap boiler. Accordingly, I was employed in cutting wick for the candles, filling the molds for cast candles, attending the shop, going of errands, etc.

I disliked the trade and had a strong inclination to go to sea, but my father declared against it; but, residing near the water, I was much in it and on it. I learned early to swim well and to manage boats; and when embarked with other boys, I was commonly allowed to govern, especially in any case of difficulty; and upon other occasions I was generally the leader among the boys and sometimes led them into scrapes.

1714-18: Youthful Inventor

About two years after writing about his boyhood abilities as a swimmer in the *Autobiography*, Franklin enlarged on his experience to his French editor.

To M. Barbeu Dubourg in France

[1773]

When I was a boy, I made two oval palettes, each about ten inches long and six broad, with a hole for the thumb, in order to retain it fast in the palm of my hand. They much resembled a painter's palettes. In swimming I pushed the edges of these forward, and I struck the water with their flat surfaces as I drew them back. I remember I swam faster by means of these palettes, but they fatigued my wrists. I also fitted to the soles of my feet a kind of sandals; but I was not satisfied with them, because I observed that the stroke is partly given by the inside of the feet and the ankles, and not entirely with the soles of the feet. . . .

1718: Printer's Apprentice

Autobiography, Part I, continued

I suppose you may like to know what kind of a man my father was. He had an excellent constitution, was of middle stature, well set and very strong. He could draw prettily, was skilled a little in music; his voice was sonorous and agreeable, so that when he played on his violin and sung withal as he was accustomed to do after the business of the day was over, it was extremely agreeable to hear.

My mother had likewise an excellent constitution. She suckled all her ten children. I never knew either my father or mother to have any sickness but that of which they died, he at eighty-nine and she at eighty-five years of age. They lie buried together at Boston, where I some years since placed a marble stone over their grave.

By my rambling digressions I perceive myself to be grown old. I used to write more methodically. But one does not dress for private company as for a public ball. Perhaps 'tis only negligence.

Candlemaking: apprentices cutting and dipping wicks

To return: I continued thus employed in my father's business for two years, that is, till I was twelve years old; and my brother John, who was bred to that business, having left my father, married and set up for himself at Rhode Island, there was every appearance that I was destined to supply his place and be a tallow chandler. But my dislike to the trade continuing, my father had apprehensions that if he did not put me to one more agreeable, I should break loose and go to sea, as my brother Josiah had done, to his great vexation.

From my infancy I was passionately fond of reading, and all the little money that came into my hands was laid out in the purchasing of books. This bookish inclination at length determined my father to make me a printer, though he had already one son of that profession. In 1717 my brother, James, returned from England with a press and letters to set up his business in Boston. I liked it much better than that of my father, but still had a hankering for the sea. To prevent the apprehended effect of such an inclination, my father was impatient to have me bound to my brother. I stood out some time, but at last was persuaded and signed the indenture, when I was yet but twelve years old. I was to serve as apprentice till I was twenty-one years of age, only I was to be allowed journeyman's wages during the last year. In a little time I made a great progress in the business and became a useful hand to my brother. I now had access to better books. An acquaintance with the apprentices of booksellers enabled me sometimes to borrow a small one, which I was careful to return soon and clean. Often I sat up in my room reading the greatest part of the night, when the book was borrowed in the evening and to be returned early in the morning, lest it should be found missing or wanted.

I now took a fancy to poetry and wrote some little pieces. My brother, supposing it might turn to account, encouraged me, and induced me to compose two occasional ballads. One was called "The Lighthouse Tragedy," and contained an account of the shipwreck of Captain Worthilake with his two daughters; the other was a "Sailor's Song on the Taking of the Famous Teach (or Blackbeard) the Pirate." They were wretched stuff, in street ballad style; and when they were printed, my brother sent me about the town to sell them. The first sold prodigiously, the event being recent and having made a great noise. This success flattered my vanity, but my father discouraged me by ridiculing my performances and telling me verse-makers were generally beggars. Thus I escaped being a poet and probably a very bad one.

But as prose writing has been of great use to me in the course of my life, and was a principal means of my advancement, I shall tell you how I acquired what little ability I may be supposed to have in that way.

There was another bookish lad in the town, John Collins by name, with whom I was intimately acquainted. We sometimes disputed, and very fond we were of argument, and very desirous of confuting one another. Persons of good sense, I have observed, seldom fall into it, except lawyers, university men, and men of all sorts who have been bred at Edinburgh. A question was once somehow or other started between Collins and me on the propriety of educating the female sex in learning and their abilities for study. He was of opinion that it was improper and that they were naturally unequal to it. I took the contrary side, perhaps a little for dispute sake. He was naturally more eloquent, having a greater plenty of words, and sometimes, as I thought, I was vanquished more by his fluency than by the strength of his reasons. As we parted without settling the point and were not to see one another again for some time, I sat down to put my arguments in writing, which I copied fair and sent to him. He answered and I replied. Three or four letters on a side had passed, when my father happened to find my papers and read them. Without entering into the subject in dispute, he took occasion to talk with me about my manner of writing, observed that though I had the advantage of my antagonist in correct spelling and pointing (which he attributed to the printing house) I fell far short in elegance of expression, in method, and in perspicuity, of which he convinced me by several instances. I saw the justice of his remarks and thence grew more attentive to my manner of writing, and determined to endeavor to improve my style.

About this time I met with an odd volume of *The Spectator*.

I thought the writing excellent and wished if possible to imitate it. With that view, I took some of the papers, and making short hints of the sentiment in each sentence, laid them by a few days, and then without looking at the book, tried to complete the papers again. Then I compared my *Spectator* with the original, discovered some of my faults, and corrected them. But I found I wanted a stock of words or a readiness in recollecting and using them, which I thought I should have acquired before that time if I had gone on making verses. Therefore I took some of the tales in *The Spectator* and turned them into verse, and after a time, when I had pretty well forgotten the prose, turned them back again. By comparing my work afterward with the original, I discovered many faults and corrected them; but I sometimes had the pleasure to fancy that in certain particulars of small consequence I had been fortunate enough to improve the method or the language, and this encouraged me to think that I might in time come to be a tolerable English writer, of which I was extremely ambitious.

The time I allotted for these exercises and for reading, was at night, or before work began in the morning, or on Sundays, when I contrived to be in the printing house, avoiding as much as I could the constant attendance at public worship which my father used to exact from me when I was under his care—and which, indeed, I continued to consider a duty, though I could not afford the time to practice it.

When about sixteen years of age I happened to meet with a book written by one Tryon, recommending a vegetable diet. I determined to go into it. My brother, being yet unmarried, did not keep house but boarded himself and his apprentices in another family. My refusing to eat flesh occasioned an inconvenience, and I was frequently chid for my singularity. I made myself acquainted with Tryon's manner of preparing some of his dishes, such as boiling potatoes or rice, making hasty pudding, and a few others; and then proposed to my brother that if he would give me weekly half the money he paid for my board, I would board myself. He instantly agreed to it, and I presently found that I could save half what he paid me. This was an additional fund for buying of books. But I had another advantage in it. My brother and the rest going from the printing house to their meals, I remained there alone, and dispatching presently my light repast (which often was no more than a biscuit or a slice of bread, a handful of raisins or a tart from the pastry cook's, and a glass of water) had the rest of the time till their return for study, in which I made the greater progress from that greater clearness of head and quicker apprehension which generally attend temperance in eating and drinking.

My brother had in 1720 or '21 begun to print a newspaper. It was the second that appeared in America and was called *The New England Courant*. The only one before it was *The Boston News-letter*. I remember his being dissuaded by some of his friends from the undertaking as not likely to succeed, one newspaper being in their judgment enough for America. At this time, 1771, there are not less than five-and-twenty. He went on, however, with the undertaking; I was employed to carry the papers to the customers, after having worked in composing the types and printing off the sheets. He had some ingenious men among his friends who amused themselves by writing little pieces for this paper, which gained it credit and made it more in demand; and these gentlemen often visited us. Hearing their conversations and their accounts of the approbation their papers were received with, I was excited to try my hand among them. But being still a boy and suspecting that my brother would object to printing anything of mine in his paper if he knew it to be mine, I contrived to disguise my hand; and writing an anonymous paper, I put it at night under the door of the printing house. It was found in the morning and communicated to his writing friends when they called in as usual. They read it, commented on it in my hearing, and I had the exquisite pleasure of finding it met with their approbation, and that in their different guesses at the author, none were named but men of some character among us, for learning and ingenuity.

1722: The Dogood Papers

Franklin's anonymous contributions to his brother's newspaper are now called after his feminine nom de plume, Silence Dogood. In the second "Dogood" letter, the sixteen-year-old Franklin continued the fanciful biography of the fictitious woman with a keen description of character.

To the Author of The New England Courant

March 26–April 2, 1722

Sir:

It may not be improper in the first place to inform your readers, that I intend once a fortnight to present them, by the help of this paper, with a short epistle, which I presume will add somewhat to their entertainment.

And since it is observed, that the generality of people, nowadays, are unwilling either to commend or dispraise what they read, until they are in some measure informed who or what the author of it is, whether he be *poor* or *rich*, *old* or *young*, a *scholar* or a *leather apron man*, etc., and give their opinion on the performance, according to the knowledge which they have of the author's circumstances, it may not be amiss to begin with a short account of my past life and present condition, that the reader may not be at a loss to judge whether or no my lucubrations are worth his reading.

At the time of my birth, my parents were on shipboard in their way from London to New England. My entrance into this troublesome world was attended with the death of my father, a misfortune, which though I was not then capable of knowing, I shall never be able to forget; for as he, poor man, stood upon the deck rejoicing at my birth, a merciless wave entered the ship, and in one moment carried him beyond reprieve. Thus was the *first* day which I saw, the *last* that was seen by my father; and thus was my disconsolate mother at once made both a *parent* and a *widow*.

When we arrived at Boston (which was not long after) I was put to nurse in a country place, at a small distance from the town, where I went to school, and passed my infancy and childhood in vanity and idleness, until I was bound out apprentice, that I might no longer be a charge to my indigent mother, who was put to hard shifts for a living.

My master was a country minister, a pious good-natured man, and a bachelor: He labored with all his might to instill virtuous and godly principles into my tender soul, well knowing that it was the most suitable time to make deep and lasting impressions on the mind, while it was yet untainted with vice, free and unbiased. He endeavored that I might be instructed in all that knowledge and learning which is necessary for our sex, and denied me no accomplishment that could possibly be attained in a country place, such as all sorts of needlework, writing, arithmetic, etc. and observing that I took a more than ordinary delight in reading ingenious books, he gave me the free use of his library, which though it was but small, yet it was well chosen, to inform the understanding rightly and enable the mind to frame great and noble ideas.

Before I had lived quite two years with this reverend gentleman, my indulgent mother departed this life, leaving me as it were by myself, having no relation on earth within my knowledge.

I will not abuse your patience with a tedious recital of all the frivolous accidents of my life, that happened from this time until I arrived to years of discretion, only inform you that I lived a cheerful country life, spending my leisure time either in some innocent diversion with the neighboring females, or in some shady retirement, with the best of company, *books.* Thus I passed away the time with a mixture of profit and pleasure, having no affliction but what was imaginary, and created in my own fancy; as nothing is more common with us women, than to be grieving for nothing, when we having nothing else to grieve for.

As I would not engross too much of your paper at once, I will defer the remainder of my story until my next letter; in the meantime desiring your readers to exercise their patience, and bear with my humors now and then, because I shall trouble them but seldom. I am not insensible of the impossibility of pleasing all, but I would not willingly displease any; and for those who will take offense where none is intended, they are beneath the notice of
Your Humble Servant, Silence Dogood

April 9–April 16, 1722

Sir:

. . . I shall conclude this with my own character, which (one would think) I should be best able to give. *Know then,* that I am an enemy to vice, and a friend to virtue. I am one of an extensive charity, and a great forgiver of *private* injuries: a hearty lover of the clergy and all good men, and a mortal enemy to arbitrary government and unlimited power. I am naturally very jealous for the rights and liberties of my country: and the least appearance of an encroachment on these invaluable privileges, is apt to make my blood boil exceedingly. I have likewise a natural inclination to observe and reprove the faults of others, at which I have an excellent faculty. I speak this by way of warning to all such whose offenses shall come under my cognizance, for I never intend to wrap my talents in a napkin. To be brief: I am courteous and affable, good-humored (unless I am first provoked), and handsome, and sometimes witty, but always,

SIR, *Your Friend, and Humble Servant,*

Silence Dogood

1723: Journeyman Printer

Autobiography, Part I, continued

Encouraged by this attempt, I wrote and sent in the same way several other [in all, 14 "Dogood"] pieces, which were equally approved, and I kept my secret till all my fund of sense for such performances was exhausted, and then I discovered it, when I began to be considered a little more by my brother's acquaintance. However, that did not quite please him as he thought that it tended to make me too vain.

This might be one occasion of the differences we began to have about this time. Though a brother, he considered himself as my master and me as his apprentice, and accordingly expected the same services from me as he would from another; while I thought he degraded me too much in some he required of me, who from a brother expected more indulgence. Our disputes were often brought before our father, and I fancy I was either generally in the right or else a better pleader, because the judgment was generally in my favor. But my brother was passionate and had often beaten me, which I took extremely amiss. Perhaps this harsh and tyrannical treatment of me might be a means of impressing me with the aversion to arbitrary power that has stuck to me through my whole life. Thinking my apprenticeship very tedious, I was continually wishing for some opportunity of shortening it, which at length offered in a manner unexpected.

One of the pieces in our newspaper on some political point which I have now forgotten, gave offense to the Assembly. He was taken up, censured, and imprisoned for a month by the Speaker's warrant, I suppose because he would not discover the author. I, too, was taken up and examined before the Council; but though I did not give them any satisfaction, they contented themselves with admonishing me and dismissed me, considering me, perhaps, as an apprentice who was bound to keep his master's secrets. During my brother's confinement, which I resented a good deal notwithstanding our private differences, I had the management of the paper, and I made bold to give our rulers some rubs in it, which my brother took very kindly, while others began to consider me in an unfavorable light as a youth that had a turn for libeling and satire. My brother's discharge was accompanied with an order from the House (and a very odd one) that "*James Franklin* should no longer print the newspaper called *The New England Courant.*" There was a consultation held in our printing house among his friends what he should do in this case. Some proposed to evade the order by changing the name of the paper. But my brother seeing inconveniences in this, came to a conclusion as a better way to let the paper be printed in the future in the name of *Benjamin Franklin;* and in order to avoid the censure of the Assembly that might fall on him as still printing it by his apprentice, he contrived and consented that my old indenture should be returned to me with a discharge on the back of it, to show in case of necessity; and in order to secure to him the benefit of my service, I should sign new indentures for the remainder of my time, which were to be kept private. A very flimsy scheme it was; however, it was immediately executed, and the paper was printed accordingly under my name for several months. At length a fresh difference arising between my brother and me, I took upon me to assert my freedom, presuming that he would not venture to produce the new indentures. It was not fair in me to take this advantage, and this I therefore reckon one of the first errata of my life. But the unfairness of it weighed little with me, when under the impressions of resentment for the blows his passion too often urged him to bestow upon me, though he was otherwise not an ill-natured man. Perhaps I was too saucy and provoking.

When he found I would leave him, he took care to prevent my getting employment in any other printing house of the town by going around and speaking to every master, who accordingly

Swimming and boating in Boston Harbor; engraving by Paul Revere

refused to give me work. I then thought of going to New York as the nearest place where there was a printer; and I was the rather inclined to leave Boston when I reflected that I had already made myself a little obnoxious to the governing party; and further that my indiscreet disputations about religion began to make me pointed at with horror by good people as an infidel or atheist. I concluded, therefore, to remove to New York, but my father now siding with my brother, I was sensible that if I attempted to go openly, means would be used to prevent me. My friend Collins therefore undertook to manage my flight. He agreed with the captain of a New York sloop for my passage, under pretense of my being a young man of his acquaintance that had got a naughty girl with child, whose parents would compel me to marry her and that I could neither appear nor come away publicly. I sold my books to raise a little money, was taken on board the sloop privately, had a fair wind, and in three days found myself at New York, near three hundred miles from my home, at the age of seventeen, without the least recommendation or knowledge of any person in the place, and with very little money in my pocket.

The inclination I had had for the sea was by this time done away, or I might now have gratified it. But having another profession and conceiving myself a pretty good workman, I offered my services to a printer of the place, old Mr. Wm. Bradford (who had been the first printer in Pennsylvania). He could give me no employment, having little to do and hands enough already. "But," he said, "my son at Philadelphia has lately lost his principal hand, Aquila Rose, by death. If you go thither I believe he may employ you."

Philadelphia was a hundred miles farther. I set out, however, in a boat for Amboy, leaving my chest and things to follow me around by sea. In crossing the bay we met with a squall that tore our rotten sails to pieces, prevented our getting into the kill, and drove us upon Long Island.

On approaching the island, we found it was in a place where there could be no landing, there being a great surf on the stony beach. So we dropped anchor, and swung out our cable toward the shore. Some people came down to the shore and halloed to us, as we did to them, but the wind was so high and the surf so loud that we could not understand each other. There were some small boats on the shore, and we made signs and called to them to fetch us, but they either did not comprehend us or it was impracticable, so they went off. Night approaching, we had no remedy but to have patience till the wind abated, and in the meantime the boatman and myself concluded to sleep if we could, and so we crowded into the hatches, and the spray breaking over the head of our boat leaked through to us, so that we were soon wet. In this manner we lay all night with very little rest; but the wind abating the next day, we made a shift to reach Amboy before night, having been thirty hours on the water without victuals or any drink but a bottle of filthy rum, the water we sailed on being salt.

In the evening I found myself very feverish and went to bed; but having read somewhere that cold water drank plentifully was good for a fever, I followed the prescription, and sweat plentifully most of the night; my fever left me, and in the morning crossing the ferry, I proceeded on my journey on foot, having fifty miles to Burlington, where I was told I should find boats that would carry me the rest of the way to Philadelphia.

It rained very hard all the day, I was thoroughly soaked, and by noon a good deal tired, so I stopped at a poor inn, where I stayed all night, beginning now to wish I had never left home. I made so miserable a figure, too, that I found by the questions asked me I was suspected to be some runaway indentured servant, and in danger of being taken up on that suspicion. However, I proceeded the next day, and got in the evening to an inn within eight or ten miles of Burlington.

I arrived the next morning at Burlington, but had the mortification to find that the regular boats were gone a little before and no other expected to go before Tuesday, this being Saturday. However, walking in the evening by the side of the river, a boat came by, which I found was going toward Philadelphia with several people in her. They took me in, and as there was no wind, we rowed all the way and arrived there about eight or nine o'clock, on the Sunday morning and landed at the Market Street wharf.

I have been the more particular in this description of my journey, and shall be so of my first entry into that city, that you may in your mind compare such unlikely beginnings with the figure I have since made there. I was in my working dress, my best clothes coming around by sea. I was dirty from my being so long in the boat; my pockets were stuffed out with shirts and stockings; I knew no one, nor where to look for lodging. Fatigued with walking, rowing, and the want of sleep, I was very hungry, and my whole stock of cash consisted in a single dollar and about a shilling in copper coin, which I gave to the boatmen for my passage. At first they refused it on account of my having rowed, but I insisted on their taking it. Man is sometimes more generous when he has little money than when he has plenty, perhaps to prevent his being thought to have but little. I walked toward the top of the street, gazing about till near Market Street, where I met a boy with bread. I have often made a meal of dry bread, and inquiring where he had bought it, I went immediately to the baker's he directed me to. I asked for biscuits, meaning such as we had in Boston, but that sort, it seems, was not made in Philadelphia. I then asked for a threepenny loaf and was told they had none. Not knowing the different prices or the names of the different sorts of bread, I told him to give me threepenny worth of any sort. He gave me accordingly three great puffy rolls.

The city of Philadelphia in 1724

I was surprised at the quantity but took it, and having no room in my pockets, walked off with a roll under each arm and eating the other. Thus I went up Market Street as far as Fourth Street, passing by the door of Mr. Read, my future wife's father, when she, standing at the door, saw me, and thought I made, as I certainly did, a most awkward, ridiculous appearance. Then I turned and went down Chestnut Street and part of Walnut Street, eating my roll all the way, and coming around, found myself again at Market Street wharf near the boat I came in, to which I went for a draught of the river water, and being filled with one of my rolls, gave the other two to a woman and her child that came down the river in the boat with us.

Thus refreshed, I walked again up the street, which by this time had many clean dressed people in it who were all walking the same way; I joined them, and thereby was led into the great meeting-house of the Quakers near the market. I sat down among them, and after looking around awhile and hearing nothing said, being very drowsy, I fell fast asleep and continued so till the meeting broke up, when someone was kind enough to rouse me. This was therefore the first house I was in or slept in, in Philadelphia.

I then walked down toward the river, and looking in the faces of everyone, I met a young Quaker man whose countenance pleased

me, and accosting him requested he would tell me where a stranger could get a lodging. He conducted me to the Crooked Billet in Water Street. There I got a dinner. And while I was eating, several questions were asked me, as from my youth and appearance I was suspected of being a runaway. After dinner my host having shown me to a bed, I lay myself on it, without undressing and slept till six in the evening, when I was called to supper. I went to bed again very early and slept very soundly till next morning. Then I dressed myself as neat as I could, and went to Andrew Bradford, the printer's. I found in the shop the old man his father, whom I had seen at New York, and who traveling on horseback, had got to Philadelphia before me. He introduced me to his son, who received me civilly, gave me a breakfast, but told me he did not at present want a hand, being lately supplied with one. But there was another printer in town lately set up, one Keimer, who perhaps might employ me; if not, I should be welcome to lodge at his house, and he would give me a little work to do now and then till fuller business should offer.

The old gentleman said he would go with me to the new printer; and when we found him, "Neighbor," said Bradford, "I have brought to see you a young man of your business; perhaps you may want such a one." He asked me a few questions, put a composing stick in my hand to see how I worked, and then said he would employ me soon, though he had just then nothing for me to do. Keimer's printing house, I found, consisted of an old damaged press and a small worn-out font of English types, which he was then using himself, composing an elegy. Keimer made verses, too, but very indifferently. He could not be said to *write* them, for his method was to compose them in the types directly out of his head. I endeavored to put his press (which he had not yet used, and of which he understood nothing) into order fit to be worked with; and promising to come and print off his elegy as soon as he should have got it ready, I returned to Bradford's, who gave me a little job to do for the present, and there I lodged and dieted. A few days after Keimer sent for me to print off the Elegy. And now he had got another pair of cases, and a pamphlet to reprint, on which he set me to work.

These two printers I found poorly qualified for their business. Bradford had not been bred to it and was very illiterate; and Keimer, though something of a scholar, was a mere compositor, knowing nothing of presswork. At this time he did not profess any particular religion, but something of all on occasion, was very ignorant of the world, and had—as I afterward found—a good deal of the knave in his composition. He did not like my lodging at Bradford's while I worked with him. He had a house, indeed, but without furniture, so he could not lodge me; but he got me a lodging at Mr. Read's, beforementioned, who was the owner of his house. And my chest and clothes being come by this time, I made rather a more respectable appearance in the eyes of Miss Read than I had done when she first happened to see me eating my roll in the street.

I began now to have some acquaintance among the young people of the town that were lovers of reading, with whom I spent my evenings very pleasantly and gained money by my industry and frugality. I lived very contented, and forgot Boston as much as I could, and did not wish it should be known where I resided except to my friend Collins, who was in my secret and kept it faithfully. At length however, an incident happened that occasioned my return home much sooner than I had intended.

I had a brother-in-law, Robert Holmes, master of a sloop that traded between Boston and Delaware. He being at New Castle, forty miles below Philadelphia, and hearing of me wrote me a letter mentioning the grief of my relations and friends in Boston at my abrupt departure, assuring me of their good will to me, and that everything would be accommodated to my mind if I would return, to which he entreated me very earnestly. I wrote an answer to his letter, thanked him for his advice, but stated my reasons for quitting Boston so fully and in such a light as to convince him that I was not so much in the wrong as he had apprehended.

Sir William Keith, governor of the province, was then at New Castle, and Captain Holmes happening to be in company with him when my letter came to hand, spoke to him of me, and showed him the letter. The Governor read it, and seemed surprised when he was told my age. He said I appeared a young man of promising parts and therefore should be encouraged. The printers at Philadelphia were wretched ones, and if I would set up there, he made no doubt I should succeed; for his part, he would procure me the public business, and do me every other service in his power. This my brother-in-law afterward told me in Boston. But I knew as yet nothing of it; when one day Keimer and I being at work together near the window, we saw the Governor and another gentleman (who proved to be Colonel French of New Castle in the province of Delaware) finely dressed, come directly across the street to our house and heard them at the door. Keimer ran down immediately, thinking it a visit to him; but the Governor inquired for me, came up, and with a condescension and politeness I had been quite unused to, made me many compliments, desired to be acquainted with me, blamed me kindly for not having made myself known to him when I first came to the place, and would have me away with him to the tavern where he was going with Colonel French to taste, as he said, some excellent Madeira. I was not a little surprised, and Keimer stared like a pig poisoned. I went, however, with the Governor and Colonel French, to a tavern the corner of Third Street, and over the Madeira he proposed my setting up my business. He stated the probabilities of my success, and both he and Colonel French assured me I should have their interest and influence to obtain for me the public business of both governments. As I expressed doubts that my father would assist me in it, Sir William said he would give me a letter to him in which he would set forth the advantages, and he did not doubt he should determine him to comply. So it was concluded I should return to Boston by the first vessel with the Governor's letter to my father. In the meantime the intention was to be kept secret, and I went on working with Keimer as usual. The Governor sent for me now and then to dine with him, which I considered a great honor, more particularly as he conversed with me in the most affable, familiar, and friendly manner.

About the end of April, 1724, a little vessel offered for Boston. I took leave of Keimer as going to see my friends. The Governor gave me an ample letter, saying many flattering things of me to my father and strongly recommending the project of my setting up at Philadelphia as a thing that would make my fortune. We struck on a shoal in going down the bay and sprung a leak; we had a blustering time at sea and were obliged to pump almost continually, at which I took my turn. We arrived safe, however, at Boston in about a fortnight. I had been absent seven months, and my friends had heard nothing of me, for my brother Holmes was not yet returned and had not written about me. My unexpected appearance surprised the family; all were, however, very glad to see me and made me welcome, except my brother. I went to see him at his printing house. I was better dressed than ever while in his service, having a genteel new suit from head to foot, a watch, and my pockets lined with near five pounds sterling in silver. He received me not very frankly, looked me all over, and turned to his work again. The journeymen were inquisitive where I had been, what sort of a country it was, and how I liked it. I praised it much and the happy life I led in it, expressing strongly my intention of returning to it; and one of them asking what kind of money we had there, I produced a handful of silver and spread it before them, which was a kind of *raree show* they had not been used to, paper being the money of Boston. Then I took an opportunity of letting them see my watch, and lastly (my brother still grum and sullen) I gave them a dollar to drink and took my leave. This visit of mine offended him extremely. For when my mother sometime after spoke to him of a reconciliation, and of her wish to see us on good terms together, and that we might live for the future as brothers, he said I had insulted him in such a manner before his people that he could never forget or forgive it. In this, however, he was mistaken.

My father received the Governor's letter with some surprise but said little of it to me for some time. Captain Holmes returning, he showed it to him, and asked him if he knew Sir William Keith and what kind of a man he was, adding that he must be of small discretion to think of setting a boy up in business who wanted yet three years to arrive at man's estate. Homes said what he could in favor of the project; but my father was decidedly against it, and at last gave a flat denial. Then he wrote a civil letter to Sir William, thanking him for the patronage he had so kindly offered me, and declining to assist me as yet in setting up, I being in his opinion too young to be trusted with the management of an undertaking so important, and for which the preparation required a considerable expenditure.

My old companion Collins, pleased with the account I gave him of my new country, determined to go thither also.

My father, though he did not approve Sir William's proposition, was yet pleased that I had been able to obtain so advantageous a character from a person of such note where I had resided, and that I had been so industrious and careful as to equip myself so handsomely in so short a time. Therefore, seeing no prospect of an accommodation between my brother and me, he gave his consent to my returning again to Philadelphia, advised me to behave respectfully to the people there, endeavor to obtain the general esteem, and avoid lampooning and libeling, to which he thought I had too much inclination, telling me that by steady industry and a prudent parsimony I might save enough by the time I was one-and-twenty to set me up, and that if I came near the matter he would help me out with the rest. This was all I could obtain, except some small gifts as tokens of his and my mother's love, when I embarked again for New York, now with their approbation and their blessing. The sloop putting in at Newport, Rhode Island, I visited my brother John, who had been married and settled there some years. He received me very affectionately, for he always loved me. A friend of his, one Vernon, having some money due to him in Pennsylvania (about thirty-five pounds currency), desired I would recover it for him, and keep it till I had his directions what to employ it in. Accordingly he gave me an order to receive it. This business afterward occasioned me a good deal of uneasiness.

At New York I found Collins, who had arrived there sometime before me, had been drunk every day and behaved himself in a very extravagant manner. He had gamed, too, and lost his money, so that I was obliged to discharge his lodgings and defray his expenses on the road and at Philadelphia—which proved a great burden to me.

We proceeded to Philadelphia. I received on the way Vernon's money, without which we could hardly have finished our journey. Collins was continually borrowing of me. At length he had got so much of it, that I was distressed to think what I should do in case of being called on to remit it.

The violation of my trust respecting Vernon's money was one of the first great errata of my life, and this showed that my father was not much out in his judgment when he considered me too young to manage business. But Sir William, on reading his letter, said he was too prudent, that there was a great difference in persons, and discretion did not always accompany years, nor was youth always without it. "But since he will not set you up, I will do it myself. Give me an inventory of the things necessary to be had from England, and I will send for them. You shall repay me when you are able; I am resolved to have a good printer here, and I am sure you must succeed." This was spoken with such an appearance of cordiality that I had not the least doubt of his meaning what he said. I had hitherto kept the proposition of my setting up a secret in Philadelphia, and I still kept it. Had it been known that I depended on the Governor, probably some friend that knew him better would have advised me not to rely on him, as I afterward heard it as his known character to be liberal of promises which he never meant to keep. Yet unsolicited as he was by me, how could I think his generous offers insincere? I believed him one of the best men in the world.

I presented him an inventory of a little printing house, amounting by my computation to about £100 sterling. He liked it but asked me if my being on the spot in England to choose the types and see that everything was good of the kind might not be of some advantage. "Then," says he, "when there you may make acquaintances and establish correspondences in the bookselling and stationery way." I agreed that this might be advantageous. "Then," says he, "get yourself ready to go with Annis," which was the annual ship and the only one at that time usually passing between London and

Philadelphia. But it would be some months before Annis sailed, so I continued working with Keimer.

I believe I have omitted mentioning that in my first voyage from Boston to Philadelphia, being becalmed off Block Island, our crew employed themselves catching cod and hauled up a great number. Till then I had stuck to my resolution to eat nothing that had had life; and on this occasion I considered, according to my Master Tryon, the taking every fish as a kind of unprovoked murder, since none of them had or ever could do us any injury that might justify this massacre. All this seemed very reasonable. But I had formerly been a great lover of fish, and when it came hot out of the frying pan, it smelled admirably well. I balanced some time between principle and inclination till recollecting that when fish were opened, I saw smaller fish taken out of their stomachs. "Then," thought I, "if you eat one another, I don't see why we mayn't eat you." So I dined upon cod very heartily and have since continued to eat as other people, returning only now and then occasionally to a vegetable diet. So convenient a thing it is to be a *reasonable creature*, since it enables one to find or make a reason for everything one has a mind to do.

Keimer and I lived on a pretty good familiar footing and agreed tolerably well, for he suspected nothing of my setting up.

I had made some courtship during this time to Miss Read. I had a great respect and affection for her, and had some reasons to believe she had the same for me; but as I was about to take a long voyage and we were both very young (only a little above eighteen), it was thought most prudent by her mother to prevent our going too far at present, as a marriage, if it was to take place, would be more convenient after my return, when I should be, as I hoped, set up in my business. Perhaps, too, she thought my expectations not so well founded as I imagined them to be.

My chief acquaintances at this time were Charles Osborne, Joseph Watson, and James Ralph—all lovers of reading. The two first were clerks to an eminent scrivener or conveyancer in the town (Charles Brockden); the other was clerk to a merchant. Osborne was sensible, candid, frank—sincere and affectionate to his friends—but in literary matters too fond of criticism. Ralph was ingenious, genteel in his manners, and extremely eloquent; I think I never knew a prettier talker. Both were great admirers of poetry and began to try their hands in little pieces. Many pleasant walks we four had together on Sundays in the woods on the banks of the Schuylkill, when we read to one another and conferred on what we read. Ralph was inclined to give himself up entirely to poetry, not doubting but he might become eminent in it and even make his fortune by it. He became, however, a pretty good prose writer. More of him hereafter. But as I may not have occasion to mention the other two, I shall just remark here that Watson died in my arms a few years after, much lamented, being the best of our set. Osborne went to the West Indies, where he became an eminent lawyer and made money but died young. He and I had made a serious agreement that the one who happened first to die should, if possible, make a friendly visit to the other and acquaint him how he found things in that separate state. But he never fulfilled his promise.

The Governor, seeming to like my company, had me frequently to his house; and his setting me up was always mentioned as a fixed thing. I was to take with me letters recommendatory to a number of his friends, besides the letter of credit, to furnish me with the necessary money for purchasing the press, types, paper, etc. For these letters I was appointed to call at different times, when they were to be ready, but a future time was still named. Thus we went on till the ship (whose departure, too, had been several times postponed) was on the point of sailing. Then when I called to take my leave and receive the letters, his secretary, Dr. Baird, came out to me and said the Governor was extremely busy in writing but would be down at New Castle before the ship, and there the letters would be delivered to me.

Ralph, though married and having one child, had determined to accompany me in this voyage. I found afterward that having some cause of discontent with his wife's relations, he proposed to leave her on their hands and never to return to America. Having taken leave of my friends and exchanged promises with Miss Read, I quitted Philadelphia in the ship, which anchored at New Castle. The Governor was there, but when I went to his lodging, his secretary came to me from him with expressions of the greatest regret that he could not then see me, being engaged in business of the utmost importance, but that he would send the letters to me on board, wished me heartily a good voyage and a speedy return, etc. I returned on board a little puzzled but still not doubting.

Understanding that Colonel French had brought on board the Governor's dispatches, I asked the captain for those letters that were to be under my care. He said all were put into the bag together; and he could not then come at them, but before we landed in England I should have an opportunity of picking them out. So I was satisfied for the present. In this passage, Mr. Denham [a Quaker merchant] contracted a friendship for me that continued during his life. The voyage was otherwise not a pleasant one, as we had a deal of bad weather.

When we came into the channel, the captain kept his word with me and gave me an opportunity of examining the bag for the Governor's letters. I found some upon which my name was put as under my care; I picked out six or seven that by the handwriting I thought might be the promised letters, especially as one of them was addressed to the King's printer, and another to some stationer. We arrived in London the 24th of December, 1724. I waited upon the stationer who came first in my way, delivering the letter as from Governor Keith. "I don't know such a person," said he. So putting the letter into my hand, he turned on his heel and left me to serve some customer. I was surprised to find these were not the Governor's letters; and after recollecting and comparing circumstances, I began to doubt his sincerity. I found my friend Denham and opened the whole affair to him. He let me into Keith's character, told me there was not the least probability that he had written any letters for me, that no one who knew him had the smallest dependence on him, and he laughed at the idea of the Governor's giving me a letter of credit, having, as he said, no credit to give. On my expressing some concern about what I should do, he advised me to endeavor getting some employment in the way of my business. "Among the printers here," said he, "you will improve yourself;

and when you return to America, you will set up to greater advantage."

But what shall we think of a Governor playing such pitiful tricks and imposing so grossly on a poor ignorant boy! It was a habit he had acquired. He wished to please everybody; and having little to give, he gave expectations. He was otherwise an ingenious, sensible man, a pretty good writer, and a good governor for the people, though not for his constituents, the Proprietaries, whose instructions he sometimes disregarded. Several of our best laws were of his planning and passed during his administration.

Ralph and I were inseparable companions. We took lodgings together in Little Britain at 3 *s.* 6 *d.* per week, as much as we could then afford. He now let me know his intentions of remaining in London and that he never meant to return to Philadelphia. He had brought no money with him, the whole he could muster having been expended in paying his passage. I had fifteen pistoles, so he borrowed occasionally of me to subsist while he was looking out for business.

For myself, I immediately got into work at Palmer's, then a famous printing house in Bartholomew Close, and here I continued near a year. I was pretty diligent, but I spent with Ralph a good deal of my earnings in going to plays and other places of amusement. We had nearly consumed all my pistoles, and now just rubbed on from hand to mouth. He seemed quite to have forgotten his wife and child, and I by degrees my engagements with Miss Read, to whom I never wrote more than one letter, and that was to let her know I was not likely soon to return. This was another of the great errata of my life which I should wish to correct if I were to live it over again. In fact, by our expenses, I was constantly kept unable to pay my passage.

I had brought over a few curiosities, among which the principal was a purse made of the asbestos, which purifies by fire. Sir Hans Sloane heard of it, came to see me, and invited me to his house in Bloomsbury Square, where he showed me all his curiosities and persuaded me to add that to the number, for which he paid me handsomely.

"Little Britain" was a street near St. Paul's Cathedral (37, upper right)

1725: The Asbestos Purse

Franklin, at nineteen, showed his interest in science and men of science in his eager dealings with Sir Hans Sloane, a distinguished English physician, who succeeded Sir Isaac Newton as president of the English Royal Society of Arts and Sciences. Sloane's collection of books, manuscripts and natural specimens was the foundation of the British Museum, where young Benjamin's "curiosity" is still in safe-keeping. In recalling the incident for his *Autobiography* fifty years later, Franklin remembered himself as more sought after and less enterprising than he actually was.

To Sir Hans Sloane in London

June 2, 1725

Sir:

Having lately been in the northern parts of America, I have brought from thence a purse made of the stone asbestos, a piece of the stone, and a piece of wood, the pithy part of which is of the same nature, and called by the inhabitants, salamander cotton. As you are noted to be a lover of curiosities, I have informed you of these; and if you have any inclination to purchase them, or see them, let me know your pleasure by a line directed for me at the Golden Fan in Little Britain, and I will wait upon you with them. I am, Sir. . . . P.S. I expect to be out of town in 2 or 3 days, and therefore beg an immediate answer.

1724: Stay in London

Autobiography, Part I, continued

In our house lodged a young woman, a milliner, who, I think, had a shop in the cloisters. She had been genteelly bred, was sensible, lively, and of a most pleasing conversation. Ralph read plays to her in the evenings, they grew intimate, she took another lodging, and he followed her. They lived together some time, but he being still out of business, and her income not sufficient to maintain them with her child, he took a resolution of going from London, to try for a country school, which he thought himself well qualified to undertake, as he wrote an excellent hand and was a master of arithmetic and accounts. This, however, he deemed a business below him, and confident of future better fortune when he should be unwilling to have it known that he was once so meanly employed, he changed his name and did me the honor to assume mine. For I soon after had a letter from him, acquainting me that he was settled in a small village in Berkshire, I think it was, where he taught reading and writing to ten or a dozen boys at sixpence per week, recommending Mrs. T. to my care and desiring me to write to him, directing for *Mr. Franklin*, schoolmaster at such a place. In the meantime Mrs. T., having on his account lost her friends and business, was often in distresses and used to send for me and borrow what money I could spare to help her out of them. I grew fond of her company, and being at this time under no religious restraint, and taking advantage on my importance to her, I attempted to take some liberties with her (another erratum), which she repulsed with a proper degree of resentment. She wrote to Ralph and acquainted him with my conduct; this occasioned a breach between us. And when he returned to London, he let me know he considered all the obligations he had been under to me as annulled—from which I concluded I was never to expect his repaying the money I had lent him or that I had advanced for him.

I now began to think of getting a little money beforehand, and expecting better employment, I left Palmer's to work at Watts's (near Lincoln's Inn Fields), a still greater printing house. Here I continued all the rest of my stay in London.

At my first admission into this printing house, I took to working at press, imagining I felt a want of the bodily exercise I had been used to in America, where presswork is mixed with the composing. I drank only water; the other workmen, near fifty in number, were great guzzlers of beer. On occasion I carried up and down stairs a large form of types in each hand, when others carried but one in both hands. They wondered to see from this and several instances that the "Water-American," as they called me, was *stronger* than themselves who drank *strong* beer.

Watts after some weeks desiring to have me in the composing room, I left the pressmen. A new *bienvenu* for drink, being five shillings, was demanded of me by the compositors. I thought it an imposition, as I had paid one to the pressmen. The master thought so, too, and forbade my paying it. I stood out two or three weeks, was accordingly considered as an excommunicate, and had so many little pieces of private malice practiced on me by mixing my sorts, transposing my pages, and breaking my matter, etc., etc., if ever I stepped out of the room—and all ascribed to the Chapel Ghost, which they said ever haunted those not regularly admitted—that notwithstanding the master's protection, I found myself obliged to comply and pay the money, convinced of the folly of being on ill terms with those one is to live with continually. I was now on a fair footing with them and soon acquired considerable influence. I proposed some reasonable alterations in their chapel [printing house] laws, and carried them against all opposition. From my example, a great many of them left their muddling breakfast of beer, bread, and cheese, finding they could with me be supplied from a neighboring house with a large porringer of hot water gruel, sprinkled with pepper, crumbed with bread, and a bit of butter in it, for the price of a pint of beer, viz., three halfpence. This was a more comfortable as well as a cheaper breakfast and kept their heads clearer.

My being esteemed a pretty good jocular, verbal satirist, supported my consequence in the society. My constant attendance recommended me to the master; and my uncommon quickness at composing occasioned my being put upon work of dispatch, which was generally better paid. So I went on now very agreeably.

My good friend Mr. Denham now told me he was about to return to Philadelphia and should carry over a great quantity of goods in order to open a store there. He proposed to take me over as his clerk to keep his books (in which he would instruct me), copy his letters, and attend the store. He added that as soon as I should be

acquainted with mercantile business he would promote me by sending me with a cargo of flour and bread, etc., to the West Indies, and
procure me commissions from others which would be profitable,
and if I managed well, would establish me handsomely. The thing
pleased me, for I was grown tired of London, remembered with
pleasure the happy months I had spent in Pennsylvania, and wished
again to see it. Therefore, I immediately agreed on the terms of
fifty pounds a year, Pennsylvania money—less, indeed, than my
then present gettings as a compositor but affording a better prospect.

I now took leave of printing, as I thought, forever, and was daily
employed in my new business—going about with Mr. Denham
among the tradesmen to purchase various articles and see them
packed up, delivering messages, calling upon workmen to dispatch,
etc.; and when all was on board, I had a few days' leisure.

Thus I passed about eighteen months in London. Most part of
the time, I worked hard at my business, and spent but little upon
myself except in seeing plays, and in books. My friend Ralph had
kept me poor. He owed me about twenty-seven pounds, which I was
now never likely to receive—a great sum out of my small earnings.
I loved him notwithstanding, for he had many amiable qualities. I
had improved my knowledge, however, though I had by no means
improved my fortune. But I had made some very ingenious acquaintance, whose conversation was of great advantage to me, and I had
read considerably.

We sailed from Gravesend on the 23rd of July, 1726.

✧1726: Observing Nature

Now twenty, Franklin traveled back across the Atlantic on
board the *Berkshire*, Henry Clark, Master, a voyage that
took fifty-one days. His journal is filled with notes of sea
life, eclipses, and marine vegetation, demonstrating the keen
observation which would win him renown as a scientist.

Journal of a Voyage U. S. 1514051

Saturday, July 23. This day we weighed anchor and fell down with the tide, there being little or no wind. In the afternoon we had a fresh gale, that brought us down to Margate, where we shall lie at anchor this night. Most of the passengers are very sick. Saw several porpoises, etc.

Sunday, July 24. This morning we weighed anchor, and coming to the Downs, we set our pilot ashore at Deal, and passed through. And now, while I write this, sitting upon the quarterdeck, I have methinks one of the pleasantest scenes in the world before me. 'Tis a fine, clear day, and we are going away before the wind with an easy, pleasant gale. We have near fifteen sail of ships in sight, and I may say in company. On the left hand appears the coast of France at a distance, and on the right is the town and castle of Dover, with the green hills and chalky cliffs of England, to which we must now bid farewell. Albion, farewell!

Saturday, August 6. This morning we had a fair breeze for some hours, and then a calm that lasted all day. In the afternoon I leaped overboard and swam around the ship to wash myself. Saw several porpoises this day.

Sunday, August 21. . . . . having a brisk gale of wind at East. Toward night a poor little bird came on board us, being almost tired to death, and suffered itself to be taken by the hand. We reckon ourselves near two hundred leagues from land, so that no doubt a little rest was very acceptable to the unfortunate wanderer, who 'tis like was blown off the coast in thick weather, and could not find its way back again. We receive it hospitably and tender it victuals and drink; but he refuses both, and I suppose will not live long. There was one came on board some days ago in the same circumstances with this, which I think the cat destroyed.

Monday, August 22. This morning I saw several flyingfish, but they were small. A favorable wind all day.

Thursday, August 25. Our company is in general very unsuitably mixed, to keep up the pleasure and spirit of conversation: and, if there are one or two pair of us that can sometimes entertain one another for half an hour agreeably, yet perhaps we are seldom in the humor for it together. I rise in the morning and read for an hour or two, perhaps, and then reading grows tiresome. Want of exercise occasions want of appetite, so that eating and drinking afford but little pleasure. I tire myself with playing at draughts, then I go to cards; nay, there is no play so trifling or childish, but we fly to it for entertainment. A contrary wind, I know not how, puts us all out of good humor; we grow sullen, silent, and reserved, and fret at each other upon every little occasion. 'Tis a common opinion among the ladies, that if a man is ill-natured he infallibly discovers it when he is in liquor. But I who have known many instances to the contrary, will teach them a more effectual method to discover the natural temper and disposition of their humble servants. Let the ladies make one long sea voyage with them, and, if they have the least spark of ill-nature in them, and conceal it to the end of the voyage, I will forfeit all my pretensions to their favor. The wind continues fair.

Friday, Sept. 2. This morning the wind changed; a little fair. We caught a couple of dolphins, and fried them for dinner. They eat indifferent well. These fish make a glorious appearance in the water; their bodies are of a bright green, mixed with a silver color, and their tails of a shining golden yellow; but all this vanishes presently after they are taken out of their element, and they change all over to a light gray. I observed that cutting off pieces of a just-caught, living dolphin for baits, those pieces did not lose their luster and fine colors when the dolphin died, but retained them perfectly. Everyone takes notice of that vulgar error of the painters, who always represent this fish monstrously crooked and deformed, when it is, in reality, as beautiful and well-shaped a fish as any that swims.

Friday, Sept. 9. This afternoon we took four large dolphins, three with a hook and line, and the fourth we struck with a fizgig. The bait was a candle with two feathers stuck in it, one on each side, in imitation of a flyingfish, which are the common prey of the dolphins. They appeared extremely eager and hungry, and snapped up the hook as soon as ever it touched the water. When we came to open them, we found in the belly of one a small dolphin, half-digested. Certainly they were half-famished, or are naturally very savage, to devour those of their own species.

Wednesday, Sept. 14. This afternoon, about two o'clock, it being fair weather and almost calm, as we sat playing draughts upon deck, we were surprised with a sudden and unusual darkness of the sun, which, as we could perceive, was only covered with a small, thin cloud; when that was passed by, we discovered that that glorious luminary labored under a very great eclipse. At least ten parts out of twelve of him were hid from our eyes, and we were apprehensive he would have been totally darkened.

Friday, Sept. 16. Calm all this day. This morning we saw a *tropic bird*, which flew around our vessel several times. It is a white fowl, with short wings; but one feather appears in his tail, and does not fly very fast. We reckon ourselves about half our voyage; latitude 38 and odd minutes. These birds are said never to be seen further north than the latitude of 40.

Sunday, September 18. We have had the finest weather imaginable all this day, accompanied with what is still more agreeable, a fair wind. Everyone puts on a clean shirt and a cheerful countenance, and we begin to be very good company. Heaven grant that this favorable gale may continue! for we have had so much of turning to windward, that the word "helm-a-lee" is become almost as disagreeable to our ears as the sentence of a judge to a convicted malefactor.

Wednesday, Sept. 21. It has been perfectly calm all this day, and very hot. I was determined to wash myself in the sea today, and should have done so had not the appearance of a shark, that mortal enemy to swimmers, deterred me: he seemed to be about five feet long, moves around the ship at some distance in a slow majestic manner, attended by near a dozen of those they call pilotfish, of different sizes; the largest of them is not so big as a small mackerel, and the smallest not bigger than my little finger. Two of these diminutive pilots keep just before his nose, and he seems to govern himself in his motions by their direction; while the rest surround him on every side indifferently. A shark is never seen without a retinue of these, who are his purveyors, discovering and distinguishing his prey for him; while he in return gratefully protects them from the ravenous hungry dolphin. They are commonly counted a very greedy fish; yet this refuses to meddle with the bait we have thrown out for him. 'Tis likely he has already made a full meal. . . .

Wednesday, Sept. 28. Variable winds and weather last night. This afternoon we took up several branches of gulf weed (with which the sea is spread all over from the Western Isles to the coast of America); but one of these branches had something peculiar in it. In common with the rest it had a leaf about three quarters of an inch long, indented like a saw, and a small yellow berry filled with nothing but wind; besides which it bore a fruit of the animal kind, very surprising to see. It was a small shellfish like a heart, the stalk by which it proceeded from the branch being partly of a gristly kind. Upon this one branch of the weed there were near forty of these vegetable animals; the smallest of them near the end contained a substance somewhat like an oyster, but the larger were visibly animated, opening their shells every moment, and thrusting out a set of unformed claws, not unlike those of a crab; but the inner part was still a kind of soft jelly. Observing the weed more narrowly, I spied a very small crab crawling among it, about as big as the head of a ten-penny nail, and of a yellowish color, like the weed itself. This gave me some reason to think that he was a native of the branch, that he had not long since been in the same condition with the rest of those little embryos that appeared in the shells, this being the method of their generation; and that consequently all the rest of this odd kind of fruit might be crabs in due time. To strengthen my conjecture, I have resolved to keep the weed in salt water, renewing it every day till we come on shore, by this experiment to see whether any more crabs will be produced or not in this manner. I remember that the last calm we had, we took notice of a large crab upon the surface of the sea, swimming from one branch of weed to another, which he seemed to prey upon; and I likewise recollect that at Boston, in New England, I have often seen small crabs with a shell like a snail's upon their backs, crawling about in the salt water; and likewise at Portsmouth in England. It is likely Nature has provided them hard shell to secure them till their own proper shell has acquired a sufficient hardness, which once perfected, they quit their old habitation and venture abroad safe in their own strength. The various changes that silkworms, butterflies, and several other insects go through, make such alterations and metamorphoses not improbable.

Friday, Sept. 30. I sat up last night to observe an eclipse of the moon, which the calendar calculated for London informed us would happen at five o'clock in the morning, September 30. It began with us about eleven last night, and continued till near two this morning, darkening her body about six digits, or one half; the middle of it being about half an hour after twelve, by which we may discover that we are in a meridian of about four hours and half from London, or 67½ degrees of longitude, and consequently have not much above one hundred leagues to run. This is the second eclipse we have had within these fifteen days.

Tuesday, October 4. Last night we struck a dolphin, and this morning we found a flyingfish dead under the windlass. He is about the bigness of a small mackerel, a sharp head, a small mouth, and a tail forked somewhat like a dolphin, but the lowest branch much larger and longer than the other, and tinged with yellow. His back and sides of a darkish blue, his belly white, and his skin very thick. His wings are of a finny substance, about a span long, reaching, when close to his body from an inch below his gills to an inch above his tail. When they fly it is straight forward (for they cannot readily turn), a yard or two above the water; and perhaps fifty yards is the furthest before they dip into the water again, for they cannot support themselves in the air any longer than while their wings continue wet. These flyingfish are the common prey of the dolphin, who is their mortal enemy. When he pursues them, they rise and fly; and he keeps close under them till they drop, and then snaps them up immediately. They generally fly in flocks, four or five, or perhaps a dozen together and a dolphin is seldom caught without one or more in his belly.

Tuesday night. Toward evening a little tired bird, something like a lark, came on board us, who certainly is an American, and 'tis likely was ashore this day. It is now calm. We hope for a fair wind.

Wednesday, October 5. This morning we saw a heron, who had lodged aboard last night. 'Tis a long-legged, long-necked bird, having, as they say, but one gut. They live upon fish, and will swallow a living eel thrice, sometimes, before it will remain in their body. The wind is west again.

Sunday, October 9. We have had the wind fair all the morning; at twelve o'clock we sounded, perceiving the water visibly changed, and struck ground at twenty-five fathoms, to our universal joy. After dinner one of our mess went up aloft to look out, and presently pronounced the long wished-for sound, LAND! LAND! In less than an hour we could decry it from the deck, appearing like tufts of trees. I could not discern it so soon as the rest; my eyes were dimmed with the suffusion of two small drops of joy.

Tuesday, October 11. This morning we weighed anchor with a gentle breeze, and passed by Newcastle, whence they hailed us and bade us welcome. It is extreme fine weather. The sun enlivens our stiff limbs with his glorious rays of warmth and brightness. The sky looks gay, with here and there a silver cloud. The fresh breezes from the woods refresh us, the immediate prospect of liberty after so long and irksome confinement ravishes us. In short all things conspire to make this the most joyful day I ever knew.

1727-31: At Home

Franklin's roots in Philadelphia were growing deeper. Undaunted by early disappointments, he was soon on his own. He joined with a few of the city's younger citizens who were not well-enough established to be eligible for membership in the gentlemen's clubs but were ambitious for themselves and their fortunes, to form an association of "leather-apron men." It served as a means for self-education and as an avenue of social and economic advancement. Franklin soon became a newspaper editor and publisher, and after his common-law marriage to Deborah, he sought new ways to better himself and his city.

Autobiography, Part I, concluded

We landed at Philadelphia the 11th of October, where I found sundry alterations. Keith was no longer Governor, being superceded by Major Gordon. I met him walking the streets as a common citizen. He seemed a little ashamed at seeing me, but passed without saying anything. I should have been as much ashamed at seeing Miss Read, had not her friends, despairing with reason of my return after the receipt of my letter, persuaded her to marry another, one Rogers, a potter, which was done in my absence. With him, however, she was never happy, and soon parted from him, refusing to cohabit with him, or bear his name, it being now said he had another wife. He was a worthless fellow, though an excellent workman. He got into debt and ran away in 1727 or '28, went to the West Indies, and died there. Keimer had got a better house, a shop well supplied with stationery, plenty of new types, and a number of hands, though none good, and seemed to have a great deal of business.

Mr. Denham took a store in Water Street, where we opened our goods. I attended the business diligently, studied accounts, and grew in a little time expert at selling. We lodged and boarded together; he counseled me as a father, having a sincere regard for me. I respected and loved him, and we might have gone on together very happily; but in the beginning of February, 1727, when I had just passed my twenty-first year, we both were taken ill. My distemper was a pleurisy, which very nearly carried me off. I forget what Mr. Denham's distemper was; it held him a long time and at length carried him off. He left me once more to the wide world.

My brother-in-law Holmes, being now at Philadelphia, advised my return to my business; and Keimer tempted me with an offer of large wages by the year to come and take the management of his printing house, that he might better attend to his stationer's shop. I had heard a bad character of him in London, from his wife and her friends, and was not for having any more to do with him. I wished employment as a merchant's clerk, but not meeting with any, I closed again with Keimer.

The Body of
B. Franklin,
Printer;
Like the Cover of an old Book,
Its Contents torn out,
And stript of its Lettering and Gilding,
Lies here, Food for Worms.
But the Work shall not be wholly lost:
For it will, as he believ'd, appear once more,
In a new & more perfect Edition,
Corrected and amended
By the Author.
He was born Jan. 6. 1706.
Died

The premature epitaph, in Franklin's handwriting

I found in his house these hands: Hugh Meredith, a Welsh Pennsylvanian, thirty years of age; bred to country work; he was honest, sensible, a man of experience, and fond of reading, but addicted to drinking. Stephen Potts, a young countryman of full age, bred to the same, of uncommon natural parts, and great wit and humor, but a little idle. These he had agreed with at extreme low wages per week, to be raised a shilling every three months, as they would deserve by improving in their business, and the expectation of these high wages to come on hereafter was what he had drawn them in with. Meredith was to work at press, Potts at bookbinding, which he by agreement was to teach them, though he knew neither one nor t'other. John ——, a wild Irishman, brought up to no business, whose service for four years Keimer had purchased from the captain of a ship, he too was to be made a pressman. George Webb, an Oxford scholar, whose time for four years he had likewise bought, intending him for a compositor (of whom more presently); and David Harry, a country boy, whom he had taken apprentice.

I soon perceived that the intention of engaging me at wages so much higher than he had been used to give was to have these raw, cheap hands formed through me, and as soon as I had instructed them, then, they being all articled to him, he should be able to do without me. I went on, however, very cheerfully, put his printing house in order, which had been in great confusion, and brought his hands by degrees to mind their business and to do it better.

John, the Irishman, soon ran away. With the rest I began to live very agreeably; for they all respected me, the more as they found Keimer incapable of instructing them and that from me they learned something daily. My acquaintance with ingenious people in the town increased. We never worked on a Saturday, that being Keimer's Sabbath. So I had two days for reading. Keimer himself treated me with great civility and apparent regard; and nothing now made me uneasy but my debt to Vernon, which I was yet unable to pay, being hitherto but a poor economist. He, however, kindly made no demand of it.

Our printing house often wanted sorts, and there was no letter foundry in America. I had seen types cast at James's in London, but without much attention to the manner. However, I now contrived a mold, made use of the letters we had, as puncheons, struck the matrices in lead, and thus supplied in a pretty tolerable way all deficiencies. I also engraved several things on occasion. I made the ink, I was warehouse man, and in short quite a *factotum*.

But however serviceable I might be, I found that my services became every day of less importance as the other hands improved in the business; and when Keimer paid me a second quarter's wages, he let me know that he felt them too heavy and thought I should make an abatement. He grew by degrees less civil, put on more the airs of master, frequently found fault, was captious, and seemed ready for an outbreaking. I went on, nevertheless, with a good deal of patience, thinking that his encumbered circumstances were partly the cause. At length a trifle snapped our connection; for a great noise happening near the courthouse, I put my head out of the window to see what was the matter. Keimer being in the street, looked up and saw me, called out to me in a loud voice and angry tone to mind my business, adding some reproachful words that nettled me the more for their publicity, all the neighbors who were looking out on the same occasion being witnesses how I was treated. He came up immediately into the printing house, continued the quarrel; high words passed on both sides, he gave me the quarter's warning we had stipulated, expressing a wish that he had not been obliged to so long a warning. I told him his wish was unnecessary for I would leave him that instant, and so taking my hat, walked out of doors, desiring Meredith, whom I saw below, to take care of some things I left, and bring them to my lodging.

Meredith came accordingly in the evening, when we talked my affair over. He had conceived a great regard for me and was very unwilling that I should leave the house while he remained in it. He dissuaded me from returning to my native country, which I began to think of. He reminded me that Keimer was in debt for all he possessed, that his creditors began to be uneasy, that he kept his shop miserably, sold often without profit for ready money, and often trusted without keeping accounts; that he must therefore fail, which would make a vacancy I might profit of. I objected my want of money. He then let me know that his father had a high opinion of me, and from some discourse that had passed between them, he was sure would advance money to set me up, if I would enter into partnership with him. "My time," said he, "will be out with Keimer in the spring; by that time we may have our press and types in from London. I am sensible I am no workman. If you like it, your skill in the business shall be set against the stock I furnish; and we will share the profits equally." The proposal was agreeable to me, and I consented. His father was in town and approved of it—the more as he saw I had great influence with his son, had prevailed on him to abstain long from dram-drinking, and he hoped might break him of that wretched habit entirely, when we came to be so closely connected. I gave an inventory to the father, who carried it to a merchant; the things were sent for; the secret was to be kept till they should arrive, and in the meantime I was to get work if I could at the other printing house. But I found no vacancy there and so remained idle a few days, when Keimer, on a prospect of being employed to print some paper money in New Jersey which would require cuts and various types that I only could supply, and apprehending Bradford might engage me and get the job from him, sent me a very civil message that old friends should not part for a few words, the effect of sudden passion, and wishing me to return. Meredith persuaded me to comply, as it would give more opportunity for his improvement under my daily instructions. So I returned, and we went on more smoothly than for some time before. The New Jersey job was obtained. I contrived a copperplate press for it, the first that had been seen in the country. I cut several ornaments and checks for the bills. We went together to Burlington, where I executed the whole to satisfaction; and he received so large a sum for the work as to be enabled thereby to keep his head much longer above water.

At Burlington I made an acquaintance with many principal people of the province. Several of them had been appointed by the Assembly a committee to attend the press and take care that no more bills were printed than the law directed. They were therefore by turns constantly with us, and generally he who attended brought with him a friend or two for company. My mind having been much more improved by reading than Keimer's, I suppose it was for that reason my conversation seemed to be more valued. They had me to their houses, introduced me to their friends, and showed me much civility.

We continued there near three months, and by that time acquired friends, afterward of great use to me, as I occasionally was to some of them. They all continued their regard for me as long as they lived.

Before I enter upon my public appearance in business, it may be well to let you know the then state of my mind with regard to my principles and morals, that you may see how far those influenced the future events of my life. My parents had early given me religious impressions, and brought me through my childhood piously. But I was scarce fifteen when, after doubting of several points, as I found them disputed in the different books I read, some books against deism fell into my hands. It happened that they wrought an effect on me quite contrary to what was intended by them, for the arguments of the deists which were quoted to be refuted appeared to me much stronger than the refutations. In short, I soon became a thorough deist. My arguments perverted some others, particularly Collins and Ralph; but each of them having afterward wronged me greatly without the least compunction, and recollecting Keith's conduct toward me (who was another freethinker) and my own toward Vernon and Miss Read (which at times gave me great trouble), I began to suspect that this doctrine, though it might be true, was not very useful.

I grew convinced that *truth*, *sincerity* and *integrity* in dealings between man and man were of the utmost importance to the felicity of life, and I formed written resolutions (which still remain in my Journal book) to practice them ever while I lived. I had, therefore, a tolerable character to begin the world with; I valued it properly and determined to preserve it.

We had not been long returned to Philadelphia, before the new types arrived from London. We settled with Keimer and left him by his consent before he heard of it. We found a house to hire near the market and took it. To lessen the rent (which was then but £24 a year, though I have since known it let for seventy) we took in Thomas Godfrey, a glazier, and his family, who were to pay a considerable part of it to us, and we to board with them. We had scarce opened our letters and put our press in order before George House, an acquaintance of mine, brought a countryman to us whom he had met in the street inquiring for a printer. All our cash was now expended in the variety of particulars we had been obliged to procure, and this countryman's five shillings, being our first fruits and coming so seasonally, gave me more pleasure than any crown I have since earned, and from the gratitude I felt toward

House, has made me often more ready than perhaps I should otherwise have been to assist young beginners.

I should have mentioned before that in the autumn of the preceding year I had formed most of my ingenious acquaintance into a club for mutual improvement which we called the Junto. We met on Friday evenings. The rules I drew up required that every member in his turn should produce one or more queries on any point of morals, politics, or natural philosophy, to be discussed by the company, and once in three months produce and read an essay of his own writing on any subject he pleased. Our debates were to be under the direction of a president, and to be conducted in the sincere spirit of inquiry after truth, without fondness for dispute or desire of victory; and to prevent warmth, all expressions of positiveness in opinion or of direct contradiction were after some time made contraband and prohibited under small pecuniary penalties.

The first members were, Joseph Breintnal, a copier of deeds for the scriveners, a good-natured, friendly, middle-aged man, a great lover of poetry—reading all he could meet with and writing some that was tolerable—very ingenious in many little knickknackeries, and of sensible conversation.

Thomas Godfrey, a self-taught mathematician, great in his way, and afterward inventor of what is now called Hadley's Quadrant. But he knew little out of his way and was not a pleasing companion, as like most great mathematicians I have met with, he expected unusual precision in everything said, or was forever denying or distinguishing upon trifles to the disturbance of all conversation. He soon left us.

Nicholas Scull, a surveyor, afterward Surveyor General, who loved books, and sometimes made a few verses.

William Parsons, bred a shoemaker, but loving reading, had acquired a considerable share of mathematics, which he first studied with a view to astrology that he afterward laughed at. He also became Surveyor General.

William Maugridge, a joiner, but a most exquisite mechanic, and a solid, sensible man.

Hugh Meredith, Stephen Potts, and George Webb I have characterized before.

Robert Grace, a young gentleman of some fortune, generous, lively, and witty, a lover of punning and of his friends.

Lastly, William Coleman, then a merchant's clerk, about my age, who had the coolest, clearest head, the best heart, and the exactest morals of almost any man I ever met with. He became afterward a merchant of great note, and one of our provincial judges. Our friendship continued without interruption to his death upward of forty years. And the club continued almost as long and was the best school of philosophy, and politics that then existed in the province; for our queries which were read the week preceding their discussion, put us on reading with attention upon the several subjects that we might speak more to the purpose; and here too, we acquired better habits of conversation, everything being studied in our rules which might prevent our disgusting each other —from hence the long continuance of the club. But my giving this account of it here is to show something of the interest I had, every one of these exerting themselves in recommending business to us.

Breintnal particularly procured us from the Quakers the printing forty sheets of their history, the rest being to be done by Keimer; and upon these we worked exceeding hard, for the price was low. It was a folio, pro patria size, in pica with long primer notes. I composed a sheet a day, and Meredith worked it off at press. It was often eleven at night, and sometimes later, before I had finished my distribution for the next day's work. For the little jobs sent in by our other friends now and then put us back. But so determined I was to continue doing a sheet a day of the folio, that one night when having imposed my forms I thought my day's work over, one of them by accident was broken and two pages reduced to *pie,* I immediately distributed and composed it over again before I went to bed. And this industry visible to our neighbors began to give us character and credit—particularly, I was told, that mention being made of the new printing office at the merchants' Every-night Club, the general opinion was that it must fail, there being already two printers in the place, Keimer and Bradford;

but Doctor Baird (whom you and I saw many years after at his native place, St. Andrew's in Scotland) gave a contrary opinion: "For the industry of that Franklin," said he, "is superior to anything I ever saw of the kind; I see him still at work when I go home from club, and he is at work again before his neighbors are out of bed." This struck the rest, and we soon after had offers from one of them to supply us with stationery; but as yet we did not choose to engage in shop business.

George Webb, who had found a female friend that lent him wherewith to purchase his time of Keimer, now came to offer himself as a journeyman to us. We could not then employ him,

Eighteenth century printers: typesetters with composing sticks (left); *journeymen spreading paper, inking type and at the press* (below)

but I foolishly let him know, as a secret, that I soon intended to begin a newspaper and might then have work for him. My hopes of success, as I told him, were founded on this: that the then only newspaper, printed by Bradford, was a paltry thing, wretchedly managed, no way entertaining, and yet was profitable to him. I therefore thought a good paper could scarcely fail of good encouragement. I requested Webb not to mention it, but he told it to Keimer, who immediately, to be beforehand with me, published proposals for printing one himself, on which Webb was to be employed. I was vexed at this, and to counteract them, not being able to commence our paper, I wrote several amusing pieces for Bradford's paper under the title of the "Busybody," which Breintnal continued some months. By this means the attention of the public was fixed on that paper, and Keimer's proposals, which we burlesqued and ridiculed, were disregarded. He began his paper, however, and before carrying it on three quarters of a year with at most only ninety subscribers, he offered it to me for a trifle; and I, having been ready some time to go on with it, took it in hand directly, and it proved in a few years extremely profitable to me.

I perceive that I am apt to speak in the singular number, though our partnership still continued; it may be that in fact the whole management of the business lay upon me. Meredith was no compositor, a poor pressman, and seldom sober. My friends lamented my connection with him, but I was to make the best of it.

Our first papers made a quite different appearance from any before in the province, a better type and better printed; but some spirited remarks of my writing struck the principal people, occasioned the paper and the manager of it to be much talked of, and in a few weeks brought them all to be our subscribers. Their example was followed by many. This was one of the first good effects of my having learned a little to scribble. Another was that the leading men, seeing a newspaper now in the hands of one who could also handle a pen, thought it convenient to oblige and encourage me. Bradford still printed the votes and laws and other public business. He had printed an address of the House to the Governor in a course, blundering manner. We reprinted it elegantly and correctly, and sent one to every member. They were sensible of the difference, it strengthened the hands of our friends in the House, and they voted us their printers for the year ensuing.

Mr. Vernon, about this time, put me in mind of the debt I owed him, but did not press me. I wrote him an ingenuous letter of acknowledgment, craved his forbearance a little longer, which he allowed me; and as soon as I was able, I paid the principal with interest and many thanks; so that erratum was in some degree corrected.

But now another difficulty came upon me which I had never the least reason to expect. Mr. Meredith's father, who was to have paid for our printing house according to the expectations given me, was able to advance only one hundred pounds currency, which had been paid; and a hundred more was due to the merchant, who grew impatient and sued us all. We gave bail but saw that if the money could not be raised in time, the suit must come to a judgment and execution, and our hopeful prospects must with us be ruined, as the press and letters must be sold for payment, perhaps at half price. In this distress two true friends, whose kindness I have never forgotten nor ever shall forget while I can remember anything, came to me separately, unknown to each other, and without any application from me, offered each of them to advance me all the money that should be necessary to enable me to take the whole business upon myself if that should be practicable; but they did not like my continuing the partnership with Meredith, who, as they said, was often seen drunk in the streets and playing at low games in alehouses, much to our discredit. These two friends were *William Coleman* and *Robert Grace*. I told them I could not propose a separation while any prospect remained of the Merediths fulfilling their part of our agreement, because I thought myself under great obligations to them for what they had done and would do if they could. But if they finally failed in their performance and our partnership must be dissolved, I should then think myself at liberty to accept the assistance of my friends.

Thus the matter rested for some time; when I said to my partner, "Perhaps your father is dissatisfied at the part you have undertaken in this affair of ours and is unwilling to advance for you and me what he would for you alone. If that is the case, tell me, and I will resign the whole to you and go about my business."

"No," said he, "my father has really been disappointed and is really unable; and I am unwilling to distress him further. I see this is a business I am not fit for. I was bred a farmer, and it was a folly in me to come to town and put myself at thirty years of age an apprentice to learn a new trade. Many of our Welsh people are going to settle in North Carolina, where land is cheap. I am inclined to go with them and follow my old employment. You may find friends to assist you. If you will take the debts of the company upon you, return to my father the hundred pounds he has advanced, pay my little personal debts, and give me thirty pounds and a new saddle, I will relinquish the partnership and leave the whole in your hands."

I agreed to this proposal. It was drawn up in writing, signed and sealed immediately. I gave him what he demanded, and he went soon after to Carolina, from whence he sent me next year two long letters containing the best account that had been given of that country, the climate, soil, husbandry, etc., for in those matters he was very judicious. I printed them in the papers, and they gave great satisfaction to the public.

As soon as he was gone, I recurred to my two friends; and because I would not give an unkind preference to either, I took half what each had offered and I wanted of one, and half of the other, paid off the company's debts, and went on with the business in my own name, advertising that the partnership was dissolved. I think this was in or about the year 1729.

About this time there was a cry among the people for more paper money. The wealthy inhabitants opposed any addition, being against all paper currency, from the apprehension that it would depreciate as it had done in New England to the injury of all creditors. We had discussed this point in our Junto, where I was on the side of an addition, being persuaded that the first small sum struck in 1723 had done much good by increasing the trade, employment, and number of inhabitants in the province.

Our debates possessed me so fully of the subject that I wrote and printed an anonymous pamphlet on it entitled *The Nature and Necessity of a Paper Currency*. It was well received by the common people in general; but the rich men disliked it, for it increased and strengthened the clamor for more money; and they happening to have no writers among them that were able to answer it, their opposition slackened, and the point was carried by a majority in the House. My friends there, who considered I had been of some service, thought fit to reward me by employing me in printing the money—a very profitable job and a great help to me. This was another advantage gained by my being able to write.

I now opened a small stationer's shop. I had in it blanks of all sorts, the correctest that ever appeared among us. I was assisted in that by my friend Breintnal. I had also paper, parchment, chapmen's books, etc. One Whitemash, a compositor I had known in London, an excellent workman, now came to me and worked with me constantly and diligently; and I took an apprentice.

I began now gradually to pay off the debt I was under for the printing house. In order to secure my credit and character as a tradesman, I took care not only to be in *reality* industrious and frugal, but to avoid the *appearance* to the contrary. I dressed plain and was seen at no places of idle diversion. I never went out fishing or shooting; a book, indeed, sometimes debauched me from my work, but that was seldom, snug, and gave no scandal; and to show that I was not above my business, I sometimes brought home the paper I purchased at the stores, through the streets on a wheelbarrow. Thus being esteemed an industrious, thriving, young man, and paying duly for what I bought, the merchants who imported stationery solicited my custom; others proposed supplying me with books, and I went on swimmingly. In the meantime Keimer's credit and business declining daily, he was at last forced to sell his printing house to satisfy his creditors [and] went to Barbados.

His apprentice, David Harry, whom I had instructed, set up in his place, having bought his materials. I was at first apprehensive of a powerful rival in Harry, as his friends were very able and had a good deal of interest. I therefore proposed a partnership to him, which he, fortunately for me, rejected with scorn. He was very proud, dressed like a gentleman, lived expensively, took much diversion and pleasure abroad, ran in debt, and neglected his business —upon which all business left him; and finding nothing to do, he followed Keimer to Barbados, taking the printing house with him.

There remained now no other competitor with me at Philadelphia but the old one, Bradford, who was rich and easy, did a little printing now and then by straggling hands, but was not very anxious about it. However, as he kept the post office, it was imagined he had better opportunities of obtaining news, his paper was thought a better distributor of advertisements than mine and therefore had many more—which was a profitable thing to him and a disadvantage to me. For though I did indeed receive and send papers by the post, yet the public opinion was otherwise; for what I did send was by bribing the riders, who took them privately— Bradford being unkind enough to forbid it, which occasioned some resentment on my part; and I thought so meanly of the practice that when I afterward came into his situation, I took care never to imitate it.

I had hitherto continued to board with Godfrey, who lived in part of my house with his wife and children, and had one side of the shop for his glazier's business, though he worked little, being always absorbed in his mathematics. Mrs. Godfrey projected a match for me with a relation's daughter, took opportunities of bringing us often together, till a serious courtship on my part ensued, the girl being in herself very deserving. The old folks encouraged me by continued invitations to supper and by leaving us together, till at length it was time to explain. Mrs. Godfrey managed our little treaty. I let her know that I expected as much money with their daughter as would pay off my remaining debt for the printing house, which I believe was not then above a hundred pounds. She brought me word they had no such sum to spare. I said they might mortgage their house in the Loan Office. The answer to this after some days was that they did not approve the match; that on inquiry of Bradford they had been informed the printing business was not a profitable one, the types would soon be worn out and more wanted; that S. Keimer and D. Harry had failed one after the other, and I should probably soon follow them; and therefore I was forbidden the house, and the daughter shut up. I declared absolutely my resolution to have nothing more to do with that family. This was resented by the Godfreys, we differed, and they removed, leaving me the whole house, and I resolved to take no more inmates. But this affair having turned my thoughts to marriage, I looked around me and made overtures of acquaintance in other places, but soon found that the business of a printer being generally thought a poor one, I was not to expect money with a wife, unless with such a one as I should not otherwise think agreeable. In the meantime that hard-to-be-governed passion of youth had hurried me frequently into intrigues with low women that fell in my way, which were attended with some expense and great inconvenience, besides a continual risk to my health by a distemper, which of all things I dreaded, though by great good luck I escaped it.

A friendly correspondence as neighbors and old acquaintances had continued between me and Miss Read's family, who all had a regard for me from the time of my first lodging in their house. I was often invited there and consulted in their affairs, wherein I sometimes was of service. I pitied poor Miss Read's unfortunate situation, who was generally dejected, seldom cheerful, and avoided company. I considered my giddiness and inconstancy when in London as in a great degree the cause of her unhappiness, though the mother was good enough to think the fault more her own than mine, as she had prevented our marrying before I went thither and persuaded the other match in my absence. Our mutual affection was revived, but there were now great objections to our union. That match was indeed looked upon as invalid, a preceding wife being said to be living in England; but this could not easily be proved because of the distance. And though there was a report of his death, it was not certain. Then, though it should be true, he had left many debts which his successor might be called upon to pay. We ventured, however, over all these difficulties, and I took her to wife, September 1, 1730. None of the inconveniences happened that we had apprehended; she proved a good and faithful helpmate, assisted me much by attending the shop; we throve together and ever mutually endeavored to make each other happy. Thus I corrected that great erratum as well as I could.

About this time our club meeting, not at a tavern, but in a little room of Mr. Grace's set apart for that purpose, a proposition was made by me that since our books were often referred to, it might be convenient to us to have them all together where we met, that upon occasion they might be consulted; and by thus clubbing our books to a common library, we should, while we liked to keep them together, have each of us the advantage of using the books of all the other members, which would be nearly as beneficial as if each owned the whole. It was liked and agreed to, and we filled one end of the room with such books as we could best spare. The number was not so great as we expected; and though they had been of great use, yet some inconveniences occurring for want of due care of them, the collection after about a year was separated, and each took his books home again.

And now I set on foot my first project of a public nature, that for a subscription library. I drew up the proposals, got them put into form by our great scrivener, Brockden, and by the help of my friends in the Junto, procured fifty subscribers of forty shillings each to begin with, and ten shillings a year for fifty years—the term our company was to continue. We afterward obtained a charter, the company being increased to one hundred. This was the mother of all the North American subscription libraries, now so numerous. It is become a great thing itself and continually goes on increasing. These libraries have improved the general conversation of the Americans, made the common tradesmen and farmers as intelligent as most gentlemen from other countries, and perhaps have contributed in some degree to the stand so generally made throughout the colonies in defense of their privileges.

Memo: Thus far was written with the intention expressed in the beginning and therefore contains several little family anecdotes of no importance to others. What follows was written many years after, and intended for the public. The affairs of the Revolution occasioned the interruption.

two

Mature Years

The American Colonies

✒ 1731: Account of My Life

More than ten years after writing the first part of his *Auto-biography*, Franklin received a copy of his manuscript from a correspondent in Philadelphia, who urged him to finish the work. Franklin was seventy years old, living in a suburb of Paris as minister plenipotentiary to France from the new United States of America. He had led the negotiations of the Treaty of Alliance with France and the Treaty of Peace with Great Britain. He consulted an associate in England and then went on the with the "Account of My Life, Begun at Passy, near Paris, 1784," accepting the suggestion that the story of his life would be an "advertisement of a rising people," an "education of the next generation" and a chance to show "how much is to be done, both to sons and fathers." Franklin no longer addressed his writing to his son, William, then in England. Father and son had not written to each other since 1775. Franklin picked up where he left off: in the year 1731, with the founding of the Philadelphia Library Company.

Autobiography, Part II

This library afforded me the means of improvement by constant study, for which I set apart an hour or two each day, and thus repaired in some degree the loss of the learned education my father once intended for me. Reading was the only amusement I allowed myself. I spent no time in taverns, games, or frolics of any kind. And my industry in my business continued as indefatigable as it was necessary. I was indebted for my printing house. I had a young family coming on to be educated, and I had two competitors to contend with for business, who were established in the place before me. My circumstances, however, grew daily easier. My original habits of frugality continuing, and my father having among his instructions to me when a boy frequently repeated a proverb of Solomon, "Seest thou a man diligent in his calling, he shall stand before kings, he shall not stand before mean men." I from thence considered industry as a means of obtaining wealth and distinction, which encouraged me, though I did not think that I should ever literally stand before kings, which, however, has since happened; for I have stood before five, and even had the honor of sitting down with one (the King of Denmark) to dinner.

We have an English proverb that says;

> "He that would thrive
> Must ask his wife."

It was lucky for me that I had one as much disposed to industry and frugality as myself. She assisted me cheerfully in my business, folding and stitching pamphlets, tending shop, purchasing old linen rags for the paper makers, etc. We kept no idle servants, our table was plain and simple, our furniture of the cheapest. For instance, my breakfast was for a long time bread and milk (no tea), and I ate it out of a twopenny earthen porringer with a pewter spoon. But mark how luxury will enter families and make a progress, in spite of principle. Being called one morning to breakfast, I found

Left, *bookbinding in the eighteenth century;* below, *special frame for stitching pages*

it in a china bowl, with a spoon of silver. They had been bought for me without my knowledge by my wife, and had cost her the enormous sum of three-and-twenty shillings, for which she had no other excuse or apology to make but that she thought *her* husband deserved a silver spoon and china bowl as well as any of his neighbors. This was the first appearance of plate and china in our house, which afterward in a course of years as our wealth increased, augmented gradually to several hundred pounds in value.

I had been religiously educated as a Presbyterian; and though some of the dogmas of that persuasion appeared to me doubtful, and I early absented myself from the public assemblies of the sect, Sunday being my studying day, I never was without some religious principles. I never doubted, for instance, the existence of the Deity, that He made the world and governed it by His providence, that the most acceptable service of God was the doing good to man, that our souls are immortal, and that all crime will be punished and virtue rewarded either here or hereafter. These I esteemed the essentials of every religion, and being to be found in all the religions we had in our country, I respected them all, though with different degrees of respect as I found them more or less mixed with other articles which without any tendency to inspire, promote, or confirm morality, served principally to divide us and make us unfriendly to one another. This respect to all, with an opinion that the worst had some good effects, induced me to avoid all discourse that might tend to lessen the good opinion another might have of his own religion; and as our province increased in people and new places of worship were continually wanted and generally erected by voluntary contribution, my mite for such purpose, whatever might be the sect, was never refused.

Though I seldom attended any public worship, I had still an opinion of its propriety and of its utility when rightly conducted, and I regularly paid my annual subscription for the support of the only Presbyterian minister or meeting we had in Philadelphia. I had some years before composed a little liturgy or form of prayer for my own private use; viz., in 1728, entitled "Articles of Belief and Acts of Religion." I returned to the use of this and went no more to the public assemblies. My conduct might be blameable, but I leave it without attempting further to excuse it, my present purpose being to relate facts and not to make apologies for them.

✍ 1738: Doubts and Beliefs

When Franklin was thirty-two, he did not make apologies for his religious feelings either, but he did explain them in a letter to his eighty-three-year-old father and his seventy-one-year-old mother.

To Josiah and Abiah Franklin in Boston

April 13, 1738

Honored Father and Mother:

I have your favor of the 21st of March in which you both seem concerned lest I have imbibed some erroneous opinions. Doubtless I have my share, and when the natural weakness and imperfection of human understanding is considered, with the unavoidable influences of education, custom, books and company, upon our ways of thinking, I imagine a man must have a good deal of vanity who believes, and a good deal of boldness who affirms, that all the doctrines he holds, are true; and all he rejects, are false. And perhaps the same may be justly said of every sect, church and society of men when they assume to themselves the infallibility which they deny to the popes and councils. I think opinions should be judged of by their influences and effects; and if a man holds none that tend to make him less virtuous or more vicious, it may be concluded he holds none that are dangerous; which I hope is the case with me. I am sorry you should have any uneasiness on my account, and if it were a thing possible for one to alter his opinions in order to please others, I know none whom I ought more willingly to oblige in that respect than yourselves: But since it is no more in a man's power *to think* than *to look* like another, methinks all that should be expected from me is to keep my mind open to conviction, to hear patiently and examine attentively whatever is offered me for that end; and if after all I continue in the same errors, I believe your usual charity will induce you rather to pity and excuse than blame me. In the meantime your care and concern for me is what I am very thankful for.

My mother grieves that one of her sons is an Arian, another an Armenian. What an Armenian or an Arian is, I cannot say that I very well know; the truth is, I make such distinctions very little my study. I think vital religion has always suffered, when orthodoxy is more regarded than virtue. And the scripture assures me, that at the last day, we shall not be examined what we *thought*, but what we *did;* and our recommendation will not be that we said *Lord, Lord*, but that we did GOOD to our fellow creatures. I am your dutiful son.

1728—: List of Virtues

Franklin had a lifelong habit of compiling lists and making "bold and arduous projects" for himself and others. He has mentioned his private "Articles of Belief and Acts of Religion," a list of qualities and beliefs for which he offered a list of "petitions" and "thanks." He also had a detailed work, dine, read, sleep and "overlook the accounts" schedule for each day, and a question to begin and end it with. He drew up a list of thirteen virtues which he wished to include in his own character and worked out an elaborate scheme to develop them, one at a time, which he tried to continue all his life.

Autobiography, Part II, concluded

. . . I included under thirteen names of virtues all that at that time occurred to me as necessary or desirable, and annexed to each a short precept which fully expressed the extent I gave to its meaning.

These names of virtues with their precepts were
1. Temperance: Eat not to dullness. Drink not to elevation.
2. Silence: Speak not but what may benefit others or yourself. Avoid trifling conversation.
3. Order: Let all your things have their places. Let each part of your business have its time.
4. Resolution: Resolve to perform what you ought. Perform without fail what you resolve.
5. Frugality: Make no expense but to do good to others or yourself; i.e., waste nothing.
6. Industry: Lose no time. Be always employed in something useful. Cut off all unnecessary actions.
7. Sincerity: Use no hurtful deceit. Think innocently and justly; and, if you speak, speak accordingly.
8. Justice: Wrong none by doing injuries or omitting the benefits that are your duty.
9. Moderation: Avoid extremes. Forbear resenting injuries so much as you think they deserve.
10. Cleanliness: Tolerate no uncleanness in body, clothes or habitation.
11. Tranquillity: Be not disturbed at trifles or at accidents common or unavoidable.
12. Chastity: Rarely use venery but for health or offspring—never to dullness, weakness, or the injury of your own or another's peace or reputation.
13. Humility: Imitate Jesus and Socrates.

My list of virtues contained at first but twelve. But a Quaker friend having kindly informed me that I was generally thought proud, that my pride showed itself frequently in conversation, that I was not content with being in the right when discussing any point, but was overbearing and rather insolent—of which he convinced me by mentioning several instances—I determined endeavoring to cure myself if I could of this vice or folly among the rest, and I added *Humility* to my list, giving an extensive meaning to the word. I cannot boast of much success in acquiring the *reality* of this virtue, but I had a good deal with regard to the *appearance* of it. I made it a rule to forbear all direct contradiction to the sentiments of others and all positive assertion of my own. And this mode, which I at first put on with some violence to natural inclination, became at length so easy and so habitual to me that perhaps for these fifty years past no one has ever heard a dogmatical expression escape me. And to this habit (after my character of integrity) I think it principally owing that I had early so much weight with my fellow citizens when I proposed new institutions or alterations in the old, and so much influence in public councils when I became a member. For I was but a bad speaker, never eloquent, subject to much hesitation in my choice of words, hardly correct in language, and yet I generally carried my point.

In reality there is perhaps no one of our natural passions so hard to subdue as *pride;* disguise it, struggle with it, beat it down, stifle it, mortify it as much as one pleases, it is still alive, and will every now and then peep out and show itself; you will see it, perhaps, often in this history; for, even if I could conceive that I had completely overcome it, I should probably be proud of my humility. (Thus far written at Passy, 1784)

1732—: Poor Richard

Back in Philadelphia, where he had been cheered and hailed by the new America, Franklin received constant requests to continue the story of his life. Among his papers and memories, and surrounded by his children and grandchildren, Franklin, eighty-two years old, started Part III of his *Autobiography*.

Autobiography, Part III

I am now about to write at home (Philadelphia), August 1788, but cannot have the help expected from my papers, many of them being lost in the war.

In 1732 I first published my *Almanac*, under the name of *Richard Saunders*; it was continued by me about twenty-five years, and commonly called *Poor Richard's Almanac*.

Poor Richard's Almanac (Preface, 1733)

Courteous Reader:

I might in this place attempt to gain thy favor, by declaring that I write almanacs with no other view than that of the public good; but in this I should not be sincere; and men are nowadays too wise to be deceived by pretenses how specious soever. The plain truth of the matter is, I am excessive poor, and my wife, good woman, is, I tell her, excessive proud; she cannot bear, she says, to sit spinning in her shift of tow, while I do nothing but gaze at the stars; and has threatened more than once to burn all my books and rattling-traps (as she calls my instruments) if I do not make some profitable use of them for the good of my family. The printer has offered me some considerable share of the profits, and I have thus begun to comply with my dame's desire.

Indeed this motive would have had force enough to have made me publish an almanac many years since, had it not been over-powered by my regard for my good friend and fellow student Mr. *Titan Leeds*, whose interest I was extremely unwilling to hurt: But this obstacle (I am far from speaking it with pleasure) is soon to be removed, since inexorable death, who was never known to respect merit, has already prepared the mortal dart, the fatal sister has already extended her destroying shears, and that ingenious man must soon be taken from us. He dies, by my calculation made at his request, on Oct. 17. 1733. 3 h. 29 m. P.M. at the very instant of the o of ☉ and ☿ : By his own calculation he will survive till the 26th of the same month. This small difference between us we have disputed whenever we have met these 9 years past; but at length he is inclinable to agree with my judgment: Which of us is most exact, a little time will now determine. As therefore these provinces may not longer expect to see any of his performances after this year, I think myself free to take up the task, and request a share of the public encouragement; which I am the more apt to hope for on this account, that the buyer of my almanac may consider himself, not only as purchasing a useful utensil, but as performing an act of charity, to his poor *Friend and Servant*.   R. SAUNDERS

Titan Leeds replies—The American Almanack (1734)

Kind Reader:

Perhaps it may be expected that I should say something concerning an almanac printed for the year 1733. Said to be writ by Poor Richard or Richard Saunders, who for want of other matter was pleased to tell his readers, that he had calculated my nativity, and from thence predicts my death to be the 17th of October, 1733. At 22 min. past 3 o'clock in the afternoon, and that these provinces may not expect to see any more of his (*Titan Leeds*) performances, and this precise predictor who predicts to a minute, proposes to succeed me in writing of almanacs; but notwithstanding his false prediction, I have by the mercy of God lived to write a diary for the year 1734, and to publish the folly and ignorance of this presumptuous author. Nay, he adds another gross falsehood in his said almanac, viz.—*That by my own Calculation, I shall survive until the 26th of the said Month* (October), which is as untrue as the former, for I do not pretend to that knowledge, although he has usurped the knowledge of the Almighty herein, and manifested himself a fool and a liar. And by the mercy of God I have lived to survive this conceited scribbler's day and minute whereon he has predicted my death; and as I have supplied my country with almanacs for three seven years by past, to general satisfaction, so perhaps I may live to write when his performances are dead. *Thus much from your annual friend, Titan Leeds.* October 18, 1733, 3 ho. 33 min. P.M.

Poor Richard's Almanac (Preface, 1734)

October 30, 1733

Courteous Readers:

Your kind and charitable assistance last year, in purchasing so large an impression of my almanacs, has made my circumstances much more easy in the world, and requires my grateful acknowledgment. My wife has been enabled to get a pot of her own, and is no longer obliged to borrow one from a neighbor; nor have we ever since been without something of our own to put in it. She has also got a pair of shoes, two new shifts, and a new warm petticoat; and for my part, I have bought a secondhand coat, so good, that I am now not ashamed to go to town or be seen there. These things have rendered her temper so much more pacific than it used to be, that I may say, I have slept more, and more quietly within this last year, than in the three foregoing years put together. Accept my hearty thanks therefor, and my sincere wishes for your health and prosperity.

In the preface to my last almanac, I foretold the death of my dear old friend and fellow-student, the learned and ingenious Mr. Titan Leeds. Whether he be really yet dead, I cannot at this present writing positively assure my readers. There is however (and I cannot speak it without sorrow), there is the strongest probability that my dear friend is *no more;* for there appears in his name, as I am assured an almanac for the year 1734, in which I am treated in a very gross and unhandsome manner; in which I am called *a false predicter, an ignorant, a conceited scribbler, a fool, and a liar.* Mr. Leeds was too well bred to use any man so indecently and so scurrilously, and moreover his esteem and affection for me was extraordinary. So that it is feared that the pamphlet may be only a contrivance of somebody or other, who hopes perhaps to sell two or three years' almanacs still, by the sole force and virtue of Mr. Leeds's name.

Poor Richard's Almanac (Preface, 1735)

October 30, 1734

Courteous Reader:

Whatever may be the music of the spheres, how great soever the harmony of the stars, 'tis certain there is no harmony among the stargazers; but they are perpetually growling and snarling at one another like strange curs, or like some men at their wives. I had resolved to keep the peace on my own part, and affront none of them and I shall persist in that resolution: but having received much abuse from Titan Leeds deceased (Titan Leeds when living would not have used me so). I say, having received much abuse from the ghost of Titan Leeds deceased, who pretends to be still living, and to write almanacs in spite of me and my predictions, I cannot help saying, that though I take it patiently, I take it very unkindly. And whatever he may pretend, 'tis undoubtedly true that he is really defunct and dead. First, because the stars are seldom disappointed. Secondly, 'twas requisite and necessary he should die punctually at that time, for the honor of astrology, the art professed both by him and his father before him. Thirdly, 'tis plain to everyone that reads his two last almanacs (for 1734 and '35) that they are not written with that *life* his performances use to be written with; the wit is low and flat, the little hints dull and spiritless; no man *living* would or could write such stuff. But lastly, I shall convince him from his own words that he is dead. For in his preface to his almanac for 1734, he says, "Saunders [Poor Richard] adds another GROSS FALSEHOOD in his almanac, viz. that by my own calculation I shall *survive* until the 26th of the said month, October 1733, which is as untrue as the former." Now if it be, as Leeds says, *untrue* and a *gross falsehood* that he survived till the 26th of October 1733, then it is certainly *true* that he died *before* that time: and if he died before that time, he is dead now, to all intents and purposes, anything he may say to the contrary notwithstanding.

Poor Richard's Almanac (Preface, 1738) by "Mistress Saunders"

Dear Readers:

My good man set out last week to visit an old stargazer of his acquaintance and see about a little place for us to settle and end our days on. He left the copy of his almanac sealed up and bid me send it to the press. I suspected something, and therefore as soon as he was gone, I opened it, to see if he had not been flinging some of his old skits [barbs] at me. Just as I thought, so it was. And truly (for want of somewhat else to say, I suppose) he had put into his preface, that his wife Bridget—was this, and that, and t'other. Cannot I have a little fault or two, but all the country must see it in print!

Upon looking over the months, I see he has put in abundance of foul weather this year; and therefore I have scattered here and there, where I could find room, some *fair, pleasant, sunshiny* etc. for the good women to dry their clothes in.

Poor Richard's Almanac (Preface, 1739)

Some people observing the great yearly demand for my Almanac, imagine I must by this time have become rich, and consequently ought to call myself *Poor Dick* no longer. But, the case is this, when I first began to publish, the printer made a fair agreement with me for my copies, by virtue of which he runs away with the greatest part of the profit. However, much good may't do him; I do not grudge it to him; he is a man I have a great regard for, and I wish his profit ten times greater than it is.

1732-37: Public Affairs

Writer, publisher, printer, newspaperman, and civic-minded citizen, Franklin used his press to stimulate interest in public projects. He made skillful appeals to his readers, exemplified by the letter, addressed to himself, on methods of fire prevention and fire fighting. Franklin's growing interest in colonial affairs was accompanied by his own increasing prosperity and self-education.

Autobiography, Part III, continued

I endeavored to make it [the *Almanac*] both entertaining and useful, and it accordingly came to be in such demand that I reaped considerable profit from it, vending annually near ten thousand. And observing that it was generally read, scarce any neighborhood in the province being without it, I considered it as a proper vehicle for conveying instruction among the common people, who bought scarce any other books. I therefore filled all the little spaces that occurred between the remarkable days in the Calendar with proverbial sentences, chiefly such as inculcated industry and frugality as the means of procuring wealth and thereby securing virtue—it being more difficult for a man in want to act always honestly, as (to use here one of those proverbs) "it is hard for an empty sack to stand upright." These proverbs, which contained the wisdom of many ages and nations, I assembled and formed into a connected discourse prefixed to the *Almanac* of 1757, as the harangue of a wise old man to the people attending an auction. The bringing all these scattered counsels thus into a focus enabled them to make greater impression. The piece, being universally approved, was copied in all the newspapers of the American continent, reprinted in Britain on a broadside to be stuck up in houses, two translations were made of it in French, and great numbers bought by the clergy and gentry to distribute gratis among their poor parishioners and tenants. In Pennsylvania, as it discouraged useless expense in foreign superfluities, some thought it had its share of influence in producing that growing plenty of money which was observable for several years after its publication.

I considered my newspaper also as another means of communicating instruction, and in that view frequently reprinted in it extracts from *The Spectator* and other moral writers, and sometimes published little pieces of my own which had been first composed for reading in our Junto. In the conduct of my newspaper I carefully excluded all libeling and personal abuse, which is of late years become so disgraceful to our country.

In 1733, I sent one of my journeymen to Charlestown, South Carolina, where a printer was wanting. I furnished him with a press and letters on an agreement of partnership, by which I was to receive one-third of the profits, paying one third of the expense.

I had begun in 1733 to study languages. I soon made myself so much a master of the French as to be able to read the books with ease. I then undertook the Italian. I afterward with a little painstaking acquired as much of the Spanish as to read their books also. I have already mentioned that I had only one year's instruction in a Latin school, and that when very young, after which I neglected that language entirely. But when I had attained an acquaintance with the French, Italian, and Spanish, I was surprised to find, on looking over a Latin Testament, that I understood so much more of that language than I had imagined; which encouraged me to apply myself again to the study of it; and I met with the more success, as those preceding languages had greatly smoothed my way.

After ten years' absence from Boston and having become more easy in my circumstances, I made a journey thither to visit my relations, which I could not sooner well afford. In returning I called at Newport to see my brother James then settled there with his printing house. Our former differences were forgotten, and our meeting was very cordial and affectionate. He was fast declining in his health and requested of me that in case of his death, which he apprehended not far distant, I would take home his son, then but ten years of age, and bring him up to the printing business. This I accordingly performed, sending him a few years to school before I took him into the office. His mother carried on the business till he was grown up, when I assisted him with an assortment of new types, those of his father being in a manner worn out. Thus it was that I made my brother ample amends for the service I had deprived him of by leaving him so early.

In 1736, I lost one of my sons, a fine boy of four years old, by the smallpox taken in the common way. I long regretted bitterly, and still regret, that I had not given it to him by inoculation. This I mention for the sake of parents who omit that operation on the supposition that they should never forgive themselves if a child died under it—my example showing that the regret may be the same either way, and therefore that the safer should be chosen.

My first promotion was my being chosen in 1736 clerk of the General Assembly. The choice was made that year without opposition; but the year following when I was again proposed (the choice, like that of the members, being annual), a new member made a long speech against me in order to favor some other candidate. I was, however, chosen, which was the more agreeable to me, as besides the pay for immediate service as clerk, the place gave me a better opportunity of keeping up an interest among the members, which secured to me the business of printing the votes, laws, paper money, and other occasional jobs for the public, that, on the whole, were very profitable.

In 1737, Colonel Spotswood, late governor of Virginia, and then postmaster general, being dissatisfied with the conduct of his deputy at Philadelphia respecting some negligence in rendering and want of exactness in framing his accounts, took from him the commission and offered it to me. I accepted it readily and found it of great advantage; for though the salary was small, it facilitated the correspondence that improved my newspaper, increased the number demanded, as well as the advertisements to be inserted, so that it came to afford me a considerable income. My old competitor's newspaper declined proportionably, and I was satisfied without retaliating his refusal, while postmaster, to permit my papers being carried by the riders.

I began now to turn my thoughts a little to public affairs, beginning, however, with small matters. The city watch was one of the first things that I conceived to want regulation. It was managed by the constables of the respective wards in turn; the constable warned a number of housekeepers to attend him for the night. Those who chose never to attend paid him six shillings a year to be excused, which was supposed to be for hiring substitutes, but was in reality much more than was necessary for that purpose and made the constableship a place of profit; and the constable for a little drink often got such ragamuffins about him as a watch that respectable housekeepers did not choose to mix with. Walking the rounds, too, was often neglected, and most of the nights spent in tippling. I thereupon wrote a paper to be read in Junto representing these irregularities but insisting more particularly on the inequality of this six-shilling tax of the constables, respecting the circumstances of those who paid it, since a poor widow housekeeper, all whose property to be guarded by the watch did not, perhaps, exceed the value of fifty pounds, paid as much as the wealthiest merchant who had thousands of pounds' worth of goods in his stores. On the whole, I proposed as a more effectual watch the hiring of proper men to serve constantly in that business; and as a more equitable way of supporting the charge, the levying a tax that should be proportioned to the property.

About this time I wrote a paper (first to be read in Junto, but it was afterward published) on the different accidents and carelessness by which houses were set on fire, with cautions against them and means proposed of avoiding them.

The Pennsylvania Gazette

February 4, 1735

Mr. Franklin:

Being old and lame of my hands, and thereby uncapable of assisting my fellow citizens, when their houses are on fire; I must beg them to take in good part the following hints on the subject of fires.

In the first place, as *an ounce of prevention is worth a pound of cure*, I would advise them to take care how they suffer living brands' ends, or coals in a full shovel, to be carried out of one room into another, or up or down stairs, unless in a warming pan shut; for scraps of fire may fall into chinks, and make no appearance till midnight; when your stairs being in flames, you may be forced (as I once was) to leap out of your windows, and hazard your necks to avoid being over-roasted.

We have at present got engines enough in the town, but I question, whether in many parts of the town, water enough can be had to keep them going for half an hour together. It seems to me some public pumps are wanting; but that I submit to better judgments.

As to our conduct in the affair of extinguishing fires, though we do not want hands or good will, yet we seem to want order and method, and therefore I believe I cannot do better than to offer for our imitation, the example of a city in a neighboring province. There is, as I am well informed, a club or society of active men belonging to each fire engine; whose business is to attend all fires with it whenever they happen; and to work it once a quarter, and see it kept in order: Some of these are to handle the fire hooks, and others the axes, which are always kept with the engine; and for this service they are considered in an abatement or exemption in the taxes. In time of fire, they are commanded by officers appointed by law, called *firewards*, who are distinguished by a red staff of five feet long, headed with a brass flame of 6 inches; and being men of prudence and authority, they direct the opening and stripping of roofs by the ax men, the pulling down burning timbers by the hookmen, and the playing of the engines, and com-

Public watchman—another of Franklin's ideas that spread

mand the making of lanes, etc. and they are empowered to require assistance for the removing of goods out of houses on fire
or in danger of fire and to appoint guards for securing such goods;
and disobedience, to these officers in any, at such times, is punished
by a fine of 40 *s.* or ten days' imprisonment. These officers, with the
men belonging to the engine, at their quarterly meetings, discourse
of fires, of the faults committed at some, the good management
in some cases at others, and thus communicating their thoughts and
experience they grow wise in the thing, and know how to command and to execute in the best manner upon every emergency.
Since the establishment of this regulation, it seems there has been
no extraordinary fire in that place; and I wish there never may be
any here.

Let others communicate their thoughts as freely as I have done
mine, and perhaps something useful may be drawn from the whole.

I am yours, &c.

A.A.

Autobiography, Part III, continued

This was much spoken of as a useful piece, and gave rise to a project which soon followed it of forming a company for the more ready extinguishing of fires, and mutual assistance in removing and securing of goods when in danger. Associates in this scheme were presently found amounting to thirty. Our articles of agreement obliged every member to keep always in good order and fit for use a certain number of leather buckets with strong bags and baskets (for packing and transporting of goods) which were to be brought to every fire; and we agreed about once a month to spend a social evening together in discoursing and communicating such ideas as occurred to us upon the subject of fires as might be useful in our conduct on such occasions. The utility of this institution soon appeared, and many more desiring to be admitted than we thought convenient for one company, they were advised to form another, which was accordingly done. And this went on, one new company after another till they became so numerous as to include most of the inhabitants who were men of property; and now at the time of my writing this (though upward of fifty years since its establishment) that which I first formed, called the Union Fire Company, still subsists; though the first members are all deceased but myself and one, who is older by a year than I am. The small fines that have been paid by members for absence at the monthly meetings have been applied to the purchase of fire engines, ladders, fire hooks, and other useful implements for each company, so that I question whether there is a city in the world better provided with the means of putting a stop to beginning conflagrations; and in fact, since those institutions, the city has never lost by fire more than one or two houses at a time, and the flames have often been extinguished before the house in which they began has been half consumed.

My business was now continually augmenting and my circumstances growing daily easier, my newspaper having become very profitable, as being for a time almost the only one in this and the neighboring provinces. I experienced, too, the truth of the observation that "after getting the first hundred pound, it is more easy to get the second:"—money itself being of a prolific nature.

The partnership at Carolina having succeeded, I was encouraged to engage in others and to promote several of my workmen who had behaved well, by establishing them with printing houses in different colonies on the same terms with that in Carolina. Most of them did well, being enabled at the end of our term (six years) to purchase the types of me and go on working for themselves, by which means several families were raised.

I had on the whole abundant reason to be satisfied with my being established in Pennsylvania. There were, however, two things that I regretted: there being no provision for defense nor for a complete education of youth, no militia nor any college. I therefore in 1743 drew up a proposal for establishing an academy; but I let the scheme lie awhile dormant. I succeeded better the next year, 1744, in proposing and establishing a Philosophical Society. The paper I wrote for that purpose will be found among my writings if not lost with many others.

✒ 1743: First Learned Society

The scientific curiosity which the twenty-year-old Franklin had exhibited on his voyage from London to Philadelphia never abated. As deputy postmaster general of the colonies, Franklin traveled and made contact with other inquiring minds. Thus, he was ready to print and circulate a proposal to form The American Philosophical Society, the oldest learned society in this country, which still operates from its headquarters near Independence Square in Philadelphia. Thomas Jefferson was among the noted Americans who followed Franklin as president of the Society.

A Proposal for Promoting Useful Knowledge among the British Plantations in America

Philadelphia, May 14, 1743

The English are possessed of a long tract of continent, from Nova Scotia to Georgia, extending north and south through different climates, having different soils, producing different plants, mines, and minerals, and capable of different improvements, manufactures, etc.

The first drudgery of settling new colonies, which confines the attention of people to mere necessaries, is now pretty well over; and there are many in every province in circumstances that set them at ease, and afford leisure to cultivate the finer arts and improve the common stock of knowledge. To such of these who are men of speculation, many hints must from time to time arise, many observations occur, which if well examined, pursued, and improved, might produce discoveries to the advantage of some or all of the British plantations, or to the benefit of mankind in general.

But as from the extent of the country such persons are widely separated, and seldom can see and converse or be acquainted with each other, so that many useful particulars remain uncommunicated, die with the discoverers, and are lost to mankind; it is, to remedy this inconvenience for the future, proposed,

That one society be formed of *virtuosi* or ingenious men, residing in the several colonies, to be called *The American Philosophical Society*, who are to maintain a constant correspondence.

That Philadelphia, being the city nearest the center of the continent colonies, communicating with all of them northward and southward by post, and with all the islands by sea, and having the advantage of a good growing library, be the center of the Society.

That a correspondence, already begun by some intended members, shall be kept up by this Society with the Royal Society of London, and with the Dublin Society.

Benjamin Franklin, the writer of this proposal, offers himself to serve the Society as their secretary, till they shall be provided with one more capable.

ℒ 1746: Colonial Defense

Autobiography, Part III, continued

With respect to defense, Spain having been several years at war against Britain and being at length joined by France, which brought us into greater danger, and the labored and long-continued endeavors of our Governor Thomas to prevail with our Quaker Assembly to pass a militia law and make other provisions for the security of the province having proved abortive, I proposed to try what might be done by a voluntary association of the people. To promote this, I first wrote and published a pamphlet, entitled *Plain Truth*, in which I stated our helpless situation in strong lights, with the necessity of union and discipline for our defense, and promised to propose in a few days an association to be generally signed for that

The first-known political cartoon in the colonies, attributed to Franklin

purpose. The pamphlet had a sudden and surprising effect. I was called upon for the instrument of association; and having settled the draft of it with a few friends, I appointed a meeting of the citizens. The house was pretty full. I had prepared a number of printed copies, and provided pens and ink dispersed all over the room. I harangued them a little on the subject, read the paper, and explained it, and then distributed the copies, which were eagerly signed, not the least objection being made.

When the company separated and the papers were collected, we found about twelve hundred signatures; and other copies being dispersed in the country, the subscribers amounted at length to upward of ten thousand. These all furnished themselves as soon as they could with arms, formed themselves into companies and regiments, chose their own officers, and met every week to be instructed in the manual exercise and other parts of military discipline. The women, by subscriptions among themselves, provided silk colors, which they presented to the companies, painted with different devices and mottoes which I supplied.

The officers of the companies composing the Philadelphia regiment, being met, chose me for their colonel; but conceiving myself unfit, I declined that station and recommended Mr. Lawrence, a fine person and man of influence, who was accordingly appointed. I then proposed a lottery to defray the expense of building a battery below the town and furnishing it with cannon. It filled expeditiously, and the battery was soon erected, the merlons being framed of logs and filled with earth. We bought some old cannon from Boston, but these not being sufficient, we wrote to England for more, soliciting at the same time our Proprietaries for some assistance, though without much expectation of obtaining it.

Meanwhile Colonel Lawrence, William Allen, Abraham Taylor, Esquires, and myself were sent to New York by the associators, commissioned to borrow some cannon of Governor Clinton. He at first refused us peremptorily; but at a dinner with his council where there was great drinking of Madeira wine, as the custom at that place then was, he softened by degrees and said he would lend us six. After a few more bumpers he advanced to ten. And at length he very good-naturedly conceded eighteen. They were fine cannon, eighteen-pounders, with their carriages, which were soon transported and mounted on our batteries, where the associators kept a nightly guard while the war lasted. And among the rest I regularly took my turn of duty there as a common soldier.

In order of time, I should have mentioned before that, having in 1742 invented an open stove for the better warming of rooms and at the same time saving fuel, as the fresh air admitted was warmed in entering, I made a present of the model to Mr. Robert Grace, one of my early friends, who having an iron furnace, found the casting of the plates for these stoves a profitable thing. Governor Thomas was so pleased with the construction of this stove that he offered to give me a patent for the sole vending of them for a term of years; but I declined it from a principle which has ever weighed with me on such occasions; viz., *that as we enjoy great advantages from the inventions of others, we should be glad of an opportunity to serve others by any invention of ours, and this we should do freely and generously.*

An ironmonger in London, however, after making some small changes in the machine, which rather hurt its operation, got a patent for it there, and made, as I was told, a little fortune by it. And this is not the only instance of patents taken out for my inventions by others, though not always with the same success, which I never contested, as having no desire of profiting by patents myself and hating disputes. The use of these fireplaces in very many houses both here in Pennsylvania and the neighboring states, has been and is a great saving of wood to the inhabitants.

Peace being concluded, I turned my thoughts again to the affair of establishing an academy. The first step I took was to associate in the design a number of active friends, of whom the Junto furnished a good part; the next was to write and publish a pamphlet entitled *Proposals Relating to the Education of Youth in Pennsylvania*. This I distributed among the principal inhabitants gratis.

1749: Colonial Education

Franklin's proposals revealed his own early attitudes toward educating the new generations. His own natural son, William, was about nineteen in 1749 when Franklin proposed as a course of study a "fair hand," arithmetic, accounts, English, geography, chronology, ancient customs, morality, history and languages (different ones for different professions or callings). He advocated also special uniforms, plain diet and frequent exercise in "running, leaping, wrestling and swimming," etc.

Proposals Relating to the Education of Youth

ADVERTISEMENT TO THE READER

It has long been regretted as a misfortune to the youth of this province, that we have no Academy, in which they might receive the accomplishments of a regular education. The following paper of hints toward forming a plan for that purpose, is so far approved by some public-spirited gentlemen, to whom it has been privately communicated, that they have directed a number of copies to be made by the press, and properly distributed, in order to obtain the sentiments and advice of men of learning, understanding, and experience in these matters; and have determined to use their interest and best endeavors, to have the scheme, when completed, carried gradually into execution; in which they have reason to believe they shall have the hearty concurrence and assistance of many who are well-wishers to their country. Those who incline to favor the design with their advice, either as to the parts of learning to be taught, the order of study, the method of teaching, the economy of the school, or any other matter of importance to the success of the undertaking, are desired to communicate their sentiments as soon as may be, by letter directed to B. Franklin, Printer, in Philadelphia.

PROPOSALS

The good education of youth has been esteemed by wise men in all ages, as the surest foundation of the happiness both of private families and of commonwealths. Almost all governments have therefore made it a principal object of their attention, to establish and endow with proper revenues, such seminaries of learning, as might supply the succeeding age with men qualified to serve the public with honor to themselves, and to their country.

Many of the first settlers of these provinces were men who had received a good education in *Europe*, and to their wisdom and good management we owe much of our present prosperity. But their hands were full, and they could not do all things. The present race are not thought to be generally of equal ability: For though the *American* youth are allowed not to want capacity; yet the best capacities require cultivation, it being truly with them, as with the best ground, which unless well tilled and sowed with profitable seed, produces only ranker weeds.

With the whole should be constantly inculcated and cultivated, that *benignity of mind*, which shows itself in *searching for* and *seizing* every opportunity *to serve* and *to oblige;* and is the foundation of what is called good breeding; highly useful to the possessor, and most agreeable to all.

The idea of what is *true merit* should also be often presented to youth, explained and impressed on their minds, as consisting in an *inclination* joined with an *ability* to serve mankind, one's country, friends and family; which *ability* is (with the blessing of God) to be acquired or greatly increased by *true learning;* and should indeed be the great *aim* and *end* of all learning.

Autobiography, Part III, continued

As soon as I could suppose their minds a little prepared by the perusal of it, I set on foot a subscription for opening and supporting an academy; it was to be paid in quotas yearly for five years; by so dividing it I judged the subscription might be larger, and I believe it was so, amounting to no less, if I remember right, than five thousand pounds.

The subscribers, to carry the project into immediate execution, chose out of their number twenty-four trustees and appointed Mr. Francis, then attorney general, and myself to draw up constitutions for the government of the academy, which being done and signed, a house was hired, masters engaged, and the schools opened, I think, in the same year, 1749.

The scholars increasing fast, the house was soon found too small, and we were looking out for a piece of ground properly situated, with intention to build, when accident threw into our way a large house ready built, which with a few alterations might well serve our purpose.

The whole care and trouble of agreeing with the workmen, purchasing materials, and superintending the work, fell upon me, and I went through it the more cheerfully, as it did not then interefere with my private business, having the year before taken a very able, industrious, and honest partner, Mr. David Hall, with whose character I was well acquainted, as he had worked for me four years. He took off my hands all care of the printing office, paying me punctually my share of the profits. This partnership continued eighteen years, successfully for us both.

Thus was established the present University of Philadelphia. I have been continued one of its trustees from the beginning (now near forty years), and have had the very great pleasure of seeing a number of the youth who have received their education in it, distinguished by their improved abilities, serviceable in public stations, and ornaments to their country.

◢1748: Retired at Forty-two

On January 1, 1748, Franklin retired from active participation in his printing business. He was forty-two years old, eager to enjoy the life of a man of leisure and to devote himself to being a philosopher—or what has since been termed a scientist.

To Cadwallader Colden in New York

September 29, 1748

I congratulate you on your return to your beloved retirement. I, too, am taking the proper measures for obtaining leisure to enjoy life and my friends, more than heretofore, having put my printing house under the care of my partner, David Hall, absolutely left off bookselling, and removed to a more quiet part of the town, where I am settling my old accounts, and hope soon to be quite master of my own time, and no longer, as the song has it, "at everyone's call but my own." If health continue, I hope to be able in another year to visit the most distant friend I have, without inconvenience.

With the same views I have refused engaging further in public affairs. The share I had in the late Association, etc., having given me a little present run of popularity, there was a pretty general intention of choosing me a representative of the city at the next election of assemblymen; but I have desired all my friends, who spoke to me about it, to discourage it, declaring that I would not serve, if chosen. Thus you see I am in a fair way of having no other tasks, than such as I shall like to give myself, and of enjoying what I look upon as a great happiness, leisure to read, study, make experiments, and converse at large with such ingenious and worthy men, as are pleased to honor me with their friendship or acquaintance, on such points as may produce something for the common benefit of mankind, uninterrupted by the little cares and fatigues of business. Among other pleasures I promise myself, that of corresponding more frequently and fully with Dr. Colden is none of the least. I shall only wish that what must be so agreeable to me may not prove troublesome to you. . . .

✐ 1748-49: Public Service

Independent and at leisure, Franklin could not refuse the calls to public office which were thrust on him. Writing his *Autobiography* in 1788, years after he had broken with his son, who remained loyal to the English crown in the American War for Independence, Franklin no longer used the warm, intimate style of Part I, which was addressed to his "Dear Son." William Franklin is mentioned, but not by name, in Part III. When William succeeded his father as clerk of the Pennsylvania Assembly, Franklin indicated some disapproval of the young man's indolence and indulgence—a note which is never sounded in the *Autobiography*.

Autobiography, Part III, continued

When I disengaged myself, as above mentioned, from private business, I flattered myself that, by the sufficient though moderate fortune I had acquired, I had found leisure during the rest of my life for philosophical studies and amusements; I purchased all Dr. Spence's apparatus, who had come from England to lecture in Philadelphia; and I proceeded in my electrical experiments with great alacrity.

But the public now considering me as a man of leisure, laid hold of me for their purposes—every part of our civil government, and almost at the same time, imposing some duty upon me. The Governor put me into the commission of the peace; the corporation of the city chose me one of the common council and soon after alderman; and the citizens at large elected me a burgess to represent them in Assembly. This latter station was the more agreeable to me, as I grew at length tired with sitting there to hear debates in which as clerk I could take no part, and which were often so uninteresting that I was induced to amuse myself with making magic squares or circles, or anything to avoid weariness. And I conceived my becoming a member would enlarge my power of doing good. I would not, however, insinuate that my ambition was not flattered by all these promotions. It certainly was. For considering my low beginning, they were great things to me. And they were still more

Deborah Franklin

*Benjamin Franklin
in his early forties*

pleasing as being so many spontaneous testimonies of the public's good opinion, and by me entirely unsolicited.

The office of justice of the peace I tried a little, by attending a few courts and sitting on the bench to hear causes. But finding that more knowledge of the common law than I possessed was necessary to act in that station with credit, I gradually withdrew from it, excusing myself by my being obliged to attend the higher duties of a legislator in the Assembly. My election to this trust was repeated every year for ten years without my ever asking any elector for his vote or signifying either directly or indirectly any desire of being chosen. On taking my seat in the House, my son was appointed their clerk.

To Mrs. Abiah Franklin in Boston

Philadelphia, April 12, 1750

Honored Mother:

We received your kind letter, and we are glad to hear you still enjoy such a measure of health, notwithstanding your great age.

As to your grandchildren, Will is now nineteen years of age, a tall, proper youth, and much of a beau. He acquired a habit of idleness on the expedition, but begins of late to apply himself to business, and I hope will become an industrious man. He imagined his father had got enough for him, but I have assured him that I intend to spend what little I have myself, if it please God that I live long enough; and, as he by no means wants sense, he can see by my going on that I mean to be as good as my word.

Sally grows a fine girl, and is extremely industrious with her needle, and delights in her book. She is of a most affectionate temper, and perfectly dutiful and obliging to her parents and to all. Perhaps I flatter myself too much, but I have hopes that she will prove an ingenious, sensible, notable, and worthy woman, like her Aunt Jenny. She goes now to the dancing school.

For my own part, at present, I pass my time agreeably enough. I enjoy, through mercy, a tolerable share of health. I read a great deal, ride a little, do a little business for myself, more for others, retire when I can, and go into company when I please; so the years roll around, and the last will come, when I would rather have it said "He lived usefully" than "He died rich."

I am your dutiful son. . . .

Autobiography, Part III, continued

The year following [1749], a treaty being to be held with the Indians at Carlisle, the Governor sent a message to the House proposing that they should nominate some of their members to be joined with some members of Council as commissioners for that purpose. The House named the Speaker (Mr. Norris) and myself; and being commissioned, we went to Carlisle and met the Indians accordingly.

1750: The Cause of Storms

Now a man of many affairs, Franklin still retained his powers of observation and his profound sense of the logic of natural events and phenomena. His scientific interests were supplemented by his travels, the growing circulation of colonial newspapers and his concise, clear and indefatigable letter-writing.

To Jared Eliot in Connecticut

February 13, 1749/1750

Dear Sir:

You desire to know my thoughts about the northeast storms beginning to leeward. Some years since, there was an eclipse of the moon at nine o'clock in the evening, which I intended to observe; but before night a storm blew up at northeast, and continued violent all night and all the next day; the sky thick-clouded, dark, and rainy, so that neither moon nor stars could be seen. The storm did a great deal of damage all along the coast, for we had accounts of it in the newspapers from Boston, Newport, New York, Maryland, and Virginia. But what surprised me was to find in the Boston newspapers an account of an observation of that eclipse made there; for I thought, as the storm came from the northeast, it must have been sooner at Boston than with us, and consequently have prevented such observation. I wrote to my brother about it, and he informed me that the eclipse was over there an hour before the storm began. Since which I have made inquiries from time to time of travelers, and of my correspondents northeastward and southwestward, and observed the accounts in the newspapers from New England, New York, Maryland, Virginia, and South Carolina; and I find it to be a constant fact that northeast storms begin to go leeward and are often more violent there than farther to windward.

As to the reason of this, I can only give you my conjectures. Suppose a great tract of country, land and sea, to wit, Florida and the Bay of Mexico, to have clear weather for several days, and to be heated by the sun, and its air thereby exceedingly rarefied. Suppose the country northeastward, as Pennsylvania, New England, Nova Scotia, and Newfoundland, to be at the same time covered with clouds, and its air chilled and condensed. The rarefied air being lighter must rise, and the denser air next to it will press into its place; that will be followed by the next denser air, that by the next, and so on. Thus, when I have a fire in my chimney, there is a current of air constantly flowing from the door to the chimney; but the beginning of the motion was at the chimney, where the air being rarefied by the fire rising, its place was supplied by the cooler air that was next to it, and the place of that by the next, and so on to the door. So the water in a long sluice or mill-race, being stopped by a gate, is at rest like the air in a calm; but as soon as you open the gate at one end to let it out, the water next the gate begins first to move, that which is next to it follows; and so, though the water proceeds forward to the gate, the motion which began there runs backward, if one may so speak, to the upper end of the race, where the water is last in motion. We have on this continent a long ridge of mountains running from northeast to southwest, and the coast runs the same course. These may, perhaps, contribute toward the direction of the winds, or at least influence them in some degree. If these conjectures do not satisfy you, I wish to have yours on the subject. . . .

✐ 1751: Colonial Affairs

Autobiography, Part III, continued

In 1751 Dr. Thomas Bond, a particular friend of mine, conceived the idea of establishing a hospital in Philadelphia—a very beneficent design for the reception and cure of poor, sick persons, whether inhabitants of the province or strangers, which has been ascribed to me but was originally and truly his. He was zealous and active in endeavoring to procure subscriptions for it; but the proposal being a novelty in America and at first not well understood, he met with little success. At length he came to me with the compliment that he found there was no such thing as carrying a public-spirited project through without my being concerned in it. "For," says he, "I am often asked by those to whom I propose subscribing, *'Have you consulted Franklin on this business? And what does he think of it?'* And when I tell them that I have not (supposing it rather out of your line), they do not subscribe but say *they will consider it.*" I inquired into the nature and probable utility of his scheme, and receiving from him a very satisfactory explanation, I not only subscribed to it myself but engaged heartily in the design of procuring subscriptions from others. Previous, however, to the solicitation, I endeavored to prepare the minds of the people by writing on the subject in the newspapers, which was my usual custom in such cases, but which Dr. Bond had omitted. The subscriptions afterward were more free and generous.

Having been for some time employed by the postmaster general

The snake, first drawn by Franklin (above), *became the colonies' symbol*

of America as his comptroller, in regulating the several offices and bringing the officers to account, I was upon his death in 1753 appointed jointly with Mr. William Hunter to succeed him by a commission from the postmaster general in England. The American office had never hitherto paid anything to that of Britain. We were to have £600 a year between us if we could make that sum out of the profits of the office. To do this, a variety of improvements were necessary; some of these were inevitably at first expensive, so that in the first four years the office became above £900 in debt to us. But it soon after began to repay us, and before I was displaced by a freak of the ministers [pp. 193–94], we had brought it to yield *three times* as much clear revenue to the Crown as the Post Office of Ireland. Since that imprudent transaction, they have received from it—not one farthing.

The business of the post office occasioned my taking a journey this year to New England, where the College of Cambridge, of their own motion, presented me with the degree of Master of Arts. Yale College in Connecticut had before made me a similar compliment. Thus without studying in any college I came to partake of their honors. They were conferred in consideration of my improvements and discoveries in the electric branch of natural philosophy.

In 1754 war with France being again apprehended, a congress of commissioners from the different colonies was by an order of the Lords of Trade to be assembled at Albany, there to confer with the chiefs of the Six Nations concerning the means of defending both their country and ours. Governor Hamilton having received this order, acquainted the House with it, requesting they would furnish proper presents for the Indians to be given on this occasion, and naming the Speaker (Mr. Norris) and myself to join Mr. John Penn and Mr. Secretary Peters as commissioners to act for Pennsylvania.

In our way thither, I projected and drew up a plan for the union of all the colonies under one government, so far as might be necessary for defense and other important general purposes. By this plan the general government was to be administered by a president general appointed and supported by the Crown and a grand council to be chosen by the representatives of the people of the several colonies met in their respective assemblies. Many objections and difficulties were started, but at length they were all overcome, and the plan was unanimously agreed to, and copies ordered to be transmitted to the Board of Trade and to the assemblies of the several provinces. Its fate was singular. The assemblies did not adopt it, as they all thought there was too much *prerogative* in it; and in England it was judged to have too much of the *democratic*. The colonies so united would have been sufficiently strong to have defended themselves; there would then have been no need of troops from England; the subsequent pretense for taxing America and the bloody contest it occasioned would have been avoided. But such mistakes are not new; history is full of the errors of states and princes.

In my journey to Boston this year, I met at New York with our new governor, Mr. Morris, just arrived there from England, with whom I had been before intimately acquainted. He brought a commission to supersede Mr. Hamilton, who, tired with the disputes his proprietary instructions subjected him to, had resigned.

1755: "Dear Katy"

Returning from Boston in January 1755, Franklin had as a traveling companion, twenty-three-year-old Catherine Ray, who was returning to her home on Block Island, off the coast of Rhode Island. Franklin's open affection for "Dear Katy" began the pattern of several other relationships with young women, who regarded him in return with all the love for a famous and indulgent ideal father.

Until this point in his fiftieth year, Franklin is not known to have corresponded with women. Several quick letters passed between Franklin and Catherine but no copies survive of these very first communications, which may have seemed indiscreet. Franklin did not meet Catherine again until 1763, by which time she was married to William Greene and the mother of the first two of her six children. After that, they saw each other only twice more, though their correspondence continued throughout Franklin's lifetime.

To Miss Catherine Ray on Block Island

Philadelphia, March 4, 1755

Dear Katy:

It gives me great pleasure to hear that you got home safe and well that day. I thought too much was hazarded, when I saw you put off to sea in that very little skiff, tossed by every wave. But the call was strong and just—a sick parent. I stood on the shore and looked after you till I could no longer distinguish you even with my glass; then returned to your sister's, praying for your safe passage. Toward evening all agreed that you must certainly be arrived before that time, the weather having been so favorable, which made me more easy and cheerful, for I had been truly concerned for you.

I left New England slowly, and with great reluctance. Short day's journeys, and loitering visits on the road for three or four weeks, manifested my unwillingness to quit a country in which I drew my first breath, spent my earliest and most pleasant days, and had now received so many fresh marks of the people's goodness and benevolence, in the kind and affectionate treatment I had everywhere met with. I almost forgot I had a *home*, till I was more than halfway toward it; till I had, one by one, parted with all my New England friends, and was got into the western borders of Connecticut, among mere strangers. Then like an old man who, having buried all he loved in this world, begins to think of heaven, I began to think of and wish for home; and as I drew nearer, I found the attraction stronger and stronger. My diligence and speed increased with my impatience. I drove on violently, and made such long stretches that a very few days brought me to my own house, and to the arms of my good old wife and children, where I remain, thanks to God, at present well and happy.

Persons subject to the *hyp* complain of the northeast wind, as increasing their malady. But since you promised to send me kisses in that wind, and I find you as good as your word, it is to me the gayest wind that blows, and gives me the best spirits. I write this during a northeast storm of snow, the greatest we have had this winter. Your favors come mixed with the snowy fleeces, which are pure as your virgin innocence, white as your lovely bosom, and—as cold. But let it warm toward some worthy young man, and may Heaven bless you both with every kind of happiness.

Philadelphia, September 11, 1755

BEGONE, business, for an hour, at least, and let me chat a little with my Katy.

You ask in your last how I do, and what I am doing, and whether everybody loves me yet, and why I make them do so.

In regard to the first I can say, thanks to God, that I do not remember I was ever better. I still relish all the pleasures of life that a temperate man can in reason desire, and through favor I have them all in my power. This happy situation shall continue as long as God pleases, who knows what is best for his creatures, and I hope will enable me to bear with patience and dutiful submission any change he may think fit to make that is less agreeable. As to the second question, I must confess (but don't you be jealous) that many more people love me now than ever did before; for since I saw you I have been enabled to do some general services to the country and to the army, for which both have thanked and praised me, and say they love me. They say so, as you used to do; and if I were to ask any favors of them, they would, perhaps, as readily refuse me; so that I find little real advantage in being beloved, but it pleases my humor.

You have spun a long thread, five thousand and twenty-two yards. It will reach almost from Rhode Island hither. I wish I had hold of one end of it, to pull you to me. But you would break it rather than come. The cords of love and friendship are longer and stronger, and in times past have drawn me farther; even back from England to Philadelphia. I guess that some of the same kind will one day draw you out of that island.

Mrs. Franklin was very proud that a young lady should have so much regard for her old husband as to send him such a present [an English cheese]. She is sure you are a sensible girl, and a notable housewife, and talks of bequeathing me to you as a legacy; but I ought to wish you a better, and hope she will live these hundred years; for we are grown old together, and if she has any faults I am so used to them that I don't perceive them. Indeed, I begin to think she has none, as I think of you. And since she is willing I should love you as much as you are willing to be loved by me, let us join in wishing the old lady a long life and a happy.

October 16, 1755

Dear Katy:

I hear you are now in Boston, gay and lovely as usual. Let me give you some fatherly advice. Kill no more pigeons than you can eat —be a good girl and don't forget your catechism.—Go constantly to meeting—or church—till you get a good husband—then stay at home, & nurse the children, and live like a Christian—Spend your spare hours in sober whist, prayers, or learning to cipher—You must practice *addition* to your husband's estate, by industry and frugality; *subtraction* of all unnecessary expenses; *multiplication* (I would gladly have taught you that myself, but you thought it was time enough, and wouldn't learn) he will soon make you a mistress of it. As to *division*, I say with Brother Paul, *Let there be no division among ye*. But as your good Sister Hubbard (my love to her) is well acquainted with *The Rule of Two*, I hope you will become an expert in the *Rule of Three*; that when I have again the pleasure of seeing you, I may find you like my grape vine, surrounded with clusters, plump, juicy, blushing, pretty little rogues, like their mama. Adieu. The bell rings, and I must go among the grave ones, and talk politics.

✒ 1755: Military Affairs

Autobiography, Part III, continued

These public quarrels were all at bottom owing to the Proprietaries, our hereditary governors, who when any expense was to be incurred for the defense of their province, with incredible meanness instructed their deputies to pass no act for levying the necessary taxes unless their vast estates were in the same act expressly exonerated; and they had even taken the bonds of these deputies to observe such instructions. The Assemblies for three years held out against this injustice, though constrained to bend at last. At length Captain Denny, who was Governor Morris's successor, ventured to disobey those instructions; how that was brought about I shall show hereafter.

But I am got forward too fast with my story; there are still some transactions to be mentioned that happened during the administration of Governor Morris.

The British government, not choosing to permit the union of the colonies as proposed at Albany and to trust that union with their defense, lest they should thereby grow too military and feel their own strength; suspicions and jealousies at this time being entertained of them, sent over General Braddock with two regiments of regular English troops for that purpose. He landed at Alexandria in Virginia and thence marched to Frederick in Maryland, where he halted for carriages. Our Assembly apprehending, from some information, that he had received violent prejudices against them, as averse to the service, wished me to wait upon him, not as from them, but as postmaster general, under the guise of proposing to settle with him the mode of conducting with most celerity and certainty the dispatches between him and the governors of the several provinces, with whom he must necessarily have continual correspondence, and of which they proposed to pay the expense. My son accompanied me on this journey.

We found the General at Frederick, waiting impatiently for the return of those he had sent through the back parts of Maryland and Virginia to collect wagons. I stayed with him several days, dined with him daily, and had full opportunity of removing all his prejudices by the information of what the Assembly had before his arrival actually done and were still willing to do to facilitate his operations. When I was about to depart, the returns of wagons to be obtained were brought in, by which it appeared that they amounted only to twenty-five, and not all of those were in serviceable condition. The General and all the officers were surprised, declared the expedition was then at an end, being impossible, and exclaimed against the ministers for ignorantly landing them in a country destitute of the means of conveying their stores, baggage, etc., not less than 150 wagons being necessary.

I happened to say I thought it was pity they had not been landed rather in Pennsylvania, as in that country almost every farmer had his wagon. The General eagerly laid hold of my words and said, "Then you, sir, who are a man of interest there, can probably procure them for us; and I beg you will undertake it." I asked what terms were to be offered the owners of the wagons, and I was desired to put on paper the terms that appeared to me necessary. This I did, and they were agreed to, and a commission and instructions accordingly prepared immediately.

I received of the General about £800 to be disbursed in advance money to the wagon owners, etc.; but that sum being insufficient, I advanced upward of £200 more, and in two weeks the 150 wagons with 259 carrying horses were on their march for the camp. [My] advertisement promised payment according to the valuation in case any wagon or horse should be lost. The owners, however, alleging they did not know General Braddock, or what dependence might be had on his promise, insisted on my bond for the performance, which I accordingly gave them.

The General was highly satisfied with my conduct in procuring him the wagons, etc., etc., and readily paid my account of disbursements, thanking me repeatedly and requesting my further assistance in sending provisions after him. I undertook this also and was busily employed in it till we heard of his defeat, advancing, for the service, of my own money upward of £ 1,000 sterling, of which I sent him an account. It came to his hands, luckily for me, a few days before the battle, and he returned me immediately an order on the paymaster for the round sum of £ 1,000, leaving the remainder to the next account. I consider this payment as good luck, having never been able to obtain that remainder—of which more hereafter.

This General was, I think, a brave man, and might probably have made a figure as a good officer in some European war. But he had too much self-confidence, too high an opinion of the validity of regular troops, and too mean a one of both Americans and Indians. George Croghan, our Indian interpreter, joined him on his march with one hundred of those people, who might have been of great use to his army as guides, scouts, etc., if he had treated them kindly; but he slighted and neglected them, and they gradually left him. In conversation with him one day, he was giving me some account of his intended progress. "After taking Fort Duquesne," said he, "I am to proceed to Niagara, and having taken that, to Frontenac, if the season will allow time, and I suppose it will; for Duquesne can hardly detain me above three or four days; and then I see nothing that can obstruct my march to Niagara." Having before revolved in my mind the long line his army must make in their march by a very narrow road to be cut for them through the woods and bushes, and also what I had read of a former defeat of 1,500 French who invaded the Illinois country, I had conceived some doubts and some fears for the event of the campaign. But I ventured only to say, "To be sure, sir, if you arrive well before Duquesne with these fine troops so well provided with artillery, the fort, though completely fortified and assisted with a very strong garrison, can probably make but a short resistance. The only danger I apprehend of obstruction to your march, is from the ambuscades of Indians, who by constant practice are dextrous in laying and executing them. And the slender line, near four miles long, which your army must make, may expose it to be attacked by surprise in its flanks, and to be cut like a thread into several pieces, which from their distance cannot come up in time to support each other." He smiled at my ignorance and replied, "These savages may indeed be a formidable enemy to your raw American militia; but upon the King's regular and disciplined troops, sir, it is impossible they should make any impression." I was conscious of an impropriety in my disputing with a military man in matters of his profession and said no more. The enemy, however, did not take the advantage of his army which I apprehended its long line of march exposed it to, but let it advance without interruption till within nine miles of the place; and then when more in a body (for it had just passed a river, where the front had halted till all were come over) and in a more open part of the woods than any it had passed, attacked its advance guard by a heavy fire from behind trees and bushes— which was the first intelligence the General had of an enemy's being near him. This guard being disordered, the General hurried the troops up to their assistance, which was done in great confusion through wagons, baggage, and cattle. And presently the fire came upon their flank; the officers, being on horseback, were more easily distinguished, picked out as marks, and fell very fast; and the soldiers were crowded together in a huddle, having or hearing no orders, and standing to be shot at till two thirds of them were killed, and then being seized with a panic the remainder fled with precipitation.

The wagoners took each a horse out of his team and scampered; their example was immediately followed by others so that all the wagons, provisions, artillery, and stores were left to the enemy. The General, being wounded, was brought off with difficulty; his secretary, Mr. Shirley, was killed by his side; and out of 86 officers, 63 were killed or wounded, and 714 men killed out of 1,100. These 1,100 had been picked men from the whole army, the rest had been left behind with Colonel Dunbar, who was to follow with the heavier part of the stores, provisions, and baggage. The fliers, not being pursued, arrived at Dunbar's camp, and the panic they brought with them instantly seized him and all his people. And though he had now above 1,000 men and the enemy who had beaten Braddock did not at most exceed 400 Indians and French together, instead of proceeding and endeavoring to recover some of the lost honor, he ordered all the stores, ammunition, etc., to be destroyed that he might have more horses to assist his flight toward the settlements and less lumber to remove. He was there met with requests from the governors of Virginia, Maryland, and Pennsylvania that he would post his troops on the frontiers so as to afford some protection to the inhabitants; but he continued his hasty march through all the country, not thinking himself safe till he arrived at Philadelphia, where the inhabitants could protect him. This whole transaction gave us Americans the first suspicion that our exalted ideas of the prowess of British regular troops had not been well founded.

In their first march, too, from their landing till they got beyond the settlements, they had plundered and stripped the inhabitants, totally ruining some poor families, besides insulting, abusing, and confining the people if they remonstrated. This was enough to put us out of conceit of such defenders, if we had really wanted any. How different was the conduct of our French friends in 1781 [during the War for Independence], who during a march through the most inhabited part of our country from Rhode Island to Virginia, near seven hundred miles, occasioned not the smallest complaint for the loss of a pig, a chicken, or even an apple!

As soon as the loss of the wagons and horses was generally known, all the owners came upon me for the valuation which I had given bond to pay. Their demands gave me a great deal of trouble. I acquainted them that the money was ready in the pay-master's hands, but the order for paying it must first be obtained from General Shirley, and that I had applied for it; but he being at a distance, an answer could not soon be received, and they must have patience. All this was not sufficient to satisfy, and some began to sue me. General Shirley at length relieved me from this terrible situation by appointing commissioners to examine the claims, and ordering payment. They amounted to near £20,000, which to pay would have ruined me.

Governor Morris, who had continually worried the Assembly with message after message before the defeat of Braddock to beat them into the making of acts to raise money for the defense of the province without taxing, among others, the proprietary estates, and had rejected all their bills for not having such an exempting clause, now redoubled his attacks, with more hope of success, the danger and necessity being greater. The Assembly however continued firm, believing they had justice on their side and that it would be giving up an essential right if they suffered the Governor to amend their money bills. In one of the last, indeed, which was for granting £50,000, his proposed amendment was only of a single word: the bill expressed "that all estates real and personal were to be taxed, those of the Proprietaries *not* excepted." His amendment was, for *not* read *only*—a small but very material alteration! However, when news of this disaster reached England, our friends there whom we had taken care to furnish with all the Assembly's answers to the Governor's messages, raised a clamor against the Proprietaries for their meanness and injustice in giving their Governor such instructions, some going so far as to say that by obstructing the defense of their province, they forfeited their right to it. They were intimidated by this, and sent orders to their receiver general to add £5,000 of their money to what-ever sum might be given by the Assembly for such purpose. This, being testified to the House, was accepted in lieu of their share of a general tax, and a new bill was formed with an exempting clause which passed accordingly. By this act I was appointed one of the commissioners for disposing of the money, £60,000. I had been active in modeling the bill and procuring its passage, and had at the same time drawn a bill for establishing and disciplining a voluntary militia, which I carried through the House without much difficulty, as care was taken in it to leave the Quakers at liberty.

While the several companies in the city and country were forming and learning their exercise, the Governor prevailed with me to take charge of our Northwestern Frontier, which was infested by the enemy, and provide for the defense of the inhabitants by raising troops, and building a line of forts. I undertook this military business, though I did not conceive myself well qualified for it. He gave me a commission with full powers and a parcel of blank commissions for officers, to be given to whom I thought fit. I had but little difficulty in raising men, having soon 560 under my command. My son, who had in the preceding war been an officer in the army raised against Canada, was my aide-de-camp, and of great use to me.

It was the beginning of January when we set out upon this business of building forts. I sent one detachment toward the Minisink, with instructions to erect one for the security of that upper part of the country; and another to the lower part, with similar instructions. And I concluded to go myself with the rest of my force to Gnadenhut, where a fort was thought more immediately necessary.

I had hardly finished this business and got my fort well stored with provisions when I received a letter from the Governor, acquainting me that he had called the Assembly and wished my attendance there. My three intended forts being now completed, and the inhabitants contented to remain on their farms under that protection, I resolved to return—the more willingly as a New England officer, Colonel Clapham, experienced in Indian war, being on a visit to our establishment, consented to accept the command. I was escorted as far as Bethlehem, where I rested a few days to recover from the fatigue I had undergone. The first night lying in a good bed, I could hardly sleep, it was so different from my hard lodging on the floor of a hut at Gnadenhut, with only a blanket or two.

Being returned to Philadelphia, I found the association went on with great success, the inhabitants that were not Quakers having pretty generally come into it, formed themselves into companies, and [had] chosen their captains, lieutenants, and ensigns according to the new law. The officers' meeting chose me to be colonel of the regiment, which I this time accepted. I forget how many companies we had, but we paraded about 1,200 well-looking men, with a company of artillery who had been furnished with six brass field pieces, which they had become so expert in the use of as to fire twelve times in a minute. The first time I reviewed my regiment, they accompanied me to my house and would salute me with some rounds fired before my door, which shook down and broke several glasses of my electrical apparatus. And my new honor proved not much less brittle, for all our commissions were soon after broken by a repeal of the law in England.

During the short time of my colonelship, being about to set out on a journey to Virginia, the officers of my regiment took it into their heads that it would be proper for them to escort me out of town as far as the lower ferry. Just as I was getting on horseback, they came to my door, between thirty and forty, mounted, and all in their uniforms. I had not been previously acquainted with the project or I should have prevented it, being naturally averse to the assuming of state on any occasion, and I was a good deal chagrined at their appearance as I could not avoid their accompanying me. What made it worse was that as soon as we began to move, they drew their swords and rode with them naked all the way. Somebody wrote an account of this to the Proprietor, and it gave him great offense. No such honor had been paid him when in the province, nor to any of his governors; and he said it was only proper to princes of the blood royal—which may be true for aught I know, who was, and still am, ignorant of the etiquette in such cases. This silly affair, however, greatly increased his rancor against me which was before considerable on account of my conduct in the Assembly respecting the exemption of his estate from taxation, which I had always opposed very warmly, and not without severe reflections on his meanness and injustice in contending for it. He accused me to the ministry as being the great obstacle to the King's service, preventing by my influence in the House the proper form of the bills for raising money; and he instanced this parade with my officers as a proof of my having an intention to take the government of the province out of his hands by force. He also applied to Sir Everard Fauckener, the postmaster general, to deprive me of my office. But it had no other effect than to procure from Sir Everard a gentle admonition.

✐ 1747-52: The Kite

Franklin's interest in electricity began during one of his early visits to Boston, where he saw demonstrations of the newly invented Leyden jar. Franklin is more widely remembered for his practical inventions such as the Franklin stove, bifocal spectacles and the lightning rod, but he was also a pure theoretical scientist. His were the original conceptions of electricity as a single fluid, and he labeled electrical charges as positive and negative, plus and minus—terms still used today. Although his first letters were treated with little respect by the Royal Society in London, Franklin kept on, making notes in his own journals, where his first identification of lightning and electricity was dated November 7, 1749.

Autobiography, Part III, continued

Before I proceed in relating the part I had in public affairs under this new Governor's [Captain Denny's] administration, it may not be amiss here to give some account of the rise and progress of my philosophical reputation.

In 1746 being at Boston, I met there with a Dr. Spence, who was lately arrived from Scotland, and showed me some electric experiments. They were imperfectly performed, as he was not very expert; but being on a subject quite new to me, they equally surprised and pleased me. Soon after my return to Philadelphia, our library company received from Mr. Peter Collinson, F.R.S., of London, a present of a glass tube, with some account of the use of it in making such experiments. I eagerly seized the opportunity of repeating what I had seen at Boston, and by much practice acquired great readiness in performing those also which we had an account of from England, adding a number of new ones. I say much practice, for my house was continually full for some time with persons who came to see these new wonders.

Obliged as we were to Mr. Collinson for the present of the tube, etc., I thought it right he should be informed of our success in using it and wrote him several letters containing accounts of our experiments. He got them read in the Royal Society, where they were not at first thought worth so much notice as to be printed in their transactions.

Early Philadelphia experiment with electricity

To Peter Collinson in London

Sir:

In my last I informed you that, in pursuing our electrical inquiries, we had observed some particular phenomena, which we looked upon to be new, and of which I promised to give you some account, though I apprehended they might possibly not be new to you, as so many hands are daily employed in electrical experiments on your side the water, some or other of which would probably hit on the same observations.

We had for some time been of opinion, that the electrical fire was not created by friction, but collected, being really an element diffused among, and attracted by other matter, particularly by water and metals. We had even discovered and demonstrated its afflux to the electrical sphere, as well as its efflux, by means of little light windmill wheels made of stiff paper vanes, fixed obliquely and turning freely on fine wire axes; also by little wheels of the same matter, but formed like water wheels. Of the disposition and application of which wheels, and the various phenomena resulting, I could, if I had time, fill you a sheet. The impossibility of electrifying one's self (though standing on wax) by rubbing the tube, and drawing the fire from it; and the manner of doing it, by passing the tube near a person or thing standing on the floor, etc., had also occurred to us some months before Mr. *Watson's* ingenious *sequel* came to hand, and these were some of the new things I intended to have communicated to you.

1. A person standing on wax, and rubbing the tube, and another person on wax drawing the fire, they will both of them (provided they do not stand so as to touch one another) appear to be electrified, to a person standing on the floor; that is, he will receive a spark on approaching each of them with his knuckle.

2. But, if the persons on wax touch one another during the exciting of the tube, neither of them will appear to be electrified.

3. If they touch one another after exciting the tube, and drawing the fire as aforesaid, there will be a stronger spark between them, than was between either of them and the person on the floor.

4. After such strong spark, neither of them discover any electricity.

These appearances we attempt to account for thus: We suppose, as aforesaid, that electrical fire is a common element, of which every one of the three persons above mentioned has his equal share, before any operation is begun with the tube. *A*, who stands on wax and rubs the tube, collects the electrical fire from himself into the glass; and his communication with the common stock being cut off by the wax, his body is not again immediately supplied. *B* (who stands on wax likewise), passing his knuckle along near the tube, receives the fire which was collected by the glass from *A*; and his communication with the common stock being likewise cut off, he retains the additional quantity received. To *C*, standing on the floor, both appear to be electrified: for he having only the middle quantity of electrical fire, receives a spark upon approaching *B*, who has an over quantity; but gives one to *A*, who has an under quantity. If *A* and *B* approach to touch each other, the spark is stronger, because the difference between them is greater: After such touch there is no spark between either of them and *C*, because the electrical fire in all is reduced to the original equality. If they touch while electrifying, the equality is never destroyed, the fire only circulating. Hence have arisen some new terms among us: we say *B* (and bodies like circumstanced) is electrified *positively*; *A*, *negatively*. Or rather, *B* is electrified *plus*; *A*, *minus*. And we daily in our experiments electrify bodies *plus or minus*, as we think proper.

To John Lining in Charleston (Excerpt from Franklin's Journal)

"*Nov.* 7, 1749. Electrical fluid agrees with lightning in these particulars: 1. Giving light. 2. Color of the light. 3. Crooked direction. 4. Swift motion. 5. Being conducted by metals. 6. Crack or noise in exploding. 7. Subsisting in water or ice. 8. Rending bodies it passes through. 9. Destroying animals. 10. Melting metals. 11. Firing inflammable substances. 12. Sulfureous smell.—The electric fluid is attracted by points.—We do not know whether this property is in lightning.—But since they agree in all the particulars wherein we can already compare them, is it not probable they agree likewise in this? Let the experiment be made. . . ."

Autobiography, Part III, continued

One paper, on the sameness of lightning with electricity, I sent to Dr. Mitchel, an acquaintance of mine and one of the members also of that Society, who wrote me word that it had been read but was laughed at by the connoisseurs. The papers, however, being shown to Dr. Fothergill, he thought them of too much value to be stifled and advised the printing of them. Mr. Collinson then gave them to [Edward] Cave for publication in his magazine; but he chose to print them separately in a pamphlet, and Dr. Fothergill wrote the preface. Cave, it seems, judged rightly for his profession; for they swelled to a quarto volume, which has had five editions and cost him nothing for copy-money.

It was, however, some time before those papers were much taken notice of in England. A copy of them happening to fall into the hands of the Count De Buffon (a philosopher deservedly of great reputation in France and indeed all over Europe), he prevailed with M. D'Alibard to translate them into French, and they were printed at Paris. My book was translated into the Italian, German, and Latin languages; and the doctrine it contained was by degrees universally adopted by the philosophers of Europe.

What gave my book the more sudden and general celebrity was the success of one of its proposed experiments made by Messrs. D'Alibard and Delor at Marly for drawing lightning from the clouds. This engaged the public attention everywhere. M. Delor, who had an apparatus for experimental philosophy and lectured in that branch of science, undertook to repeat what he called the "Philadelphia experiments," and after they were performed before the King and court, all the curious of Paris flocked to see them. I will not swell this narrative with an account of that capital experiment, or of the infinite pleasure I received in the success of a similar one I made soon after with a kite at Philadelphia, as both are to be found in the histories of electricity.

From Joseph Priestley's "History and Present State of Electricity" (1767)

The greatest discovery which Dr. Franklin made concerning electricity, and which has been of the greatest practical use to mankind, was that of the perfect similarity between electricity and lightning. As every circumstance relating to so capital a discovery as this (the greatest, perhaps, that has been made in the whole compass of

philosophy, since the time of Sir Isaac Newton) cannot but give pleasure to all my readers, I shall endeavor to gratify them with the communication of a few particulars which I have from the best authority [probably Franklin himself].

The Doctor, after having published his method of verifying his hypothesis concerning the sameness of electricity with the matter of lightning, was waiting for the erection of a spire in Philadelphia to carry his views into execution, not imagining that a pointed rod

The kite experiment: decorative panel of a Philadelphia fire engine

of a moderate height could answer the purpose, when it occurred to him that, by means of a common kite, he could have a readier and better access to the regions of thunder than by any spire whatever. Preparing, therefore, a large silk handkerchief and two cross sticks of a proper length on which to extend it, he took the opportunity of the first approaching thunderstorm to take a walk into a field, in which there was a shed convenient for his purpose. But, dreading the ridicule which too commonly attends unsuccessful attempts in science, he communicated his intended experiment to nobody but his son, who assisted him in raising the kite.

The kite being raised, a considerable time elapsed before there was any appearance of its being electrified. One very promising cloud had passed over it without any effect, when, at length, just as he was beginning to despair of his contrivance, he observed some loose threads of the hempen string to stand erect and to avoid one another, just as if they had been suspended on a common conductor. Struck with this promising appearance, he immediately presented his knuckle to the key, and (let the reader judge of the exquisite pleasure he must have felt at that moment) the discovery was complete. He perceived a very evident electric spark. Others succeeded, even before the string was wet, so as to put the matter past all dispute, and when the rain had wet the string, he collected electric fire very copiously. This happened in June 1752, a month after the electricians in France had verified the same theory, but before he heard of anything they had done.

Besides this kite, Dr. Franklin had afterward an insulated iron rod to draw lightning into his house, in order to make experiments whenever there should be a considerable quantity of it in the atmosphere, and that he might not lose any opportunity of that nature, he connected two bells with this apparatus, which gave him notice, by their ringing, whenever his rod was electrified.

1757: Mission to London

Franklin's mission was to have the King's rule substituted for the proprietorship of the Penns. He undertook the perilous sea crossing with his son, William, leaving his wife and daughter behind. Mrs. Franklin was a timid traveler, and there is no record of her venturing farther than the outskirts of New York to see her husband off. Franklin could not know at this point that he would be away for seven years. He made little effort, it seems, to overcome his wife's fear of traveling so that she could accompany him.

Autobiography, Part III, continued

Dr. Wright, an English physician then at Paris, wrote to a friend who was of the Royal Society an account of the high esteem my experiments were in among the learned abroad, and of their wonder that my writings had been so little noticed in England. The Society on this resumed the consideration of the letters that had been read to them, and the celebrated Dr. Watson drew up a summary account of them and of all I had afterward sent to England on the subject, which he accompanied with some praise of the writer. And some members of the Society in London, particularly the very ingenious Mr. Canton, having verified the experiment of procuring lightning from the clouds by a pointed rod and acquainted them with the success, they soon made me more than amends for the slight with which they had before treated me. Without my having made any application for that honor, they chose me a member and voted that I should be excused the customary payments, which would have amounted to twenty-five guineas, and ever since have given me their transactions gratis. They also presented me with the Gold Medal of Sir Godfrey Copley for the year 1753.

Our new Governor, Captain Denny, brought over for me the beforementioned medal from the Royal Society, which he presented to me at an entertainment given him by the city. He accompanied it with very polite expressions of his esteem for me, having, as he said, been long acquainted with my character. After dinner, when the company, as was customary at that time, were engaged in drinking, he took me aside into another room and acquainted me that he had been advised by his friends in England to cultivate a friendship with me, as one who was capable of giving him the best advice, and of contributing most effectually to the making his administration easy. He said much to me also of the Proprietor's good dispositions toward the province and of the advantage it would be to us all, and to me in particular, if the opposition that had been so long continued to his measures were dropped and harmony restored between him and the people, in effecting which it was thought no one could be more service-able than myself, and I might depend on adequate acknowledg-ments and recompenses, etc., etc.

My answers were to this purpose: that my circumstances, thanks to God, were such as to make proprietary favors unnecessary to me; and that being a member of the Assembly, I could not pos-sibly accept of any; that, however, I had no personal enmity to the Proprietary; and that whenever the public measures he pro-posed should appear to be for the good of the people, no one would espouse and forward them more zealously than myself; and that he might rely on everything in my power to make his admin-istration as easy to him as possible, hoping at the same time that he had not brought with him the same unfortunate instructions his predecessor had been hampered with. On this he did not then explain himself. But when he afterward came to do business with the Assembly, they appeared again; the disputes were renewed; and I was as active as ever in the opposition, being the penman first of the request to have a communication of the instructions and then of the remarks upon them, which may be found in the Votes of the Time and in the historical review I afterward pub-lished. But between us personally no enmity arose; we were often together; he was a man of letters, had seen much of the world, and was very entertaining and pleasing in conversation. He gave me the first information that my old friend Jas. Ralph was still alive, that he was esteemed one of the best political writers in England, and had obtained a pension of three hundred a year; that his reputation was indeed small as a poet, [Alexander] Pope having damned his poetry in the *Dunciad*, but his prose was thought as good as any man's.

The Assembly finally, finding the Proprietaries obstinately persisted in manacling their deputies with instructions inconsistent not only with the privileges of the people but with the service of the Crown, resolved to petition the King against them, and appointed me their agent to go over to England to present and support the petition. The House had sent up a bill to the Governor granting a sum of £60,000 for the King's use (£10,000 of which was subjected to the orders of the then General, Lord Loudon), which the Governor in compliance with his instructions absolutely refused to pass. I had agreed with Captain Morris, of the packet at New York, for my passage, and my stores were put on board, when Lord Loudon arrived at Philadelphia, expressly, as he told me, to endeavor an accommodation between the Governor and Assembly, that his Majesty's service might not be obstructed by their dissensions.

But in the meantime the packet had sailed with my sea stores, which was some loss to me, and my only recompense was his Lordship's thanks for my service, all the credit of obtaining the accommodation falling to his share.

He set out for New York before me; and as the time for dispatching the packet boats was in his disposition and there were two then remaining there, one of which he said was to sail very soon, I requested to know the precise time that I might not miss her by any delay of mine.

This daily expectation of sailing, and all the three packets going down to Sandy Hook to join the fleet there, the passengers thought it best to be on board, lest by a sudden order the ships should sail and they be left behind. There, if I remember right, we were about six weeks, consuming our sea stores and obliged to procure more.

To Mrs. Deborah Franklin in Philadelphia

Trenton, April 5, 1757

My dear Child:

We found the roads much better than we expected and got here well before night. About a dozen of our friends accompanied us quite hither, to see us out of the province, and we spent a very agreeable evening together. I leave home, and undertake this long voyage more cheerfully, as I can rely on your prudence in the management of my affairs, and education of my dear child; and yet I cannot forbear once more recommending her to you with a father's tenderest concern. My love to all. Billy presents his duty and love to all. I am your affectionate husband. . . .

New York, Friday, May 27, 1757, Afternoon

My dear Debby:

All the packets are to sail together with the fleet, but when that will be is yet uncertain. For yesterday came in three privateers with several prizes, and by them there is advice that the French fleet, which was in the West Indies, is gone to the northward; and now 'tis questioned whether it will be thought prudent for these transports to sail till there is certain advice that the grand fleet is arrived from England. This, however, is only town talk.

I have been very low-spirited all day. This tedious state of uncertainty and long waiting has almost worn out my patience. I know not when I have spent time so uselessly as since I left Philadelphia.

I left my best spectacles on the table. Please to send them to me.

New York, June 2, 1757

My dear Child:

. . . It is now said we are all to go on board tomorrow, and fall down to the Hook. I hope it will be so, for, having now nothing to do, my stay here is extremely tedious. . . .

I hope my dear Sally will behave in every thing to your satisfaction, and mind her learning and improvement. As my absence
will make your house quieter and lessen your business, you will
have more leisure to instruct her and form her. I pray God to
bless you both, and that we may once more have a happy meeting.
God preserve, guard and guide you.

Autobiography, Part III, concluded

At length the fleet sailed, the General and all his army on board,
bound to Lewisburg with intent to besiege and take that for-
tress; all the packet boats in company, ordered to attend the
General's ship, ready to receive his dispatches when they should
be ready. We were out five days before we got a letter with leave
to part, and then our ship quitted the fleet and steered for England.

We were several times chased in our passage, but outsailed
everything and in thirty days had soundings. We had a good
observation, and the captain judged himself so near our port
(Falmouth) that if we made a good run in the night, we might
be off the mouth of the harbor in the morning, and by running
in the night might escape the notice of the enemy's privateers,
who often cruised near the entrance of the Channel. Accordingly,
all the sail was set that we could possibly make, and the wind
being very fresh and fair, we stood right before it and made
great way. The captain after his observation, shaped his course,
as he thought, so as to pass wide of the Scilly Rocks; but it seems
there is sometimes a strong current setting up St. George's Channel
which deceives seamen. This was probably also the cause of what
happened to us. We had a watchman placed in the bow to whom
they often called, "Look well out before, there"; and he as often
answered, "Aye, aye!" But perhaps had his eyes shut and was half
asleep at the time, they sometimes answering, as is said, mechan-
ically. For he did not see a light just before us which had been
hid by the studding sails from the man at helm and from the rest

of the watch, but by an accidental yaw of the ship was discovered and occasioned a great alarm—we being very near it, the light appearing to me as large as a cartwheel. It was midnight, and our captain fast asleep. But Captain Kennedy jumping upon deck and seeing the danger, ordered the ship to wear around, all sails standing; an operation dangerous to the masts, but it carried us clear, and we avoided shipwreck, for we were running right upon the rocks on which the lighthouse was erected. This

English fleet near Lewisburg, 1758,
during French and Indian War

deliverance impressed me strongly with the utility of lighthouses and made me resolve to encourage the building some of them in America, if I should live to return thither.

In the morning it was found by the soundings, etc., that we were near our port, but a thick fog hid the land from our sight. About nine o'clock the fog began to rise and seemed to be lifted up from the water like the curtain at a theater, discovering underneath the town of Falmouth, the vessels in its harbor, and

the fields that surrounded it. This was a most pleasing spectacle to those who had been long without any other prospect than the uniform view of a vacant ocean! And it gave us the more pleasure, as we were now freed from the anxieties which had arisen.

I set out immediately, with my son, for London, and we only stopped a little by the way to view Stonehenge on Salisbury Plain, and Lord Pembroke's house and gardens, with the very curious antiquities, at Wilton.

We arrived in London the 27th of July, 1757.

✐ 1757: Craven Street

The edition of Benjamin Franklin's *Autobiography* edited by his grandson, William Temple Franklin and published in 1818, ends at this point in 1757. The following pages written in Franklin's hand, sometimes referred to as *Autobiography IV*, were discovered by John Bigelow and published as part of a whole new edition in 1868.

Franklin found lodgings at 7 (later 36) Craven Street, Strand, in the house of Margaret Stevenson, which became his home in London for all of the eighteen years that he was there. Mrs. Stevenson and her eighteen-year-old daughter, Mary, better known as Polly, became his lifelong friends. In addition to his son, William, Franklin was accompanied by a Negro slave, Peter. William Franklin was enrolled in the Middle Temple to study for the bar.

Autobiography, Part IV

As soon as I was settled in a lodging Mr. Charles had provided for me, I went to visit Dr. Fothergill, to whom I was strongly recommended and whose counsel respecting my proceedings I was advised to obtain. He was against an immediate complaint to government and thought the Proprietaries should first be personally applied to.

Franklin disobeyed his doctor's orders to sit for this miniature.

To Mrs. Deborah Franklin in Philadelphia

London, November 22, 1757

My dear Child:

During my illness, which continued near eight weeks, I wrote you several little letters, as I was able. The last was by the packet which sailed from Falmouth above a week since. In that I informed you that my intermittent fever, which had continued to harass me by frequent relapses, was gone off, and I have ever since been gathering strength and flesh. My doctor, Fothergill, who had forbid me the use of pen and ink, now permits me to write as much as I can without overfatiguing myself, and therefore I sit down to write more fully than I have hitherto been able to do.

The 2d of September I wrote to you that I had had a violent cold and something of a fever, but that it was almost gone. However, it was not long before I had another severe cold, which continued longer than the first, attended by great pain in my head, the top of which was very hot and, when the pain went off, very sore and tender. These fits of pain continued sometimes longer than at others; seldom less than twelve hours, and once thirty-six hours. I was now and then a little delirious; they cupped me on the back of the head, which seemed to ease me for the present; I took a great deal of bark, both in substance and infusion, and too soon thinking myself well, I ventured out twice, to do a little business and forward the service I am engaged in, and both times got fresh cold and fell down again. My good doctor grew very angry with me for acting contrary to his cautions and directions, and obliged me to promise more observance for the future. He attended me very carefully and affectionately; and the good lady of the house [Mrs. Stevenson] nursed me kindly. Billy was also of great service to me, in going from place to place, where I could not go myself, and Peter was very diligent and attentive. I took so much bark in various ways that I began to abhor it; I dared not vomit, for fear of my head; but at last I was seized one morning with a vomiting and purging, the latter of which continued the greater part of the day, and I believe was a kind of crisis to the distemper, carrying it clear off; for ever since I feel quite lightsome, and am every day gathering strength; so I hope my seasoning is over, and that I shall enjoy better health during the rest of my stay in England.

December 3d. I write by little and little as I can find time. I have now gone through all your agreeable letters, which give me fresh pleasure every time I read them. Last night I received another, dated October 16, which brings me the good news that you and Sally were got safe home.

I hear there has a miniature painter gone over to Philadelphia, a relation to John Reynolds. If Sally's picture is not done to your mind by the young man, and the other gentleman is a good hand and follows the business, suppose you get Sally's done by him, and send it to me with your small picture, that I may here get all our little family drawn in one conversation piece. I am sorry to hear of the general sickness; I hope it is over before this time.

I was as much disappointed in my intention of writing by that packet as you were in not receiving letters by her, and it has given me a great deal of vexation. I wrote to you by way of New York the day after my arrival in London, which I do not find you have received.

I do not use to be a backward correspondent, though my sickness has brought me behindhand with my friends in that respect. Had I been well I intended to have gone around among the shops, and bought some pretty things for you and my dear good Sally (whose little hands you say eased your headache) to send by this ship, but I must now defer it to the next, having only got a crimson satin cloak for you, the newest fashion, and the black silk for Sally; but Billy sends her a scarlet feather, muff, and tippet, and a box of fashionable linen for her dress.

It is now twelve days since I began to write this letter, and I still continue well, but have not yet quite recovered my strength, flesh, or spirits. I every day drink a glass of infusion of bark in wine, by way of prevention, and hope my fever will no more return. On fair days, which are but few, I venture out about noon. The agreeable conversation I meet with among men of learning, and the notice taken of me by persons of distinction, are the principal things that soothe me for the present under this painful absence from my family and friends. Yet those would not keep me here another week, if I had not other inducements—duty to my country, and hopes of being able to do it service.

Pray remember me kindly to all that love us, and to all that we love. 'Tis endless to name names. I am, my dear child, your loving husband. . . .

✒ 1757-60: The Proprietors

Autobiography, Part IV, continued

After some days, Dr. Fothergill having spoken to the Proprietaries, they agreed to a meeting with me at Mr. T. Penn's house in Spring Garden. The conversation at first consisted of mutual declarations of disposition to reasonable accommodation, but I suppose each party had its own ideas of what should be meant by *reasonable*. We then went into consideration of our several points of complaint which I enumerated. The Proprietaries justified their conduct as well as they could, and I the Assembly's. We now appeared very wide, and so far from each other in our opinions as to discourage all hope of agreement.

The Conversation with the Penns, described in a Letter soon after the Event

London, January 14, 1758

. . . "But," says I, "your father's charter expressly says that the Assembly of Pennsylvania shall have all the powers and privileges of an assembly according to the rights of free-born subjects of England, and as is usual in any of the British plantations in America." "Yes," says he, "but if my father granted privileges he was not by royal charter empowered to grant, nothing can be claimed by such grant." I said: "If then your father had no right to grant the privileges he pretended to grant, and published all over Europe as granted, those who came to settle in the province on the faith of that grant, and in expectation of enjoying the privileges contained in it, were deceived, cheated, and betrayed." He answered that they should have themselves looked to that; that the royal charter was no secret; they who came into the province on his father's offer of privileges, if they were deceived, it was their own faults, and that he said with a kind of triumphing, laughing insolence, such as a low jockey might do when a purchaser complained that he had cheated him in a horse. I was astonished to see him thus meanly give up his father's character, and conceived at that moment a more cordial and thorough contempt for him than I ever before felt for any man living, a contempt that I cannot express in words; but I believe my countenance expressed it strongly, and that his brother, who was looking at me, must have observed it. However, finding myself grow warm, I made no other answer to this than that the poor people were no lawyers themselves and, confiding in his father, did not think it necessary to consult any.

Autobiography, Part IV, concluded

However, it was concluded that I should give them the heads of our complaints in writing, and they promised then to consider them. I did so soon after; but they put the paper into the hands of their solicitor, Ferdinand John Paris, who managed for them all their law business, and wrote for them all their papers and messages in their dispute with the Assembly. He was a proud, angry man; and as I had occasionally in the answers of the Assembly treated his papers with some severity, they being really weak in point of argument, and haughty in expression, he had conceived a mortal enmity to me, which discovering itself whenever we met, I declined the Proprietary's proposal that he and I should discuss the heads of complaint between our two selves and refused treating with anyone but them.

The paper lay unanswered a year wanting eight days, during which time I made frequent demands of an answer from the Proprietaries. What it was, I never learned, for they did not communicate it to me. But during this delay, the Assembly prevailed with Governor Denny to pass an act taxing the proprietary estate in common with the estates of the people, which was the grand point in dispute.

When this act, however, came over, the Proprietaries counseled by Paris determined to oppose its receiving the royal assent. Accordingly, they petitioned the King in Council, and a hearing was appointed, in which two lawyers were employed by them against the act and two by me in support of it. They alleged that the act was intended to load the proprietary estate in order to spare those of the people, and that if it were suffered to continue in force and the Proprietaries, who were in odium with the people, left to their mercy in proportioning the taxes, they would inevitably be ruined.

We replied that the act had no such intention and would have no such effect, that the assessors were honest and discreet men, under an oath to assess fairly and equitably, and that any advantage each of them might expect in lessening his own tax by augmenting that of the Proprietaries was too trifling to induce them to perjure

William Penn, the first Proprietor, signs a treaty with the Indians.

themselves. This is the purport of what I remember as urged by both sides, except that we insisted strongly on the mischievous consequences that must attend a repeal; for that the money, £100,000, being printed and given to the King's use, expended in his service, and now spread among the people, the repeal would strike it dead in their hands, to the ruin of many.

On this Lord Mansfield, one of the Council, rose, and beckoning to me, took me into the clerks' chamber, while the lawyers were pleading, and asked me if I was really of opinion that no injury would be done the proprietary estate in the execution of the act.

I said, "Certainly."

"Then," says he, "you can have little objection to enter into an engagement to assure that point."

I answered, "None at all." He then called in Paris, and after some discourse his Lordship's proposition was accepted on both sides; a paper to the purpose was drawn up by the clerk of the Council, which I signed when Lord Mansfield returned to the council chamber, where finally the law was allowed to pass. For one year's tax having been levied by the act before the order of Council arrived, they appointed a committee to examine the proceedings of the assessors, and on this committee they put several particular friends of the Proprietaries. After a full inquiry they unanimously signed a report that they found the tax had been assessed with perfect equity. The Assembly looked on my entering into the first part of the engagement as an essential service to the province, since it secured the credit of the paper money then spread over all the country; and they gave me their thanks when I returned.

But the Proprietaries were enraged at Governor Denny for having passed the act and turned him out, with threats of suing him for breach of instructions which he had given bond to observe. He, however, having done it at the instance of the General and for his Majesty's service, and having some powerful interest at court, despised the threats, and they were never put in execution.

three

Colonial Agent
London

1757: Away from Home

Franklin had many friendships in London, where his fame as the genius of electricity made him perhaps the best known of all Americans. For fourteen years he had exchanged letters with William Strahan, the prospering printer of Samuel Johnson's dictionary, David Hume's history, and later, the works of Adam Smith and Edward Gibbon. Before he sailed, Franklin sent advance notice: "If a fat old fellow should come to your printing house and request a little smouting [job work] depend upon it 'tis your affectionate friend and humble servant." Strahan's and Franklin's letters spun out affectionate plans to marry Sally Franklin, aged six, to William Strahan, three years her elder. Strahan suggested to Franklin that he move his family to London.

To Mrs. Deborah Franklin in Philadelphia

London, July 27, 1757

My dear Child:

We arrived here well last night, only a little fatigued with the last day's journey, being 70 miles. I have just seen Mr. Strahan, who is well with his family. Billy (son William) is with me here at Mr. Collinson's and presents his duty to you and love to his sister. My love to all. I am, my dear child, your loving husband.

London, January 14, 1758

Dear Debby:

The New York paper you sent me was the latest that came, and of use to our friend Strahan. He has offered to lay me a considerable wager, that a letter he has wrote to you will bring you immediately over hither; but I tell him I will not pick his pocket; for I am sure there is no inducement strong enough to prevail with you to cross the seas. I should be glad if I could tell you when I expected to be at home, but that is still in the dark; it is possible I may not be able to get away this summer; but I hope, if I stay another winter,

*Colonial agent
in London, 1759*

it will be more agreeable than the greatest part of the time I have hitherto spent in England. But however I must bring my business to some conclusion.

I received Sally's letter but cannot now write to her. I am not yet quite so hearty as before my illness; but I think I am daily stronger and better, so I hope I have had my seasoning; but much writing still disorders me.

From William Strahan
to Mrs. Deborah Franklin in Philadelphia

London, December 13, 1757

Dear Madam:

I had for many years conceived a very high, and now find, a very just opinion of Mr. Franklin; this I was naturally led to by the concurring testimony of everybody who knew him (for the voice of his enemies, if he had any, never reached me). But though the notion I had formed of him, in my own mind, before I had the pleasure of seeing him, was really as far as it went, just enough; I must confess it was very unequal to what I now know his singular merit deserves.

I own it is somewhat odd to entertain a lady, with the character of her husband, who must herself, of all others, be the least ignorant in that particular. But as all who know me, know that I cannot help speaking my sentiments freely, on any subject that strikes me in a great degree, so I choose to write my mind in regard to Mr. Franklin, before all others to you, because you are the most unexceptionable judge of the truth and propriety of what I say, and because I am persuaded you will listen to me, not only with patience, but with pleasure; and indeed, whatever your own personal qualities may be, however amiable and engaging in my mind, your being the choice of such a man, must add greatly to your honor, to be the wife of one who has so much ability, inclination and success. To be the bosom friend of one who is equally fitted to promote any kind of domestic happiness, must as necessarily be the constant spring of the most substantial comfort to you.

For my own part, I never saw a man who was, in every respect, so perfectly agreeable to me. Now madam, as I know the ladies here consider him in exactly the same light I do, upon my word I think you should come over, with all convenient speed to look after your interest; not but that I think him as faithful to his Joan, as any man breathing; but who knows what repeated and strong temptations may in time, and while he is at so great a distance from you, accomplish. Besides what a delightful expedition would this be to Miss Franklin, and how much must it amuse and improve her, to see and live a while in this great city. I know you will object to the length of the voyage and the danger of the seas, but truly this is more terrible in apprehension than in reality; of all the ways of traveling it is the easiest; and as for the danger, there has not a soul been lost between Philadelphia and this, in my memory.

I leave it to your friend to write you every thing from this place, you would desire to know. But I cannot take my leave of you without informing you that Mr. F. has the good fortune to lodge with a very discreet good gentlewoman, who is particularly careful of him, who attended him during a very severe cold with an assiduity, concern and tenderness which perhaps, only yourself could equal: so that I don't think you could have a better substitute till you come over, to take him under your own protection.

My wife joins me in kindest compliments to you and dear Miss. I wish you a speedy and happy meeting with your friends on this side of the water, which will give great pleasure to

William Strahan

To Mrs. Deborah Franklin in Philadelphia

London, January 21, 1758

My dear Child:

I seize a minute or two just to let you know we are well, that is, I am well, compared to what I have been during a great part of the time since my arrival, and I hope with the spring to recover my full strength. Billy is quite hearty, and presents his duty, love, etc.

I begin to think I shall hardly be able to return before this twelve months. I am for doing effectually what I came about; and I find it requires both time and patience. You may think, perhaps, that I can find many amusements here to pass the time agreeably. 'Tis true, the regard and friendship I meet with from persons of worth, and the conversation of ingenious men, give me no small pleasure; but at this time of life, domestic comforts afford the most solid satisfaction, and my uneasiness at being absent from my family, and longing desire to be with them, make me often sigh in the midst of cheerful company.

My love to my dear Sally. I confide in you the care of her and her education. I promise myself the pleasure of finding her much improved at my return.

London, February 19, 1758

My dear Child:

Last night I received yours of the 1st and 6th of January, which gave me the great pleasure of hearing that you and my little family were well. I hope you continue so and that I shall have the happiness to find you so.

I hope Sally applies herself closely to her French and music and that I shall find she has made great proficiency. Sally's last letter to her brother is the best wrote that of late I have seen of hers. I only wish she was a little more careful of her spelling. I hope she continues to love going to church.

I have made your compliments to Mrs. Stevenson. She is indeed very obliging, takes great care of my health, and is very diligent when I am any way indisposed, but yet I have a thousand times wished you with me, and my little Sally with her ready hands and feet to do and go, and come, and get what I wanted. There is a great difference in sickness between being nursed with that tender attention, which proceeds from sincere love.

[Remainder of letter lists shipment of two cases, which included assorted china, silver, linens, carpeting, tablecloths, sheeting, bedticking, some music, optical instruments and something French and new, called a "blanket," which could replace "a quilt or a counterpane."]

London, June 10, 1758

My dear Child:

I was down at Cambridge with Billy; so being very kindly entertained there in the colleges, we did not hurry so soon home as we might have done. I think nobody ever had more faithful correspondents than I have in (Mr. Hughes and) you. I have now before me your letters of Jan. 15, 22, 29 & 31. Feb. 3, 4 & 6. March 12. April 3, 9, 17 & 23, which is the last. It is impossible for me to get or keep out of your debts. I received the bill of exchange you got of Mr. Nelson and it is paid. It gives me concern to receive such frequent accounts of your being indisposed; but we both grow in years, and must expect our constitutions, though tolerably good in themselves, will by degrees give way to the infirmities of age.

I have no prospect of returning till next spring, so you will not expect me. But pray remember to make me as happy as you can, by sending some pippins for myself and friends, some of your small hams and some cranberries.

Billy is of the Middle Temple and will be called to the bar either this term or next. I write this in answer to your particular inquiry. I am glad you like the cloak I sent you. The black silk was sent by our friend, Mr. Collinson. I never saw it. Your answer to Mr. Strahan was just what it should be. I was much pleased with it. He fancied his rhetoric and art would certainly bring you over.

I think I have now gone through your letters, which always give me great pleasure to receive and read, since I cannot be with you in person.

P.S. Mrs. Stevenson and her daughter desire me to present their respects and offer their service to you and to Sally.

London, March 5, 1760

My dear Child:

I received the enclosed some time since from Mr. Strahan. I afterward spent an evening in conversation with him on the subject. He was very urgent with me to stay in England, and prevail with you to remove hither with Sally. He proposed several advantageous schemes to me which appeared reasonably founded. His family is a very agreeable one: Mrs. Strahan a sensible and good woman, the children of amiable characters, and particularly the young man, [who is] sober, ingenious, and industrious, and a [desirable] person. In point of circumstances there can be no objection, Mr. Strahan now living a way as to lay up a thousand pounds every year from the profits of his business, after maintaining his family and paying all charges. I gave him, however, two reasons why I could not think of removing hither: one, my affection to Pennsylvania, and long established friendships and other connections there; the other, your invincible aversion to crossing the seas. And without removing hither, I could not think of parting with my daughter to such a distance. I thanked him for the regard shown to us in the proposal, but gave him no expectation that I should forward the letters. So you are at liberty to answer or not, just as you think proper. Let me however, know your sentiments. You need not deliver the letter to Sally, if you do not think it proper.

My best respects to Mr. Hughes, Mr. Bartram, and all inquiring friends. I am your ever loving husband. . . .

London, 1760

My dear Child:

Yesterday I received your letter of February 10th, in which you mention that it was some months since you heard from me. During my journey I wrote several times to you, and since my return some very long letters that might have been with you before your last to me; but I suppose the severe winter on your coast, among other delays, has kept the vessels out.

I have now the pleasure to acquaint you, that our business draws near a conclusion, and that in less than a month we shall have a hearing, after which I shall be able to fix a time for my return.

London, June 27, 1760

My dear Child:

I wrote a line to you by the packet to let you know we were well. I am concerned that so much trouble should be given you by idle reports concerning me. Be satisfied, my dear, that while I have my senses, and God vouchsafes me His protection, I shall do nothing unworthy the character of an honest man, and one that loves his family.

The dried venison was very acceptable, and I thank you for it. We have it constantly shaved to eat with our bread and butter for breakfast, and this week saw the last of it. The bacon still holds out, for we are choice of it. Some rashers of it yesterday relished a dish of green peas. Mrs. Stevenson thinks there was never any in England so good.

I think you will not complain this year, as you did last, of being so long without a letter. I have wrote to you very frequently; and shall not be so much out of the way of writing this summer as I was last.

London, March 24, 1762

My dear Child:

I condole with you most sincerely on the death of our good mother [Mrs. Read, mother of Mrs. Franklin], being extremely sensible of the distress and affliction it must have thrown you into. Your comfort will be, that no care was wanting on your part toward her, and that she had lived as long as this life could afford her any rational enjoyment. 'Tis, I am sure, a satisfaction to me, that I cannot charge myself with having ever failed in one instance of duty and respect to her during the many years that she called me son. The circumstances attending her death were indeed unhappy in some respects; but something must bring us all to our end, and few of us shall see her length of days.

We are all well and Billy presents his duty. Mr. Strahan has received your letter, and wonders he has not been able to persuade you to come over.

1760: British Canada

On September 13, 1759, Generals Montcalm and Wolfe fought each other to the death on the Plains of Abraham before the city of Quebec in Canada. The English were victorious and soon Canada became part of England's possessions in North America.

To Lord Kames in Scotland

London, January 3, 1760

My dear Lord:

You have been pleased kindly to desire to have all my publications. I had daily expectations of procuring some of them from a friend to whom I formerly sent them when I was in America, and postponed writing to you, till I should obtain them; but at length he tells me he cannot find them. Very mortifying this to an author, that his works should so soon be lost! So I can only send you my

Observations on the Peopling of Countries, which happens to have been reprinted here; *The Description of the Pennsylvania Fireplace*, a machine of my contriving; and some little sketches that have been printed in the *Grand Magazine*, which I should hardly own, did I not know that your friendly partiality would make them seem at least tolerable.

No one can more sincerely rejoice than I do on the reduction of Canada; and this is not merely as I am a colonist, but as I am a Briton. I have long been of opinion, that the *foundations of the future grandeur and stability of the British Empire lie in America;* and though, like other foundations, they are low and little seen, they are, nevertheless, broad and strong enough to support the greatest political structure that human wisdom ever yet erected. I am, therefore, by no means for restoring Canada. If we keep it, all the country from the St. Lawrence to the Mississippi will in another century be filled with British people. Britain itself will become vastly more populous, by the immense increase of its commerce; the Atlantic sea will be covered with your trading ships; and your naval power, thence continually increasing, will extend your influence around the whole globe, and awe the world! If the French remain in Canada, they will continually harass our colonies by the Indians, and impede if not prevent their growth; your progress to greatness will at best be slow, and give room for many accidents that may forever prevent it. But I refrain, for I see you begin to think my notions extravagant, and look upon them as the ravings of a mad prophet.

✑1762: William's Marriage

Franklin hoped that his son, William, might marry Polly Stevenson, daughter of the landlady of the Craven Street house where he lived. But events turned out otherwise. Repeating the elder Franklin's past, young William fathered a son out of wedlock, who was to be accepted into the family as William Temple Franklin. Two years later in September, 1762, William Franklin married Elizabeth Downes, of the West Indies, a few weeks after his father had left England. Waiting in Portsmouth to board a vessel for home, Franklin wrote of his disappointment to Polly.

To Miss Mary Stevenson in London

Portsmouth, August 11, 1762

My dear Polly:

This is the best paper I can get at this wretched inn, but it will convey what is entrusted to it as faithfully as the finest. It will tell my Polly how much her friend is afflicted that he must, perhaps never again, see one for whom he has so sincere an affection joined to so perfect an esteem; who he once flattered himself might become his own, in the tender relation of a child, but can now entertain such pleasing hopes no more. Will it tell her *how much* he is afflicted? No, it cannot.

Adieu, my dearest child. I will call you so. Why should I not call you so, since I love you with all the tenderness, all the fondness of a father? Adieu. May the God of all goodness shower down his choicest blessings upon you, and make you infinitely happier than that event could have made you.

1762: Return to America

The idea of living in England had taken on a strong appeal for Franklin and he had almost made up his mind to do so after one last voyage to America. But once more back in Philadelphia, excited by his enthusiastic welcome, he did not mention the subject again until a year later, when his own troubles started mounting. Franklin openly missed his English friends, but soon the idea of "an old tree being transplanted" seemed to have faded.

To William Strahan in London

Portsmouth, Monday, August 23, 1762

Dear Sir:

I have been two nights on board expecting to sail, but the wind continuing contrary, am just now on shore again, and have met with your kind letter of the 20th. The attraction of reason is at present for the other side of the water, but that of inclination will be for this side. You know which usually prevails. I shall probably make but this one vibration and settle here forever. Nothing will prevent it, if I can, as I hope I can, prevail with Mrs. F. to accompany me, especially if we have a peace.

Philadelphia, December 2, 1762

Dear Straney:

I got home well the 1st of November and had the happiness to find my little family perfectly well. My house has been full of a succession of [my friends] from morning to night, ever since my arrival, congratulating me on my return with the utmost cordiality and affection. My fellow citizens, while I was on the sea, had at the annual election chosen me unanimously, as they had done every year while I was in England, to be their representative in Assembly and would, they say, if I had not disappointed them by coming privately to town before they heard of my landing, have met me with 500 horse. Excuse my vanity in writing this to you.

Mrs. Franklin and Sally desire their compliments and thanks to you all for your kindness to me while in England.

To Miss Mary Stevenson in London

Philadelphia, March 25, 1763

My dear Polly:

Your pleasing favor of November 11 is now before me. It found me, as you supposed it would, happy with my American friends and family about me; and it made me more happy in showing me that I am not yet forgotten by the dear friends I left in England. And, indeed, why should I fear they will ever forget me, when I feel so strongly that I shall ever remember them!

Of all the enviable things England has, I envy it most its people. Why should that petty island, which, compared to America, is but a stepping stone in a brook, scarce enough of it above water to keep one's shoes dry; why, I say, should that little island enjoy, in almost every neighborhood, more sensible, virtuous, and elegant minds than we can collect in ranging a hundred leagues of our vast forests? But 'tis said the arts delight to travel westward. You have effectually defended us in this glorious war [French and Indian War, 1754–1763], and in time you will improve us. After the first cares for the necessaries of life are over, we shall come to think of the embellishments. Already, some of our young geniuses begin to lisp attempts at painting, poetry, and music.

Nothing can please me more than to see your philosophical improvements when you have leisure to communicate them to me; I still owe you a long letter on that subject, which I shall pay.

To William Strahan in London

Boston, August 8, 1763

Dear Friend:

I have received here your favor of May 3, and postscript of May 10, and thank you cordially for the sketch you give me of the present state of your political affairs. If the stupid, brutal opposition your good King [George III] and his measures have lately met with should, as you fear, become general, surely you would not wish me to come and live among such people; you would rather remove hither, where we have no savages but those we expect to be such. But I think your madmen will erelong come to their senses; and when I come I shall find you generally wise and happy. That I have not the propensity to sitting still that you apprehend, let my present journey witness for me, in which I have already traveled eleven hundred and forty miles on this continent since April, and shall make six hundred and forty miles more before I see home. No friend can wish me more in England than I do myself. But before I go, everything I am concerned in must be so settled here as to make another return to America unnecessary.

To Miss Mary Stevenson in London

Philadelphia, March 14, 1764

Dear Polly:

I believe you were right in dissuading your good mother from coming hither. The proposal was a hasty thought of mine, in which I considered only some profit she might make by the adventure and the pleasure to me and my family from the visit, but forgot poor Polly, and what her feelings must be on the occasion, and perhaps did not sufficiently reflect, that the inconveniences of such a voyage, to a person of her years and sex, must be more than the advantages could compensate.

Let me hear from you as often as you can afford it. You can scarce conceive the pleasure your letters give me. But I write so little, that I have no claim to much from you. Business, public and private, devours all my time. I must return to England for repose. With such thoughts I flatter myself, and need some kind friend to put me often in mind that *old trees cannot safely be transplanted.*

✍1762-64: Colony Beset

Two eventful years followed Franklin's return to America. His affairs with the post office, his son's appointment as Royal Governor of New Jersey, the massacre of the Indians in the back country of Pennsylvania, his election defeat, etc., are recounted in a long letter, written after his return to England. Governor William Franklin of New Jersey had official residences in Burlington and Amboy, where he and his new lady lived.

William Franklin,
Royal Governor
of New Jersey

To Lord Kames in Scotland

London, June 2, 1765

My dear Lord:

You require my history from the time I set sail for America. I left England about the end of August 1762, in company with ten sail of merchant ships, under a convoy of a man-of-war.

On the 1st of November, I arrived safe and well at my own home, after an absence of near six years; found my wife and daughter well; the latter grown quite a woman, with many amiable accomplishments acquired in my absence; and my friends as hearty and affectionate as ever, with whom my house was filled for many days, to congratulate me on my return.

In February following my son arrived with my new daughter; for, with my consent and approbation, he married soon after I left England a very agreeable West India lady with whom he is very happy. I accompanied him to his government, where he met with the kindest reception from the people of all ranks, and has lived with them ever since in the greatest harmony. A river only parts that province and ours, and his residence is within seventeen miles of me, so that we frequently see each other.

In the spring of 1763 I set out on a tour through all the northern colonies to inspect and regulate the post offices in the several provinces. In this journey I spent the summer, traveled about sixteen hundred miles, and did not get home till the beginning of November.

The Assembly sitting through the following winter, and warm disputes arising between them and the governor, I became wholly engaged in public affairs; for, besides my duty as an assemblyman, I had another trust to execute, that of being one of the commissioners appointed by law to dispose of the public money appropriated to the raising and paying an army to act against the Indians, and defend the frontiers.

And then in December, we had two insurrections of the back inhabitants of our province, by whom twenty poor Indians were murdered that had, from the first settlement of the province, lived among us under the protection of our government.

This gave me a good deal of employment; for as the rioters threatened further mischief, and their actions seemed to be approved by an increasing party, I wrote a pamphlet entitled *A Narrative of The Late Massacres in Lancaster County* (which I think I sent to you) to strengthen the hands of our weak government by rendering the proceedings of the rioters unpopular and odious. This had a good effect; and afterward, when a great body of them with arms marched toward the capital, in defiance of the government, with an avowed resolution to put to death a hundred and forty Indian converts then under its protection, I formed an association at the governor's request, for his and their defense, we having no militia.

Near a thousand of our citizens accordingly took arms; Governor Penn made my house for some time his headquarters, and did everything by my advice; so that for about forty-eight hours, I was a very great man; as I had been once some years before, in a time of public danger.

But the fighting face we put on, and the reasonings we used with the insurgents (for I went at the request of the governor and council, with three others, to meet and discourse with them) having turned them back and restored quiet to the city, I became a less man than ever; for I had, by these transactions, made myself many enemies among the populace; and the governor (with whose family our public disputes had long placed me in an unfriendly light, and the services I had lately rendered him not being of the kind that make a man acceptable), thinking it a favorable opportunity, joined the whole weight of the proprietary interest to get me out of the Assembly; which was accordingly effected at the last election, by a majority of about twenty-five in four thousand voters.

✒ 1764: Justice for All

The French and Indian War had just ended (1763) between England and France, but war went on between the American colonists and the Indians, particularly between the newer settlers pushing out toward the frontiers. The brutal massacre of twenty peaceful Indians by the self-named Paxton Boys in 1763 was connected with the continuing warfare with hostile tribes, but it also involved the antagonisms between the Scotch-Irish newcomers to Pennsylvania and the old, prosperous Quaker community in Philadelphia. Franklin's pamphlet, which his old partner, David Hall, did not print, was an emotional appeal; it helped cool the passion and bitterness but gained him more enemies than friends. It reveals his own principles of humanity and indicates his growing feelings against slavery and the slave trade.

A Narrative of the Late Massacres in Lancaster County

January 30?, 1764

These Indians were the remains of a tribe of the Six Nations, called Conestoga Indians. On the first arrival of the English in Pennsylvania, messengers from this tribe came to welcome them, with presents of venison, corn and skins; and the whole tribe entered into a treaty of friendship with the first Proprietor, William Penn, which was to last "as long as the sun should shine, or the waters run in the rivers."

There are some (I am ashamed to hear it) who would extenuate the enormous wickedness of these actions, by saying, "The inhabitants of the frontiers are exasperated with the murder of their relations, by the enemy Indians, in the present war." It is possible; but though this might justify their going out into the woods, to seek for those enemies and avenge upon them those murders; it can never justify their turning in to the heart of the country, to murder their friends.

If an Indian injures me, does it follow that I may revenge that

Attack on Franklin in an early Philadelphia cartoon

injury on all Indians? It is well known that Indians are of different tribes, nations and languages, as well as white people. In Europe, if the French, who are white people, should injure the Dutch, are they to revenge it on the English, because they too are white people? The only crime of these poor wretches seems to have been, that they had a reddish-brown skin, and black hair; and some people of that sort, it seems, had murdered some of our relations. If it be right to kill men for such a reason, then, should any man, with a freckled face and red hair, kill a wife or child of mine, it would be right for me to revenge it by killing all the freckled red-haired men, women and children, I could afterward anywhere meet with.

We pretend to be Christians, and, from the superior light we enjoy, ought to exceed heathens, Turks, Saracens, Moors, [African] Negroes and Indians, in the knowledge and practice of what is right. I will endeavor to show, by a few examples from books and history, the sense those people have had of such actions.

Will it be permitted me to adduce, on this occasion, an instance of the honor in a poor unenlightened African Negro. I find it in Captain Seagrave's account of his voyage to Guinea. He relates that a New England sloop, trading there in 1752, left their second mate, William Murray, sick on shore, and sailed without him. Murray was at the house of a black, named Cudjoe, with whom he had contracted an acquaintance during their trade. He recovered and the sloop being gone, he continued with his black friend, till some other opportunity should offer of his getting home. In the meanwhile, a Dutch ship came into the road and some of the blacks going on board her, were treacherously seized and carried off as slaves. Their relations and friends, transported with sudden rage, ran to the house of Cudjoe to take revenge, by killing Murray. Cudjoe stopped them at the door, and demanded what they wanted?

"The white men," said they, "have carried away our brothers and sons, and we will kill all white men; give us the white man that you keep in your house, for we will kill him."

"Nay," said Cudjoe, "the white men that carried away your brothers are bad men; kill them when you can catch them, but this white man is a good man, and you must not kill him."

"But he is a white man," they cried, "the white men are all bad, and we will kill them all."

"Nay," says he, "you must not kill a man, that has done no harm, only for being white. This man is my friend, my house is his fort, and I am his soldier. I must fight for him. You must kill me, before you can kill him. What good man will ever come again under my roof, if I let my floor be stained with a good man's blood!"

Now I am about to mention something of Indians, I beg that I may not be understood as framing apologies for *all* Indians. I am far from desiring to lessen the laudable spirit of resentment in my countrymen against those now at war with us, so far as it is justified by their perfidy and inhumanity. I would only observe that the Six Nations, as a body, have kept faith with the English ever since we knew them, now near an hundred years.

✐ 1764: Tension with Britain

Two points of view in Pennsylvania were in sharp conflict: one favored the continued proprietorship of the Penn family; the other desired to see the province governed directly by the English king. Franklin long held that the Crown would provide better government. But changes in England's overall policy toward its colonies were being proposed which were a worry and a threat to America, the first signs of the storms ahead.

To Peter Collinson in London

Philadelphia, April 30, 1764

Dear Friend:

By the enclosed papers you will see that we are all to pieces again; and the general wish seems to be a king's government. If that is not to be obtained, many talk of quitting the province, and among them your old friend, who is tired of these contentions, and longs for philosophic ease and leisure.

I suppose by this time the wisdom of your Parliament has determined in the points you mention, of trade, duties, troops, and fortifications in America.

Our opinions or inclinations, if they had been known, would perhaps have weighed but little among you. We are in your hands as clay in the hands of the potter; and so in one more particular than is generally considered: for as the potter cannot waste or spoil his clay without injuring himself, so I think there is scarce anything you can do that may be hurtful to us but what will be as much or more so to you. This must be our chief security; for interest with you we have but little.

Therefore what you get from us in taxes you must lose in trade. The cat can yield but her skin. And as you must have the whole hide, if you first cut thongs out of it, 'tis at your own expense. The same in regard to our trade with the foreign West India islands. If you restrain it in any degree, you restrain in the same proportion our power of making remittances to you, and of course our demand for your goods; for you will not clothe us out of charity. In time perhaps mankind may be wise enough to let trade take its own course, find its own channels, and regulate its own proportions, etc.

1764: Return to London

In spite of Franklin's defeat, the Pennsylvania Assembly voted to send him to London as agent for the province to work out a change of government from the proprietorship of the Penns to rule by the English king. Franklin did not realize that he would not be back for twelve years as he left behind advice for his family and affairs. After a fairly swift voyage, he took up his lodgings once again in Craven Street, London, with Mrs. Margaret Stevenson.

To Miss Sarah Franklin in Philadelphia

Reedy Island, 7 at night
November 8, 1764

My dear Sally:

My dear child, the natural prudence and goodness of heart God has blessed you with make it less necessary for me to be particular in giving you advice. I shall therefore only say, that the more attentively dutiful and tender you are toward your good mamma, the more you will recommend yourself to me. But why should I mention *me*, when you have so much higher a promise in the commandments that such conduct will recommend you to the favor of God.

Go constantly to church, whoever preaches. I wish you would never miss the prayer days. For the rest, I would only recommend to you in my absence, to acquire those useful accomplishments, arithmetic and bookkeeping. We expect to be at sea tomorrow, if this wind holds, after which I shall have no opportunity of writing to you, till I arrive (if it please God I do arrive) in England.

To Mrs. Deborah Franklin in Philadelphia

Saint Helen's Road, Isle of Wight,
December 9, 1764, 5 P.M.

My dear Debby:

This line is just to let you know that we have this moment come to an anchor here and that I am going ashore at Portsmouth and hope to be in London on Tuesday morning. We have had terrible weather, and I have often been thankful that our dear Sally was not with me. Tell our friends that the kind prayer they put up for thirty days fair wind for me was favorably heard and answered, we being just 30 days from land to land.

I am, thanks to God, very well and hearty. Thank all my friends for their favors, which contributed so much to the comfort of my voyage. I have not time to name names; you know whom I love and honor. Say all the proper things for me to everybody.

London, December 27, 1764

My dear Child:

I can only write a line or two, just to let you know that I am now almost well, though for 10 or 12 days I have been severely handled by a most violent cold that has worried me extremely.

P. S. Mrs. Stevenson desires her compliments.

London, February 9, 1765

My dear Child:

I have been so hurried of late, that I could not write much by this packet. One letter to the Speaker [Pennsylvania Assembly], and one to you, are all I shall be able to make out. Thanks to God, I am got perfectly well, my cough quite gone. Mrs. Stevenson has bought the things you wrote for. She presents her compliments & wishes you would come over & bring Sally.

I hope to be able to return about the end of summer.

London, February 14, 1765

My dear Child:

Let no one make you uneasy with their idle or malicious stories or scribblings, but enjoy yourself and friends, and the comforts of life that God has bestowed on you, with a cheerful heart. Let Sally divert you with her music.

A few months, I hope, will finish affairs here to my wish, and bring me to that retirement and repose with my little family, so suitable to my years, and which I have so long set my heart upon.

1765: The Stamp Act

Franklin's mission to change the government of Pennsylvania was soon lost in the larger struggle of the whole relationship between Great Britain and her colonies. The most difficult questions related to taxation and the regulation of trade. The

Stamp Act raised enormous resistance in America, which astounded Franklin: expecting the tax to be enforced, he had a friend made collector. The result was an angry Philadelphia crowd which stormed Franklin's house.

To Charles Thomson in America

London, July 11, 1765

Dear Friend:

Depend upon it, my good neighbor, I took every step in my power to prevent the passing of the Stamp Act. Nobody could be more concerned in interest than myself to oppose it sincerely and heartily. But the tide was too strong against us. The nation was provoked by American claims of independence, and all parties joined in resolving by this act to settle the point. We might as well have

The repeal of the Stamp Act, 1776; English cartoon

hindered the sun's setting. That we could not do. But since it is down, my friend, and it may be long before it rises again, let us make as good a night of it as we can. We may still light candles. Frugality and industry will go a great way toward indemnifying us. Idleness and pride tax with a heavier hand than kings and parliaments. If we can get rid of the former, we may easily bear the latter.

To Mrs. Deborah Franklin in Philadelphia

London, February 22, 1766

My dear Child:

I am excessively hurried, being every hour that I am awake either abroad to speak with members of Parliament or taken up with people coming to me at home concerning our American af-

fairs, so that I am much behindhand in answering my friends' letters. But though I cannot by this opportunity write to others, I must not omit a line to you, who kindly write me so many. I am well. It is all I can say at present, except that I am just made very happy by a vote of the Commons for the repeal of the Stamp Act. . . .

1767: Father from Afar

Sally Franklin, aged twenty-three, had been asked in marriage by Richard Bache, a thirty-year-old merchant, born in Yorkshire, who came to Philadelphia after Franklin had already left. William Franklin seemed to have thought him a fortune hunter and so informed his father. By this time, Franklin's partnership in his printing business with David Hall had expired after continuing for eighteen years, leaving the Franklin household somewhat reduced in income. Concerned about the business reverses of his daughter's suitor, Franklin suggested that Sally postpone her decision by journeying to London.

To Mrs. Deborah Franklin in Philadelphia

London, June 22, 1767

My dear Child:

It seems now as if I should stay here another winter, and therefore I must leave it to your judgment to act in the affair of your daughter's match as shall seem best. If you think it a suitable one, I suppose the sooner it is completed the better. In that case I would only advise that you do not make an expensive feasting wedding, but conduct everything with frugality and economy, which our circumstances now require to be observed in all our expenses. For since my partnership with Mr. Hall is expired, a great source of our income is cut off, and if I should lose the post office, which among the many changes here is far from being unlikely, we should be reduced to our rents and interest of money for a subsistence, which will by no means afford the chargeable housekeeping and entertainments we have been used to.

For my own part, I live here as frugally as possible not to be destitute of the comforts of life, making no dinners for anybody, and contenting myself with a single dish when I dine at home, and yet such is the dearness of living here, in every article, that my expenses amaze me. I see, too, by the sums you have received in my absence, that yours are very great, and I am very sensible that your situation naturally brings you a great many visitors, which occasion an expense not easily to be avoided, especially when one has been long in the practice and habit of it. But when people's incomes are lessened, if they cannot proportionately lessen their outgoings, they must come to poverty. If we were young enough to begin business again, it might be another matter; but I doubt we are past it, and business not well managed ruins one faster than no business. In short, with frugality and prudent care we may subsist decently on what we have, and leave it entire to our children; but without such care we shall not be able to keep it together; it will melt away like butter in the sunshine, and we may live long enough to feel the miserable consequences of our indiscretion.

I know very little of the gentleman or his character, nor can I at this distance. I hope his expectations are not great of any fortune to be had with our daughter before our death. I can only say that if he proves a good husband to her and a good son to me, he shall find me as good a father as I can be; but at present I suppose you would agree with me that we cannot do more than fit her out handsomely in clothes and furniture, not exceeding in the whole five hundred pounds of value. For the rest, they must depend, as you and I did, on their own industry and care, as what remains in our hands will be barely sufficient for our support, and not enough for them when it comes to be divided at our decease.

Having lately bought a piece of fine pocket handkerchiefs, I send you four of them, being half the piece; and shall look out for the quilts you mention—that is, Mrs. Stevenson will—and for the muff for Sally. None of the things are yet come on shore.

Our Polly's [Mary Stevenson] match is quite broke off. The difference was about money matters. I am not displeased at it, as I did not much like the man, thinking him a mean-spirited mercenary fellow and not worthy so valuable a girl as she is in every respect: person, fortune, temper, and excellent understanding.

I am glad to hear that Sally keeps up and increases the number of her friends. The best wishes of a fond father for her happiness always attend her. . . .

London, August 5, 1767

My dear Child:

I am glad you go sometimes to Burlington [residence of Governor William Franklin]. The harmony you mention in our family and among our children gives me great pleasure. In your last letters you say nothing concerning Mr. Bache. The misfortune that has lately happened to his affairs though it may not lessen his character as an honest or a prudent man, will probably induce him to forbear entering hastily into a state that must require a great addition to his expense, when he will be less able to supply it. If you think that in the meantime it will be some amusement to Sally to visit her friends here and return with me, I should have no objection to her coming over. I think too it might be some improvement to her.

I long to see you & be with you.

✑1768: Politics in London

The agitation in the colonies, the threats of boycott of English manufactures, led to efforts in England to work out a solution. There was some talk of appointing Franklin to office in the English Ministry. Franklin was still not sure how he himself felt about the basic principles of the bond between the colonies and the mother country, but he tended toward the idea of separate states with a common loyalty to the Crown. Franklin seemed much concerned about his son's relationships with the Colonial Office and the English ministers in London.

To Governor William Franklin in New Jersey

London, January 9, 1768

Dear Son:

I am told there has been a talk of getting me appointed undersecretary to Lord Hillsborough [Minister for American Affairs]; but with little likelihood, as it is a settled point here, that I am too much of an American. I am in very good health, thanks to God. Your affectionate father.

London, March 13, 1768

Dear Son:

I have received all together your letters of January 6, 21 and 22. It has been a great while that I had not heard from you. The purpose of settling the new colonies seems at present to be dropped, the change of American administration not appearing favorable to it. There seems rather to be an inclination to abandon the posts in the back country as more expensive than useful.

As to my own sentiments, I am weary of suggesting them to so many different inattentive heads though I must continue to do it while I stay among them.

I can tell you there are many here to whom the news of such a war [with the Indians] would give pleasure; who speak of it as a thing to be wished; partly as a chastisement to the colonies, and partly to make them feel the want of protection from this country, and pray for it. For it is imagined that we could not possibly defend ourselves against the Indians without such assistance, so little is the state of America understood here.

I am not yet master of the idea . . . the New England writers have of the relation between Britain and her colonies. I know not what the Boston people mean by the "subordination" they acknowledge in their Assembly to Parliament, while they deny its powers to make laws for them . . . it being difficult to draw lines between duties for regulations and those for revenue.

The more I have thought and read on the subject, the more I find myself confirmed in the opinion, that no middle doctrine can be well maintained, I mean not clearly with intelligible arguments. Something might be made of either of the extremes; that Parliament has a power to make *all laws* for us, or that it has a power to make *no laws* for us; and I think the arguments for the latter more numerous and weighty than those of the former. Supposing that doctrine established, the colonies would then be so many separate states, only subject to the same king.

Mr. Grenville complained in the House, that the governors of New Jersey, New Hampshire, East and West Florida, had none of them obeyed the orders sent them, to give an account of the manufactures carried on in their respective provinces. Upon hearing this, I went after the House was up, and got a sight of the reports made by the other governors. They are all much in the same strain, that there are no manufactures of any consequence.

These accounts are very satisfactory here, and induce the Parliament to despise and take no notice of the Boston resolution. I wish you would send your account before the meeting of the next Parliament. You have only to report a glasshouse for coarse window glass and bottles, and some domestic manufacture of linen and woolen for family use, that do not half clothe the inhabitants, all the finer goods coming from England and the like.

London, July 2, 1768

Dear Son:

Since my last I have received yours of May 10, dated at Amboy, which I shall answer particularly by next week's packet. I purpose now to take notice of that part wherein you say it was reported at Philadelphia I was to be appointed to a certain office here, which my friends all wished, but you did not believe it for the reasons I had mentioned. Instead of my being appointed to a new office, there has been a motion made to deprive me of that I now hold, and I believe for the same reason, though that was not the reason given out, viz., my being too much of an American; but as it came from Lord Sandwich, our new postmaster general, who is of the Bedford party and a friend of Mr. Grenville, I have no doubt that the reason he gave out, viz., my nonresidence, was only the pretense, and that the other was the true reason; especially as it is the practice in many other instances to allow the nonresidence of American officers who spend their salaries here, provided care is taken that the business be done by deputy or otherwise.

The first notice I had of this was from my fast friend, Mr. Cooper, secretary of the treasury. He told me that the Duke of Grafton [the prime minister] had mentioned to him to say to me that, though my going to my post might remove the objection, yet if I choose rather to reside in England, my merit was such in his opinion as to entitle me to something better here, and it should not be his fault if I was not well provided for. I told Mr. Cooper that, without having heard any exception had been taken to my residence here, I was really preparing to return home and expected to be gone in a few weeks; that, having lived long in England and contracted a friendship and affection for many persons here, it could not but be agreeable to me to remain among them some time longer, if not for the rest of my life; and that there was no nobleman to whom I could, from sincere respect for his great abilities and amiable qualities, so cordially attach myself, or to whom I should so willingly be obliged for the provision he mentioned, as to the Duke of Grafton, if his Grace should think I could, in any station where he might place me, be serviceable to him and to the public.

You see by the nature of this whole letter that it is to yourself only. It may serve to prepare your mind for any event that shall happen.

If Mr. Grenville comes into power again, in any department respecting America, I must refuse to accept of anything that may seem to put me in his power, because I apprehend a breach between the two countries; and that refusal might give offense.

So that, you see, a turn of a die may make a great difference in our affairs. We may be either promoted or discarded; one or the other seems likely soon to be the case, but it is hard to divine which. I am myself grown so old as to feel much less than formerly the spur of ambition; and if it were not for the flattering expectation that by being fixed here I might more effectually serve my country, I should certainly determine for retirement without a moment's hesitation. I am, as ever, your affectionate father. . . .

✍ 1768: Still Away

Franklin, now sixty-three, had been in London since 1757 without Deborah—with the exception of two years back in America. His letters to his wife shifted from suggestions of a swift return to hints of a longer and longer stay away from her. Franklin's relationship with his wife seemed distant and as far apart as the ocean that separated them. For Deborah, lonely and unhappy in Philadelphia, from which she rarely budged, her husband had a few gifts, some bare words of affection, but none of the warmth, chattiness and intimacy of his letters to other women. Deborah was made agent of the family's affairs, which were expanding in Philadelphia, and she was cruelly criticized when she blundered. Franklin's intimate ties with his landlady, Mrs. Stevenson, could only sharpen Deborah's loneliness and jealousies.

To Mrs. Deborah Franklin in Philadelphia

London, October 5, 1768

My dear Child:

It feels very strange to me to have ships and packets come in, and no letters from you. But I do not complain of it, because I know the reason is, my having written to you that I was coming home.

I have made no very long journey this summer as usual, finding myself in very good health, a greater share of which I believe few enjoy at my time of life, but we are not to expect it will always be sunshine.

December 21, 1768

My dear Child:

I have now before me your favors of Oct. 1, 18, 23, 30, and Nov. 5, which I shall answer in order.

I wonder to hear that my friends were backward in bringing you my letters when they arrived, and think it must be a mere imagination of yours, the effect of some melancholy humor you happened then to be in.

You say in yours of Oct. 18, "For me to give you any uneasiness about your affairs here, would be of no service, and I shall not at this time enter on it." I am made by this to apprehend that something is amiss, and perhaps have more uneasiness from the uncertainty, than I should have had if you had told me what it was. I wish therefore you would be explicit in your next. Upon what you write me now about the watches, I shall, if I can afford it send you another for yourself, I say if I find I can afford it; for I understand the balance of the post office account which I must pay here, is greatly against me, owing to the large sums you have received. I do not doubt your having applied them properly, and I only mention it, that if I do not send you a watch, it will not be through neglect or for want of regard, but because I cannot spare the cash, for I shall not like to leave debts behind me here.

As you ask me, I can assure you, that I do really intend, God willing, to return in the summer. I am glad that you find so much reason to be satisfied with Mr. Bache. I hope all will prove for the best.

I hope the cold you complain of in two of your letters went off without any ill consequences. We are, as you observe, blessed with a great share of health considering our years now 63. For my own part, I think of late that my constitution rather mends: I have had but one touch of the gout, and that a light one, since I left you; it was just after my arrival here, so that this is the 4th winter I have been free. Walking a great deal tires me less than it used to do. I feel stronger and more active. Yet I would not have you think that I fancy I shall grow young again. I know that men of my bulk often fail suddenly: I know that according to the course of nature I cannot at most continue much longer, and that the living even of another day is uncertain. I therefore now form no schemes, but such as are of immediate execution; indulging myself in no future prospect except one, that of returning to Philadelphia, there to spend the evening of life with my friends and family.

London, June 10, 1770

My dear Child:

I received your kind letters of March 12 and April 24. I think you are the most punctual of all my correspondents; and it is often a particular satisfaction to me to hear from you, when I have no letter from anyone else. As to myself, I had from Christmas till Easter, a disagreeable giddiness hanging about me, which however did not hinder me from being about and doing business. In the Easter holidays being at a friend's house in the country, I was taken with a sore throat, and came home half strangled. I was bled largely and purged two or three times. On Friday came a fit of gout, from which I had been free five years. I was confined about three weeks; since which I am perfectly well, the giddiness and every other disagreeable symptom having quite left me. I hope your health is likewise by this time reestablished. . . .

From Deborah Franklin to Benjamin Franklin, London

November 20, 1769

. . . yister day I reseved yours dated September the 9 . . . my disorder was for this reson my distres for my dear Debbey misforten and her being removed so far from her friend and such a helpeles famely and before I had got the better of that our Cusin Betsey macum was taken ill and so much distresst so soon that added to my one [own] dis satisfied distresed att your staying so much longer that I loste all my resey lushon and the very disma . . . bouth Salley and my self live so very lonley that I had got into verey low staite and got into so unhapey a way that I could not sleep a long time good old Mr. Whorton did come sometimes to

aske how we did and asked us to cume to spend a day att his house
. . . and while thair I lost all my memery I cold not tell aney
thing but stayed all day but verey sleepey and as soon as I got to
bed I sleep all night and semd [seemed?] quite hapey and esey and
I shold a got better but Salley was surprised att my sleepinge as I
did . . . [I] supmited to be bleeded and took somthing agonste
my one [own] judgment to oblige Salley as shee was in such a
Condison as shee was, I had no head ake or fever the Dr sed my
blood was verey good but sed he wold sende to you I beg[g]ed
him not but it gave me much onesey nes a boute it or I wold not a
lett you to a knowe a boute it   I still sleep verey well and sleep as
soon as night but did loos my apeytite and loos my memery . . .
and then wold be better agen for some time after but this time I
was verey ill for . . . days verey mortely and thanke god while I
semed to recover my memerey and thanke god I have my memery
in sume meshur returned I did grow verey thin so much that Billey
sed he had never seen so much changes in me and *since* the wether
I have grone better and recovered my coller agen I am in hopes I
shall get better agen to see you it was not only sickness but two
much disquiet of mind but I had taken up a resey lushon never to
make any complainte to you or give you aney disquiet to you . . .

✐1770: Troops in Boston

The winds in London concerning the colonies kept shifting.
It was not realized by either side of the Atlantic that the
colonists were slowly becoming less and less British. On
March 5, 1770, the so-called Boston massacre occurred. A
squad of British troops, quartered in the city at the request of
the unpopular governor, Thomas Hutchinson, after repeated
provocation, fired on an unruly crowd, killing five citizens.

To Joseph Galloway in Philadelphia

London, June 11, 1770

Dear Sir:

   The Parliament is up without repealing the tea duty: but it is generally given out & understood that it will be done next winter. Lord North, I have reason to believe, was for doing it now; but

was overruled. A general act is talked of, revising all the acts for regulating trade in America, wherein every thing that gives just cause of offense to the colonists may be omitted, and the tea with its odious preamble may be dropped, without hurting the honor of Parliament, which it seems was apprehended if it had been repealed this year. But it is by no means certain yet that such an act will take place.—The act intended at the beginning of the session, and

At the Governor's request, British troops are landed in Boston, 1768.

alluded to in the King's speech, for punishing the combinations of merchants not to import, etc. was never brought forward. I flatter myself I may have had some share in discouraging it, by representing the difficulties & even impracticabilities of carrying such an act into execution in the colonies, showing that government here would by such a measure only expose its own weakness and imprudence in a fresh instance, and produce an effect contrary to that intended, rendering the agreements more general and more firmly adhered to, by souring still farther the minds of the people.—Toward the conclusion of the session Governor Pownall made another speech and motion relating to the military power kept up in America, a copy of which I send you enclosed. It is a curious question, how far it is agreeable to the British Constitution, for the king who is sovereign over different states, to march the troops he has raised by authority of Parliament in one of the states, into another state, and quarter them there in time of peace, without the consent of the Parliament of that other state. Should it be concluded that he may do this, what security has Great Britain, that a future king, when the colonies shall become more powerful, may not raise armies there, transport them hither, and quarter them here without consent of Parliament, perhaps to the prejudice of their liberties, and even with a view of subverting them?—The House got over Mr. Pownall's motion, by a declaration of the Ministry that the several matters contained in it were already under consideration of his Majesty's law servants, and that everything would be done conformable to the law and the Constitution; that the troops would not be returned to Boston, unless called for by the civil power, etc.

On the whole, there seems a general disposition in the nation (a particular faction excepted) to be upon good terms with the colonies, and to leave us in the enjoyment of all our rights. It is universally thought that no future impositions on America will ever be attempted here; only it is not to be expected that Parliament should formally renounce its claim; that, they say, would be inconsistent with its dignity, etc. And yet I think all this is not quite to be relied on. There is a malice against us in some powerful people, that discovers itself in all their expressions when they speak of us; and incidents may yet arise on either side of the water that may give them advantage, and prevent those healing measures that all good men wish to take place.

✍1771: Family Finances

Franklin was concerned about his income. The revenues from his Philadelphia properties went to support his wife. In London he lived on his salaries from the post office and as agent for the colonies of Pennsylvania, Massachusetts, New Jersey and Georgia, which were often late in being paid. Governor Franklin, drew on his father each year for funds to keep up his station. There was a plan proposed which could have netted them both a fortune. Vast lands in what is now West Virginia had been ceded by the Indians to the English. The Grand Ohio Company, later to be known as the Walpole Company, involved a first request for 2,500,000 acres, later enlarged to 20,000,000 acres, which offered investors an opportunity for fabulous returns. The list of investors, limited to seventy-two, included Benjamin Franklin and his son, William, as well as many English statesmen, politicians and noblemen. Franklin gave up his shares in this venture in 1774.

To Governor William Franklin in New Jersey

London, April 20, 1771

Dear Son:

It is long since I have heard from you. The last packet brought me no letter, and there are two packets now due. It is supposed that the long easterly winds have kept them back. We have had a severe and tedious winter here. There is not yet the smallest appearance of spring. Not a bud has pushed out, nor a blade of grass. The turnips that used to feed the cattle have been destroyed by the frost. The hay in most parts of the country is gone, and the cattle perishing for want, the lambs dying by thousands, through cold and scanty nourishment.

The Ohio affair seems now near a conclusion. And if the present Ministry stand a little longer, I think it will be completed to our satisfaction. I would, however, advise you not to say anything of our prospect of sucess till the event appears, for many things happen between the cup & the lip . . .

To Mrs. Deborah Franklin in Philadelphia

May 1, 1771

My dear Child:

The bill on Sir Alexander Grant for £30 which you so kindly sent me enclosed, came safe to hand. I am obliged too to Mr. Hall for enabling you on a pinch to buy it. But I am sorry you had so much trouble about it; and the more so, as it seems to have occasioned some disgust in you against Messrs. Foxcrofts, [joint deputy postmaster general and brother] for not supplying you with money to pay for it. That you may not be offended with your neighbors without cause; I must acquaint you with what it seems you did not know, that I had limited them in their payments to you, to the sum of thirty pounds per month, for the sake of our more easily settling, and to prevent mistakes. This making 360 pounds a year, I thought, as you have no house rent to pay yourself, and receive the rents of 7 or 8 houses besides, might be sufficient for the maintenance of your family. I judged such a limitation the more necessary, because you never have sent me any account of your expenses, and think yourself ill-used if I desire it; and because I know you were not very attentive to money matters in your best days, and I apprehend that your memory is too much impaired for the management of unlimited sums, without danger of injuring the future fortune of your daughter and grandson. If out of more than £500 a year, you could have saved enough to buy those bills it might have been well to continue purchasing them. But I do not like your going about among my friends to borrow money for that purpose, especially as it is not at all necessary. And therefore I once more request that you would decline buying them for the future. And I hope you will no longer take it amiss of Messrs. Foxcrofts that they did not supply you. If what you receive is really insufficient for your support, satisfy me by accounts that it is so, and I shall order more.

I am much pleased with the little histories you give me of your fine boy [Franklin's grandson, Benjamin Franklin Bache], which are confirmed by all that have seen him. I hope he will be spared and continue the same pleasure and comfort to you, and that I shall ere long partake with you in it. My love to him, and to his papa and mama. Mrs. Stevenson too is just made very happy by her daughter's being safely delivered of a son; the mother and child both well.

1771: Journey with a Child

On a visit to his friend Bishop Jonathan Shipley in the summer of 1771, Franklin wrote the first part of his *Autobiography* in thirteen days or less. Returning to London, he took back to school the youngest daughter of the household, Catherine or Kitty, aged eleven.

To Mrs. Jonathan Shipley at Twyford

London, August 12, 1771

Dear Madam:

This is just to let you know that we arrived safe and well in Marlborough Street about six, where I delivered up my charge.

The above seems too short for a letter; so I will lengthen it by a little account of our journey. The first stage we were rather pensive. I tried several topics of conversation, but none of them would hold. But after breakfast we began to recover spirits and had a good deal of chat. Will you hear some of it? We talked of her brother, and she wished he was married. And don't you wish your sisters married too? Yes. All but Emily; I would not have her married. Why? Because I can't spare her, I can't part with her. The rest may marry as soon as they please, so they do but get good husbands. We then took upon us to consider for 'em what sort of husband would be fitted for every one of them. We began with Georgiana. She thought a country gentleman that loved traveling and would take her with him, that loved books and would hear her read to him. I added that had a good estate and was a member of Parliament and loved to see an experiment now and then. This she agreed to. So we set him down for Georgiana and went on to Betsy. Betsy, says I, seems of a sweet, mild temper, and if we should give her a country squire, and he should happen to be of a rough, passionate turn, and be angry now and then, it might break her heart! O none of 'em must be so; for then they would not be good husbands. To make sure of this point, however, for Betsy, shall we give her a bishop? O no, that won't do. They all declare against the Church, and against the Army; not one of them will marry either a clergyman or an officer; that they are resolved upon. What can be the reason for that? Why, you know that when a clergyman or an officer dies, the income goes with 'em; and then what is there to maintain the family? There's the point. Then suppose we give her a good, honest, sensible city merchant who will love her dearly and is very rich? I don't know but that may do. We proceeded to Emily, her dear Emily. I was afraid we should hardly find anything good enough for Emily; but at last, after first settling that if she did marry, Kitty was to live a good deal with her, we agreed that as Emily was very handsome we might expect an earl for her. So having fixed her, as I thought, a countess, we went on to Anna Maria. She, says Kitty, should have a rich man that has a large family and a great many things to take care of; for she is very good at managing, helps my Mama very much, can look over bills, and order all sorts of family business. Very well, and as there is a grace and dignity in her manner that would become the station, what do you think of giving her a duke? O no! I'll have the duke for Emily. You may give the earl to Anna Maria if you please: but Emily shall have the duke. I contested this matter some time; but at length was forced to give up the point, leave Emily in possession of the duke, and content myself with the earl for Anna Maria. And now what shall we do for Kitty? We have forgot her, all this time. Well, and what will you do for her? I suppose that though the rest have resolved against the Army, she may not yet have made so rash a resolution. Yes, but she has: Unless now, an old one, an old general that has done fighting, and is rich, such a one as General Rufane. I like him a good deal; you must know that I like an old man, indeed I do. And somehow or other all the old men take to me; all that come to our house like me better than my other sisters. I go to 'em and ask 'em how they do, and they like it mightily; and the maids take notice of it, and say when they see an old man come, there's a friend of yours, Miss Kitty. But then as you like an old general, hadn't you better take him while he's a young officer, and let him grow old upon your hands, because then you'll like him better and better every year as he grows older and older. No, that won't do. He must be an old man of 70 or 80, and take me when I am about 30. And then you know I may be a rich young widow.

We dined at Staines. She was Mrs. Shipley, cut up the chicken pretty handily (with a little direction), and helped me in a very womanly manner. Now, says she when I commended her, my father never likes to see me or Georgiana carve, because we do it, he says, so badly. But how should we learn if we never try? We drank good Papa and Mama's health, and the healths of the duchess, the countess, the merchant's lady, the country gentleman, and our Welsh brother. This brought their affairs again under consideration. I doubt, says she, we have not done right for Betsy. I don't think a merchant will do for her. She is much inclined to be a fine gentlewoman; and is indeed already more of the fine gentlewoman, I think, than any of my other sisters; and therefore she shall be a viscountess.

Thus we chatted on and she was very entertaining quite to town.

I have now made my letter as much too long as it was at first too short. The Bishop would think it too trifling, therefore don't show it him. I am afraid too that you will think it so and have a good mind not to send it. Only it tells you Kitty is well at school, and for that I let it go. My love to the whole amiable family, best respects to the Bishop, and 1000 thanks for all your kindnesses, and for the happy days I enjoyed at Twyford.

With the greatest esteem and respect, I am, Madam, your most obedient humble servant. . . .

✐ 1772: Family Affairs

Franklin met his new son-in-law in London and seemed pleased enough to make him a gift of two hundred pounds to launch his business in Philadelphia, where he proposed the young man establish himself. Franklin made no move to overindulge the young businessman. Franklin, who had not yet seen his grandson in Philadelphia, delighted in comparing experiences with his "godson," Billy, the child of Polly Stevenson, now Hewson, in London. Deborah's health was failing and Sally Bache was taking over the management of the Philadelphia household.

From Deborah Franklin to Benjamin Franklin, London

[1772?]

My dear Child:

I reseved yours by the packit it gives me much pleshuer to hear that you air well and happey I was in hopes that a packit or a vesill wold arived before this wente . . . as I was in hopes that [it] wold in forme when you intend to returne agen to your one home I conte write to you as I am so very unfitt to express my self and not a bell to due as I yousd for that illness I hed was a polsey all thou I donte shake my memery failes me I conte expres my self as I yousd to due I did tell your friend Dr Small when he was heare that I had thoute it was a polsey my write hand is verey weak some times I am not abel to try on my close I am verey low sperreted that it is verey trubl sume to tell what I wold say it wold be of . . . I have bin verey un well for 5 or 6 days I donte make aney complaint to you. I saw yisterday that several vesils from N York and frome this place to Ingland I belive Dr Small was in one of them I hope he is safe arived at home and well Mr. Beache ses that he is a good mon I hope Capt Falkner is safe arive and well . . . I must aske in faver for sume muslim for Salley to worke for her self I have one my self but have not wore it . . . let me know if you shold return home this fall I heard that Mrs. Write has seen you but when shee wente I did not know when shee wente or I shold a given her a letter. . . . I observe with pleshuer you tell me a boote the dear child you tell me and the pleshuer his grandmama takes of her and I have been told with so much pleshuer of your grand dafter in their plase shee is a fine young lady shee is the verey pickter of her father a fine child in dead.

To Mrs. Sarah Bache in Philadelphia

London, January 29, 1772

Dear Sally:

I received your agreeable letters of Oct. 11 and Nov. 5. I met with Mr. Bache at Preston, where I stayed two or three days, being very kindly entertained by his mother and sisters, whom I liked much. He came to town with me, and is now going home to you. I have advised him to settle down to business in Philadelphia, where he will always be with you. I am of opinion, that almost any profession a man has been educated in, is preferable to an office held at pleasure, as rendering him more independent, more a freeman, and less subject to caprices of superiors. And I think, that in keeping a store, if it be where you dwell, you can be service-

Sarah Franklin Bache

able to him as your mother was to me: for you are not deficient in capacity, and I hope are not too proud.

You might easily learn accounts, and you can copy letters, or write them very well upon occasion. By industry & frugality you may get forward in the world, being both of you yet young. And then what we may leave you at our death may be a pretty addition, though of itself far from sufficient to maintain & bring up a family. It is one of the more importance for you to think seriously of this, as you may have a number of children to educate. Till my return you need be at no expense for rent, etc., as you are all welcome to continue with your mother, and indeed it seems to be your duty to attend her, as she grows infirm, and takes such delight in your company and the child's. This saving will be a help in your progress. And for your encouragement I can assure you that there is scarce a merchant of opulence in your town, whom I do not remember a young beginner with as little to go on with, & no better prospects than Mr. Bache. That his voyage hither might not be quite fruitless, I have given him £ 200 sterling; with which I wish you good luck.

I hope you will attend to what is recommended to you in this letter, it proceeding from sincere affection, after due consideration, with the knowledge I have of the world and my own circumstances. I am much pleased with the account I receive from all hands of your dear little boy. I hope he will be continued a blessing to us all. Though I long to see my family, I am glad you did not come over, as the expense would have been great, and I think I shall not continue here much longer. It is a pleasure to me that the little thing I sent you proved agreeable.

To Mrs. Deborah Franklin in Philadelphia

London, May 5, 1772

My dear Child:

I received your kind letter of March 2. I hope Mr. Bache is with you and his family by this time as he sailed from the Downs the latter end of February. My love to him and Sally and young master, who I suppose is master of the house. Tell him that Billy Hewson is as much thought of here as he can be there. . . .

London, January 6, 1773

My dear Child:

I feel still some regard for this sixth of January, as my old nominal birthday, though the change of style [to the Gregorian calendar, 1752] has carried the real day forward to the 17th, when I shall be, if I live till then, 67 years of age. It seems but the other day since you and I were ranked among the boys & girls, so swiftly does time fly! We have however great reason to be thankful that so much of our lives has passed so happily; and that so great a share of health and strength remains, as to render life yet comfortable.

I rejoice to hear that you all continue well. But you have so used me to have something pretty about the boy, that I am a little disappointed in finding nothing more of him than that he is gone up to Burlington. Pray give me in your next as usual, a little of his history. . . .

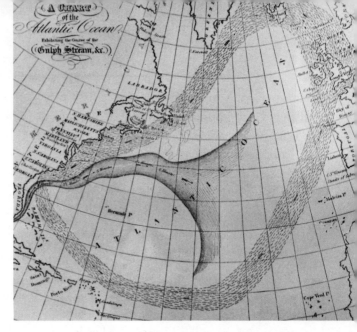

The Gulf Stream, drawn from Franklin's notes

London, February 2, 1773

My dear Child:

I know you love to have a line from me by every packet so I write, though I have little to say, having had no letter from you since my last, of Jan. 6.

In return for your history of your *grandson*, I must give you a little of the history of my *godson*. He is now 21 months old, very strong and healthy, and begins to speak a little and even to sing. He was with us a few days last week, grew fond of me, and would not be contented to sit down to breakfast without coming to call *pa*, rejoicing when he had got me into my place. It makes me long to be at home to play with Ben. . . .

To Mrs. Sarah Bache in Philadelphia

London, April 6, 1773

Dear Sally:

I am glad you have undertaken the care of the housekeeping as it will be an ease to your mother, especially if you can manage to her approbation; *that* may perhaps be at first a difficulty. It will be of use to you if you get a *habit* of keeping exact accounts, and it will be some satisfaction to me to see them. I long to be with you all, and to see your son. I pray God to bless him and you.

1772: Father and Son

Franklin continued to send reports to his son, Governor William, about general affairs between England and the colonies and particularly about the slow and secret progress of their investment prospects in the Grand Ohio Company. Prospects must have seemed fair enough for Franklin to suggest to his son a will in favor of the growing boy, Temple, who was at school in England. William's request for additional salary as governor seems to have found little response and his father seemed less than eager to pursue it for him. The older Franklin shows more than a little irritation over his son's request that he exert political influence to get some advantage out of the collection of duties and customs by the British in America. But, still a father, the elder Franklin shows concern for his son's health and urges his famous exercise regimen. There is also a hint, perhaps playful, of a rivalry for honors between father and son.

To Governor William Franklin in New Jersey

London, August 17, 1772

Dear Son:

At length we have got rid of Lord Hillsborough, and Lord Dartmouth takes his place, to the great satisfaction of all the friends of America. You will hear it said among you, I suppose, that the interest of the Ohio planters has ousted him; but the truth is, what I wrote you long since, that all his brother ministers disliked him extremely, and wished for a fair occasion of tripping up his heels; so, seeing that he made a point of defeating our scheme, they made another of supporting it on purpose to mortify him, which they knew his pride could not bear. I do not mean they would have done this if they had thought our proposal bad in itself, or his opposition well founded; but I believe if he had been on good terms with them they would not have differed with him for so small a matter. The King, too, was tired of him and of his administration, which had weakened the affection and respect of the colonies for the royal government, of which (I may say it to you) I used proper means from time to time that his Majesty should have due information and convincing proofs. More of this when I see you.

The King's dislike made the others more firmly united in the resolution of disgracing Hillsborough, by setting at nought his famous report. But now that business is done, perhaps our affair may be less regarded in the cabinet, and suffered to linger, and possibly may yet miscarry. Therefore let us beware of every word and action that may betray a confidence in its success, lest we render ourselves ridiculous in case of disappointment. We are now pushing for a completion of the business; but the time is unfavorable, everybody gone or going into the country, which gives room for accidents.

P.S. The regard Lord Dartmouth has always done me the honor to express for me, gives me room to hope being able to obtain more in favor of our colonies upon occasion than I could for some time past.

London, August 19, 1772

Dear Son:

In yours of May 14 you acquaint me with your indisposition, which gave me great concern. The resolution you have taken to use more exercise is extremely proper and I hope you will steadily perform it. It is of the greatest importance to prevent diseases, since the cure of them by physic is so very precarious.

In considering the different kinds of exercise, I have thought that the *quantum* of each is to be judged of, not by time or by distance, but by the degree of warmth it produces in the body. Thus, when I observe if I am cold when I get into a carriage in a morning I may ride all day without being warmed by it; that if on horseback my feet are cold I may ride some hours before they become warm, but if I am ever so cold on foot I cannot walk an hour briskly without glowing from head to foot by the quickened circulation; I have been ready to say (using round numbers without regard to exactness, but merely to mark a great difference) that there is more exercise in *one* mile's riding on horseback than in *five* in a coach; and more in *one* mile's walking on foot than in *five* on horseback; to which I may add that there is more in walking *one* mile up and down stairs than in *five* on a level floor. The two latter exercises may be had within doors when the weather discourages going abroad; and the last may be had when one is pinched for time, as containing a great quantity of exercise in a handful of minutes. The dumbbell is another exercise of the latter compendious kind. By the use of it I have in forty swings quickened my pulse from sixty to one hundred beats in a minute, counted by a second-watch; and I suppose the warmth generally increases with quickness of pulse.

London, August 19, 1772

Dear Son:

I received yours of June 30. I am vexed that my letter to you, written at Glasgow, miscarried; not so much that you did not receive it as that it is probably in other hands. It contained some accounts which were for you only.

As to my situation here, nothing can be more agreeable, especially as I hope for less embarrassment from the new minister [Lord Dartmouth]: a general respect paid me by the learned, a number of friends and acquaintance among them with whom I have a pleasing intercourse; a character of so much weight that it has protected me when some in power would have done me injury, and continued me in an office they would have deprived me of; my company so much desired that I seldom dine at home in winter, and could spend the whole summer in the country houses of inviting friends if I chose it. Learned and ingenious foreigners that come to England almost all make a point of visiting me; for my reputation is still higher abroad than here. Several of the foreign ambassadors have assiduously cultivated my acquaintance, treating me as one of their *corps*, partly I believe from the desire they have, from time to time, of hearing something of American affairs, an object become of importance in foreign courts, who begin to hope Britain's alarming power will be diminished by the defection of her colonies; and partly that they may have an opportunity of introducing me to the gentlemen of their country who desire it. The King, too, has lately been heard to speak of me with great regard.

These are flattering circumstances; but a violent longing for home sometimes seizes me, which I can no otherwise subdue but by promising myself a return next spring or next fall, and so forth. As to returning hither, if I once go back, I have no thoughts of it. I am too far advanced in life to propose three voyages more. I have some important affairs to settle at home, and considering my double expenses here and there, I hardly think my salaries fully compensate the disadvantages. The late change, however, being thrown into the balance determines me to stay another winter.

August 22. I find I omitted congratulating you on the honor of your election into the Society for Propagating the Gospel. There you match indeed my Dutch honor. But you are again behind, for last night I received a letter from Paris, of which the enclosed is an extract, acquainting me that I am chosen *Associé Etranger* (foreign member) of the Royal Academy there. There are but eight of these *Associés Etrangers* in all Europe, and those of the most distinguished names for science. The vacancy I have the honor of filling was made by the death of the late celebrated Van Swieten of Vienna. This mark of respect from the first academy in the world, which Abbé Nollet, one of its members, took so much pains to prejudice against my doctrines, I consider as a kind of victory without ink shed, since I never answered him. I am told he has but one of his sect now remaining in the Academy. All the rest who have in any degree acquainted themselves with electricity, are, as he calls them, *Franklinists*. Yours, etc. . . .

London, November 3, 1772

Dear Son:

I wrote to you per the October packet, and have not since had any line from you. Lord Dartmouth came to town last week, and had his first levee on Wednesday, at which I attended. He received me very politely in his room, only Secretary Pownall present, expressing some regret that he happened to be from home when I was near him in the country, where he had hoped for the pleasure of seeing me, etc. I said I was happy to see his Lordship in his present situation, in which for the good of both countries I hoped he would long continue; and I begged leave to recommend my son to his protection, who, says I, is one of your governors in America. The Secretary then put in—*and a very good governor he is.* Yes, says my Lord, he has been a good governor, and has kept his province in good order during times of difficulty. I then said that I came at present only to pay my respects, and should wait on his Lordship another day on business; to which he said he should always be ready to hear me and glad to see me. I shall attend his levee again today, on some New England affairs, and hope we may now go on more smoothly; but time will show.

As the Boards are met again, the Ohio affair will again be put forward as soon as Mr. Walpole comes to [town?], who went lately into Norfolk. I am almost settled in my new apartment; but removing, and sorting my papers, and placing my books and things has been a troublesome job. I am amazed to see how books have grown upon me since my return to England. I brought none with me, and have now a roomful: many collected in Germany, Holland, and France, and consisting chiefly of such as contain knowledge that may hereafter be useful to America.

My love to Betsey concludes at present from your affectionate father. . . .

London, April 6, 1773

Dear Son:

Possibly indeed the ideas of the court may change; for I think I see some alarm at the discontents in New England, and some appearance of softening in the disposition of government, on the idea that matters have been carried too far. But all depends upon circumstances and events. We govern from hand to mouth. There seems to be no wise regular plan . . . I saw Lord Dartmouth about 2 weeks since. He mentioned nothing to me of your application for additional salary, nor did I to him, for I do not like it. I fear it will embroil you with your people.

The Parliament is like to sit till the end of June. I had thoughts of returning home about that time. The Boston Assembly's answer to the Governor's speech [Governor Thomas Hutchinson] which I have just received, may possibly produce something here to occasion my longer stay.

London, July 14, 1773

Dear Son:

I am glad to find by yours of May 4 that you have been able to assist Josiah Davenport [Franklin's nephew] a little, but vexed that he and you should think of putting me upon a solicitation, which it is impossible for me to engage in. I am not upon terms with Lord North for any relation of mine. And detesting as I do the whole system of American customs, believing that they will one day bring on a breach, through the indiscretion and insolence of those concerned in the collection, I should never wish to see one so near to me in that business. . . .

I am glad you stand so well with Lord Dartmouth. I am likewise well with him, but he never spoke to me of augmenting your salary. He is truly a good man, and wishes sincerely a good understanding with the colonies, but does not seem to have the strength equal to his wishes.

West Wycombe, Lord Le Despencer's, August 3, 1773

Dear Son:

I am come hither to spend a few days and breathe a little fresh air. As to the Ohio affair, it is scarcely likely to be got through this summer, for reasons I have already given you.

Temple is just returned to school from his summer vacation. He always behaves himself so well, as to increase my affection for him every time he is with me.

As you are likely to have a considerable landed property, it would

"Bostonians in Distress,"
a sympathetic
English view

be well to make your will, if you have not already done it, and secure that property to him. Our friend Galloway will advise you in the manner. Whatever he may come to possess, I am persuaded he will make a good use of it, if his temper and understanding do not strangely alter. . . .

1773: Hutchinson Letters

In 1768–69, Thomas Hutchinson, later to become governor of Massachusetts, wrote six letters in secret to British ministers, in which he advocated strong and forceful measures against the colonists. Andrew Oliver, later to be lieutenant governor, wrote an additional four. When they fell into

Franklin's hands in London, he realized that some of Britain's unpopular repressive measures, for example the landing of the British troops at Boston, were not suggested in London but by native Americans. His anger against England cooled and he felt similar furies in America would also abate. Secretly he sent the originals to Boston, where his conditions that they not be copied or published were disregarded. As Franklin predicted, the Boston reaction turned against the Governor and Lieutenant Governor and the Assembly voted a petition to the King for their removal, which Franklin expected to present peaceably. Governor William Franklin, who seemingly entertained some friendship for his fellow governor, differed with his father, siding more strongly with the English government.

Still unmindful of the fact that political thunderbolts were building up over the Hutchinson letters, Franklin continued his affairs. His works were increasingly popular in France and England and his reputation was growing similarly. He turned his sharpest pen and nimblest wit to satirizing the English claims against the American colonies.

To Mrs. Deborah Franklin in Philadelphia

London, September 1, 1773

My dear Child:

There is a new translation of my book at Paris and printed there, being the 3d edition in French. A fifth edition is now printing here. To the French edition, they have prefixed a print of me, which, though a copy by that of Chamberlain, has got so French a countenance, that you would take me for one of that lively nation. I think you do not mind such things or I would send you one. . . .

To Governor William Franklin in New Jersey

London, September 1, 1773

Dear Son:

I have now before me yours of July 5 and 6. I think the resolutions of the New England townships must have the effect they seem intended for, viz. to show that the discontents were really general and their sentiments concerning their rights unanimous, and not the fiction of a few demagogues, as their governors used to represent them here.

It is said here, that the famous Boston letters [the Hutchinson letters] were sent chiefly, if not all, to the late Mr. Whately. They fell into my hands, and I thought it my duty to give some principal people there a sight of them, very much with this view, that when they saw the measures they complained of took their rise in a great degree from the representations and recommendations of their own countrymen, their resentment against Britain on account of these measures might abate, as mine had done, and a reconciliation more easily obtained. In Boston they concealed who sent them, the better to conceal who received and communicated them. And perhaps it is as well, that it should continue a secret. Being of that country [Boston] myself, I think those letters more heinous than you seem to think them; but you had not read them all, nor perhaps the Council's remarks on them. I have written to decline their agency, on account of my return to America. Dr. Lee succeeds me. I only keep it while I stay, which perhaps will be another winter.

London, October 6, 1773

Dear Son:

I wrote to you on the 1st of last month, since which I have received yours of July 29 from New York. I know not what letters of mine Governor H[utchinson] could mean as advising the people to insist on their independency. But whatever they were, I suppose he has sent copies of them hither, having heard some whisperings about them. I shall, however, be able at any time to justify everything I have written; the purport being uniformly this, that they should carefully avoid all tumults and every violent measure, and content themselves with verbally keeping up their claims and holding forth their rights whenever occasion requires; secure that, from the growing importance of America, those claims will erelong be attended to and acknowledged.

From a long and thorough consideration of the subject, I am

indeed of opinion that the Parliament has no right to make any law whatever, binding on the colonies; that the King, and not the King, Lords, and Commons collectively, is their sovereign; and that the King, with their respective Parliaments, is their only legislator. I know your sentiments differ from mine on these subjects. You are a thorough government man, which I do not wonder at, nor do I aim at converting you. I only wish you to act uprightly and steadily, avoiding that duplicity which in Hutchinson adds contempt to indignation. If you can promote the prosperity of your people and leave them happier than you found them, whatever your political principles are, your memory will be honored.

I have written two pieces here lately for the *Public Advertiser*, on American affairs, designed to expose the conduct of this country toward the colonies in a short, comprehensive, and striking view, and stated, therefore, in out-of-the-way forms, as most likely to take the general attention. The first was called "Rules by Which a Great Empire May Be Reduced to a Small One"; the second, "An Edict of the King of Prussia." I sent you one of the first, but could not get enough of the second to spare you one, though my clerk went the next morning to the printer's and wherever they were sold. They were all gone but two. In my own mind I preferred the first, as a composition, for the quantity and variety of the matter contained and a kind of spirited ending of each paragraph. But I find that others here generally prefer the second.

I am not suspected as the author except by one or two friends; and have heard the latter spoken of in the highest terms, as the keenest and severest piece that has appeared here for a long time.

What made it the more noticed here was that people in reading it were, as the phrase is, *taken in*, till they had got half through it, and imagined it a real edict, to which mistake I suppose the king of Prussia's *character* must have contributed.

London, January 5, 1774

Dear Son:

My return will interfere with nobody's interest or influence in public affairs, as my intention is to decline all interest in them, and every active part and to content myself with communicating the knowledge of them which my situation may have furnished me with. For being now about entering my sixty-ninth year, and having lived so great a part of my life to the public, it seems but fair that I should be allowed to live the small remainder to myself and my friends.

Our friend [John] Temple, as you will see by the papers, has been engaged in a duel, about an affair in which he had no concern. As the combat was interrupted and understood to be unfinished, I thought it incumbent on me to do what I could for preventing further mischief, and so declared my having transmitted the letters in question. This has drawn some censure upon myself, but as I grow old, I grow less concerned about censure, when I am satisfied I am acting rightly; and I have the pleasure of having exculpated a friend, who lay undeservedly under an imputation to his dishonor.

I am now seriously preparing for my departure to America. I purpose sending my luggage, books, instruments etc. by All or Falconer, and taking my passage to New York in one of the spring or summer packets, partly for settling some business with the post office, and partly that I may see you on my way to Philadelphia. . . .

1774: In the Cockpit

In his letter to his son of October 6, 1773, Franklin hinted at the suggestion of the sympathy that the New Jersey Governor felt for his Massachusetts colleague. "I do not wonder that Hutchinson should be dejected," he wrote as if in response to his son's comment. "It must be an uncomfortable thing to live among people who he is conscious universally detest him." The affair of the Hutchinson letters continued to smolder. Franklin, without realizing it, gave his enemies a powerful weapon by publicly acknowledging his part in forwarding the letters. Three days after his letter to his son, dated January 5, 1774, Franklin was summoned to appear before the Privy Council. Events moved fast. At the end of the month, Franklin stood silently, dressed in a simple blue coat, before a conclave of ministers in the "Cockpit" and was attacked and abused. He was called a "thief" by the vituperative spokesman for the English government. His "crime" was admitting what all ministers were guilty of—making public use of private letters. But here was a chance to get rid of Franklin and to punish him for his tenacious battle for America's rights. Governor Hutchinson's nephews and sons were also agents in Boston for the East India Company, which was acquiring a monopoly of the tea trade. Other tea merchants were outraged, and the situation exploded in the Boston Tea Party, December 16, 1773, the news of which had just aroused London.

To Thomas Cushing in Boston

London, February 15, 1774

Sir:

I wrote a line to you by the last packet, just to acquaint you there had been a hearing on our petition [to remove the governor and lieutenant governor]. I shall now give you the history of it as succinctly as I can.

We had long imagined that the King would have considered that petition as he had done the preceding one, in his cabinet, and have given an answer without a hearing, since it did not pray

punishments or disabilities on the governors. But on Saturday the 8th of January, in the afternoon, I received notice from the clerk of the council that the Lords of the Committee for Plantation Affairs would, on the Tuesday following at twelve, meet at the Cockpit to take into consideration the petition referred to them by his Majesty, and that my attendance was required.

On Monday, very late in the afternoon, I received another notice, that Mr. [Israel] Mauduit, agent for the governor and lieutenant governor, had asked and obtained leave to be heard by counsel on the morrow in their behalf. This very short notice seemed intended to surprise us. On Tuesday we attended at the Cockpit, and, the petition being read, I was called upon for what I had to offer in support of it. I said that with the petition of the House of Representatives I had received their resolutions which preceded it, and a copy of the letters on which those resolutions were founded, which I would lay before their Lordships in support of the petition.

The resolutions were accordingly read; but when the letters were taken up, Mr. [Alexander] Wedderburn, the solicitor general, brought there as a counsel for the governors, began to object and inquire how they were authenticated, as did also some of the Lords. I said the authentications were annexed. They wanted to know the nature of them. I said that would appear when they were read,

In the Cockpit:
Franklin stands
straight and silent

and prayed they would hear them. Lord Chief Justice De Grey asked whom the letters were directed to; and taking them in his hand, observed there was no address prefixed to any of them. I said that though it did not appear to whom they were directed, it appeared who had written them; their names were subscribed; the originals had been shown to the gentlemen themselves, and they had not denied their handwriting; and the testifications annexed proved these to be true copies.

With difficulty I obtained leave to have the authentications read; and the solicitor general proceeding to make observations as counsel for the governors, I said to their Lordships that it was some surprise to me to find counsel employed against the petition; I said I had intended merely to lay the papers before their Lordships, without making a single comment on them. But this did not satisfy; he chose to be heard by counsel. So finally I had leave to be heard by counsel also in behalf of the petition. The solicitor general, finding his cavils against the admission of the letters were not supportable, at last said that, to save their Lordships' time, he would admit the copies to be true transcripts of the originals, but he should reserve to himself a right, when the matter came on again, of asking certain questions, such as how the Assembly came into possession of them, through what hands, and by what means they were procured. The day appointed for the hearing was the 29th of January.

A report now prevailed through the town that I had been grossly abused by the solicitor general at the council board. But this was premature. He had only intended it, and mentioned that intention. I heard, too, from all quarters, that the ministry and all the courtiers were highly enraged against me for transmitting those letters. I was called an incendiary, and the papers were filled with invectives against me. Hints were given me that there were some thoughts of apprehending me, seizing my papers, and sending me to Newgate. I was well informed that a resolution was taken to deprive me of my place; it was only thought best to defer it till after the hearing, I suppose, because I was there to be so blackened that nobody should think it injustice. Many knew, too, how the petition was to be treated, and I was told, even before the first hearing, that it was to be rejected with some epithets, the Assembly to be censured, and some honor done the governors. How this could be known one cannot say. It might be only conjecture.

The transactions relating to the tea had increased and strengthened the torrent of clamor against us. No one had the least expectation of success to the petition.

While my mind was taken up with this business I was harassed with a subpoena from the chancellor to attend his court the next day, at the suit of Mr. William Whately concerning the letters. This man was under personal obligations to me, such as would have made it base in him to commence such a suit of his own motion against me without any previous notice, claim, or demand; but if he was capable of doing it at the instance of the ministry, whose banker he is for some pension money, he must be still baser.

The briefs being prepared and perused, our counsel, therefore thought it was more advisable to state as facts the general discontent of the people, that the governors had lost all credit with them, and were become odious, etc.; facts of which the petition was itself full proof, because otherwise it could not have existed; and then show that it must in such a situation be necessary for his Majesty's service, as well as the peace of the province, to remove them. By this opinion, great part of the brief became unnecessary.

Notwithstanding the intimations I had received, I could not believe that the solicitor general would be permitted to wander from the question before their Lordships into a new case, the accusation of another person for another matter, not cognizable before them, who could not expect to be there so accused and therefore could not be prepared for his defense. And yet all this happened, and in all probability was preconcerted; for all the courtiers were invited, as to an entertainment, and there never was such an appearance of privy councilors on any occasion, not less than thirty-five, besides an immense crowd of other auditors.

The hearing began by reading my letter to Lord Dartmouth, enclosing the petition, then the petition itself, the resolves, and lastly the letters, the solicitor general making no objections nor asking any of the questions he had talked of.

The solicitor general then went into what he called a history of the province for the last ten years, and bestowed plenty of abuse upon it, mingled with encomium on the governors. But the favorite part of his discourse was leveled at your agent, who stood there the butt of his invective ribaldry for near an hour, not a single Lord adverting to the impropriety and indecency of treating a public messenger in so ignominious a manner, who was present only as the person delivering your petition, with the consideration of which no part of *his* conduct had any concern. If he had done a wrong in obtaining and transmitting the letters, that was not the tribunal where he was to be accused and tried. The cause was already before the chancellor. Not one of their Lordships checked and recalled the orator to the business before them, but on the contrary, a very few excepted, they seemed to enjoy highly the entertainment and frequently burst out in loud applauses. This part of his speech was thought so good that they have since printed it in order to defame me everywhere, and particularly to destroy my reputation on your side of the water; but the grosser parts of the abuse are omitted, appearing, I suppose, in their own eyes too foul to be seen on paper; so that the speech, compared to what it was, is now perfectly decent. My friends advise me to write an answer, which I purpose immediately.

Their Lordships' Report, which I send you, is dated the same day. It contains a severe censure, as you will see, on the petition and the petitioners; and, as I think, a very unfair conclusion from my silence that the charge of surreptitiously obtaining the letters was a true one; though the solicitor, as appears in the printed speech, had acquainted them that the matter was before the chancellor; and my counsel had stated the impropriety of my answering there to charges then trying in another court. In truth I came by them honorably, and my intention in sending them was virtuous, if an endeavor to lessen the breach between two states of the same empire be such, by showing that the injuries complained of by one of them did not proceed from the other but from traitors among themselves.

It may be supposed that I am very angry on this occasion, and therefore I did purpose to add no reflections of mine on the treatment the Assembly and their agent have received, lest they should be thought the effects of resentment and a desire of exasperating. But indeed what I feel on my own account is half lost in what I feel for the public. When I see that all petitions and complaints of grievances are so odious to government that even the mere pipe which conveys them becomes obnoxious, I am at a loss to know how peace and union are to be maintained or restored between the different parts of the Empire. Grievances cannot be redressed unless they are known; and they cannot be known but through complaints and petitions. If these are deemed affronts, and the messengers punished as offenders, who will henceforth send petitions? And who will deliver them? It has been thought a dangerous thing in any state to stop up the vent of griefs. Wise governments have therefore generally received petitions with some indulgence, even when but slightly founded. Those who think themselves injured by their rulers are sometimes, by a mild and prudent answer, convinced of their error. But where complaining is a crime, hope becomes despair.

The day following I received a written notice from the secretary of the general post office, that his Majesty's postmaster general *found it necessary* to dismiss me from my office of deputy postmaster general in North America. The expression was well chosen, for in truth they were *under a necessity* of doing it; it was not their own inclination; they had no fault to find with my conduct in the office; they knew my merit in it, and that if it was now an office of value it had become such chiefly through my care and good management; that it was worth nothing when given to me; it would not then pay the salary allowed me, and unless it did I was not to expect it; and that it now produces near three thousand pounds a year clear to the treasury here. They had besides a personal regard for me.

With my best wishes for the prosperity of the province, I have the honor to be, sir, etc. . . .

To Governor William Franklin in New Jersey

London, February 2, 1774

Dear Son:

This line is just to acquaint you that I am well, and that my office of Deputy Postmaster is taken from me. As there is no prospect of your being ever promoted to a better government, and that you hold has never defrayed its expenses, I wish you were well settled in your farm. 'Tis an honester and a more honorable, because a more independent employment. You will hear from others the treatment I have received. I leave you to your own reflections and determinations upon it, and remain ever your affectionate father.

To Richard Bache in Philadelphia

London, February 17, 1774

Dear Son:

I received yours of Nov. 20, 30, Dec. 28 & Jan. 1. Before this gets to hand you will have heard that I am displaced and consequently have it no longer in my power to assist you in your views relating to the Post Office, and as things are I would not wish to see you concerned in it. For I conceive that the dismissing me merely for not being corrupted by the office to betray the interests of my country, will make it some disgrace among us to hold such an office.

I am now fixed to return homeward in or about May next. I hope to have the great pleasure of finding you all well and happy. It will not be worthwhile to write me any letters that cannot be expected to arrive here before the middle of that month.

To Governor William Franklin in New Jersey

February 18, 1774

Some tell me that it is determined to displace you likewise, but I do not know it as certain. I only give you the hint, as an inducement to you to delay awhile your removal to Amboy, which in that case would be an expense and trouble to no purpose. Perhaps they may expect that your resentment of their treatment of me may induce you to resign, and save them the shame of depriving you when they ought to promote. But this I would not advise you to do. Let them take your place if they want it, though in truth I think it is scarce worth your keeping, since it has not afforded you sufficient to prevent your running every year behindhand with me. But one may make something of an injury, nothing of a resignation.

To Mrs. Deborah Franklin in Philadelphia

London, April 28, 1774

My dear Love:

I hoped to have been on the sea in my return by this time; but I find I must stay a few weeks longer, perhaps for the summer ships. Thanks to God, I continue well and hearty; and I hope to find you so, when I have the happiness once more of seeing you. . . . My blessings to the children.

1774: Death of Deborah

Even after the violent abuse of the Cockpit, Franklin still tarried in England. His correspondence with his wife lagged as she failed in health. His concern for his grandson, Temple, in a warm affectionate letter to his royalist son, reveals his wish to keep the young man from "precarious dependencies," suggesting his grandfather's and father's government services. Franklin's last known letter to his wife was dated on September 10, the month he told his son he might be on the high seas bound for home.

To Mrs. Deborah Franklin in Philadelphia

London, July 22, 1774

My dear Child:

I have had no line from you by several late opportunities. I flatter myself it is owing not to indisposition, but to the opinion of my having left England, which indeed I hope soon to do. Mr. Dillwyn tells me he never saw so fine a child as your youngest grandson: Has he eclipsed poor Ben? of whose pretty history I used to receive so many folio pages in your letters.

To Governor William Franklin in New Jersey

West Wycombe, August 1, 1774

Dear Son:

Methinks 'tis time to think of a profession for Temple (who is now upward of fourteen), that the remainder of his education may have some relation to it. I have thought he may make an expert lawyer, as he has a good memory, quick parts, and ready elocution. He would certainly make an excellent painter, having a vast fondness for drawing, which he pursues with unwearied industry, and has made great proficiency. But I do not find that he thinks of it as a business. The only hint of inclination he has given is that of being a surgeon; but it was slightly mentioned. It is indeed my wish that he might learn some art by which he could at any time procure a subsistence; and after that, if anything better could be done for him, well and good. But posts and places are precarious dependencies. I would have him a free man. Upon the whole, in my opinion, we should turn him to the law, as a profession reputable in itself; and as the knowledge he may gain in that study will qualify him for other employments and be serviceable to him if he were to be only a mere gentleman.

If I return this year it will probably be in the September packet. But I begin to have some doubts.

With love to Betsey, I am ever your affectionate father. . . .

To Mrs. Deborah Franklin in Philadelphia

London, September 10, 1774

It is now nine long months since I received a line from my dear Debby. I have supposed it owing to your continual expectation of my return; I have feared that some indisposition has rendered you unable to write; I have imagined anything rather than admit a supposition that your kind attention toward me was abated. And yet when so many other old friends have dropped a line to me now & then at a venture, taking the chance of finding me here or not as it might happen, why might I not have expected the same comfort from you, who used to be so diligent and faithful a correspondent, as to omit scarce any opportunity?

This will serve to acquaint you that I continue well, thanks to God.—It would be a great pleasure to me to hear that you are so. My love to our children, and believe me ever

Your affectionate Husband

From Governor Franklin to his Father in London

Philadelphia, December 24, 1774

Hon'rd Father:

I came here on Thursday last to attend the funeral of my poor old mother, who died the Monday noon preceding. Mr. Bache sent his clerk express to me on the occasion, who reached Amboy on Tuesday evening, and I set out early the next morning, but the weather being very severe and snowing hard, I was not able to reach here till about 4 o'clock on Thursday afternoon, about half an hour before the corpse was to be moved for interment. Mr. Bache and I followed as chief mourners; your old friend H. Roberts and several other of your friends were carriers, and a very respectable number of the inhabitants were at the funeral. I don't mention the particulars of her illness, as you will have a much fuller account from Mr. Bache than I am able to give. Her death was no more than might be reasonably expected after the paralytic stroke she received some time ago, which greatly affected her memory and understanding. She told me when I took leave of her on my removal for Amboy, that she never expected to see you unless you returned this winter, for that she was sure she should not live till next summer. I heartily wish you had happened to have come over in the fall, as I think her disappointment in that respect preyed a good deal on her spirits. . . .

I hope to see you and [Temple] in the spring, and that you will spend some time with me at Amboy, where I shall always have an apartment at your services. Your dutiful son . . .

✒1774:   Efforts   for   Peace

Despite the personal humiliation and abuse heaped on him, Franklin was still ready to counsel moderation if the bond between England and America could be preserved. Many in England, too, sought ways to effect a reconciliation, but Franklin's suggestions were mostly unacceptable to a government really out of touch with the real state of affairs in the colonies. America, too, was impatient. Any spark could explode the powder keg, as it was soon to do.

To Thomas Cushing in Boston

October 6, 1774

Sir:

Since my last to you which went per Captain Foulger, the Parliament by a sudden & unexpected resolution in the Cabinet, has been dissolved. Various are the conjectures as to the motives; among which one is that some advices from Boston, importing the impossibility of carrying on government there under the late acts of Parliament, have made it appear necessary that a new election should be got through before any ferment arises here among the manufacturers, which if it happened during the election (as might be expected if the old Parliament had gone on to finish its term) would probably have been a means of outing many of the Court candidates. As yet it does not appear that there is any intention of changing measures: But all intelligent men are of opinion, that if the American Congress should resolve on the nonconsumption of the manufactures of Britain, this Ministry must go out, and their late measures be all reversed. As such a resolution, firmly adhered to would in a peaceable and justifiable way do everything for us that we can wish, I am grieved to hear of mobs & violence, and the pulling down the houses, which our friends cannot justify, and which give great advantage against us to our enemies.

And when the result of the Congress arrives, and the measures they resolve to pursue (which I confide will be wise & good, entered into with unanimity, and persisted in with firmness) come to be known and considered here, I am persuaded our friends will be multiplied, and our enemies diminished so as to bring on an accommodation in which our undoubted rights shall be acknowledged and established.—This, for the common welfare of the British Empire, I most ardently wish. But I am in perpetual anxiety lest the mad measure of mixing soldiers among a people whose minds are in such a state of irritation, may be attended with some sudden mischief; for an accidental quarrel, a personal insult, an imprudent order, an insolent execution of even a prudent one, or 20 other things, may produce a tumult, unforeseen, and therefore impossible to be prevented in which such a carnage may ensue, as to make a breach that can never afterward be healed.—

1775: Loss of a Son

On his way back to Philadelphia on board the Pennsylvania packet, Franklin on March 22, 1775, began to write a full account of the "misunderstandings between Great Britain and America," which was later described as "Negotiation to Prevent the War." It was addressed, like the *Autobiography*, Part I, to "Dear Son," who was still the royal governor of New Jersey. But instead of following his father into the service of the rising America, Governor Franklin remained a Loyalist and a Tory. Joseph Galloway, who had been Franklin's agent in Pennsylvania, also sided against his countrymen. Governor Franklin's contention that some obligation was due to the British Ministry was turned down by his father in a letter that ended the correspondence between the two Franklins, so far as it is known, until 1784, nine years later. Franklin's letters are silent about this rupture in his "little family."

To Governor William Franklin in New Jersey

May 7, 1775

I don't understand it as any favor to me or to you, the being continued in an office by which, with all your prudence, you cannot avoid running behindhand if you live suitably to your station. While you are in it I know you will execute it with fidelity to your master, but I think independence more honorable than any service, and that in the state of American affairs which, from the present arbitrary measures, is likely soon to take place, you will find yourself in no comfortable situation and perhaps wish you had soon disengaged yourself. . . .

1775: Return Home

On April 19, 1775, at Concord and Lexington in Massachusetts open warfare began and the War for Independence was on. Franklin was at sea, returning home. For one week, he kept testing the temperature of the water, two to four times a day, to add to his knowledge of the Gulf Stream. On May 5th he reached Philadelphia and learned of the bloody outbreaks a few weeks before.

To Bishop Jonathan Shipley in London

Philadelphia, July 7, 1775

I found at my arrival all America from one end of the twelve united provinces, to the other, busily employed in learning the use of arms. The attack upon the country people near Boston by the army had roused everybody and exasperated the whole continent. The tradesmen of this city were in the field twice a day, at five in the morning and six in the afternoon, disciplining with the utmost diligence, all being volunteers. We have now three battalions, a troop of light horse and a company of artillery, who have made surprising progress. The same spirit appears everywhere, and the unanimity is amazing.

The day after my arrival, I was unanimously chosen by our Assembly, then sitting, an additional delegate to the Congress, which met the next week. The numerous visits of old friends and the public business have since devoured all my time; for we meet at nine in the morning and often sit till four. I am also upon a Committee of Safety appointed by the Assembly, which meets at six, and sits till near nine. The members attend closely without being bribed to it, by either salary, place, or pension, or the hopes of any: which I mention for your reflection on the difference between a new virtuous people, who have public spirit, and an old corrupt one, who have not so much as an idea that such a thing exists in nature. There has not been a dissenting voice among us in any resolution for defense, and our army, which is already formed, will soon consist of above twenty thousand men.

THE AMERICAN RIFLE MEN.

You will have heard before this reaches you of the defeat the ministerial troops met with in their first sortie; the several small advantages we have since had of them, and the more considerable affair of the 17th, when after two severe repulses they carried the unfinished trenches of the post we had just taken on a hill near Charlestown. They suffered greatly, however, and I believe are convinced by this time that they have men to deal with, though unexperienced and not yet well armed. In their way to this action, without the least necessity, they barbarously plundered and burned a fine, undefended town opposite to Boston, called Charlestown, consisting of about four hundred houses, many of them elegantly built; some sick, aged, and decrepit poor persons, who could not be carried off in time, perished in the flames. In all our wars, from our first settlement in America to the present time, we never received so much damage from the Indian *savages* as in this one day from these. Perhaps ministers may think this a means of disposing us to reconciliation. I feel and see everywhere the reverse. Most of the little property I have consists of houses in the seaport towns, which I suppose may all soon be destroyed in the same way, and yet I think I am not half so reconcilable now as I was a month ago.

The Congress will send one more petition to the King, which I suppose will be treated as the former was, and therefore will probably be the last; for though this may afford Britain one chance more of recovering our affections and retaining the connection, I think she has neither temper nor wisdom enough to seize the golden opportunity. When I look forward to the consequences, I see an end to all commerce between us; on our seacoasts she may hold some fortified places as the Spaniards do on the coast of Africa, but can penetrate as little into the country; a very numerous fleet, extending fifteen hundred miles at an immense expense, may prevent other nations trading with us; but as we have or may have within ourselves everything necessary to the comfort of life, and generally import only luxuries and superfluities, her preventing our doing that will in some respects contribute to our prosperity. By the present stoppage of our trade we save between four and five millions per annum, which will do something toward the expense of the war. What *she* will get by it, I must leave to be computed by her own political arithmeticians. These are some of my present ideas which I throw out to you in the freedom of friendship. Perhaps I am too sanguine in my opinion of our abilities for the defense of our country after we shall have given up our seaports to destruction, but a little time will show.

General Gage, we understand, entered into a treaty with the inhabitants of Boston whom he had confined by his works, in which treaty it was agreed that if they delivered their arms to the selectmen, their own magistrates, they were to be permitted to go out with their *effects*.

As soon as they had so delivered their arms, he seized them and caviled about the meaning of the word *effects*, which he said was only wearing apparel and household furniture, and not merchandise or shop goods, which he therefore detains. And the continual injuries and insults they met with from the soldiery made them glad to get out by relinquishing all that kind of property. How much those people have suffered, and are now suffering rather than submit to what they think unconstitutional acts of Parliament is really amazing. Two or three letters I send you enclosed may give you some, though a faint, idea of it. Gage's perfidy has now made him universally detested. When I consider that all this mischief is done my country by Englishmen and Protestant Christians, of a nation among whom I have so many personal friends, I am ashamed to feel any consolation in a prospect of revenge; I choose to draw it rather from a confidence that we shall sooner or later obtain reparation. I have proposed therefore to our people that they keep just accounts, and never resume the commerce or the union till satisfaction is made. If it is refused for twenty years, I think we shall then be able to take it with interest.

Your excellent advice was that if we must have a war, let it be carried on as between nations who had once been friends and wish to be so again. In this ministerial war against us, all Europe is conjured not to sell us arms or ammunition, that we may be found defenseless and more easily murdered. The humane Sir W.

Draper, who had been hospitably entertained in every one of our colonies, proposes in his papers called the *Traveller*, to excite the domestic slaves you have sold us to cut their masters' throats. Dr. Johnson, a Court pensioner, in his *Taxation no Tyranny*, adopts and recommends that measure, together with another of hiring the Indian savages to assassinate our planters in the back settlements. They are the poorest and most innocent of all people; and the Indian manner is to murder and scalp men, women, and children. This book I heard applauded by Lord Sandwich in Parliament, and all the ministerial people recommended it. Lord Dunmore and Governor Martin have already, we are told, taken some steps toward carrying one part of the project into execution, by inciting an insurrection among the blacks. And Governor Carleton, we have certain accounts, has been very industrious in engaging the

Cartoon for 1775: English policy inflames America

Indians to begin their horrid work. This is making war like nations who never had been friends and never wish to be such while the world stands. You see I am warm; and if a temper naturally cool and phlegmatic can, in old age, which often cools the warmest, be thus heated, you will judge by that of the general temper here, which is now little short of madness. We have, however, as yet asked no foreign power to assist us, nor made any offer of our commerce to other nations for their friendship. What another year's persecution may drive us to is yet uncertain.

I drop this disagreeable subject; and will take up one that I know must afford you and the good family, as my friends, some pleasure. It is the state of my own family, which I found in good health: my children affectionately dutiful and attentive to everything that can be agreeable to me; with three very promising grandsons, in whom I take great delight. So that were it not for our public troubles and the being absent from so many that I love in England, my present felicity would be as perfect as in this world one could well expect it. I enjoy, however, what there is of it, while it lasts, mindful at the same time that its continuance is like other earthly goods, uncertain. Adieu, my dear friend, and believe me ever, with sincere and great esteem, yours most affectionately. . . .

✑1776: To His Grandson

Franklin's Tory son was held prisoner for two years in Connecticut, both on parole and behind bars at the Litchfield jail. William Temple Franklin, living in the governor's mansion at Amboy, wished to visit his father and sought permission from his grandfather. Franklin refused, calming the lad's fears that the refusal was based on any suspicions of Tory espionage. Franklin may have been unsure of the boy's attachment to his father, and to keep him at his side, he summoned him to Philadelphia for something important secretly in the making.

Philad. July 5. 1775

Mr. Strahan;

You are a Member of Parliament, and one of that Majority which has doomed my Country to Destruction.—You have begun to burn our Towns, and murder our People.—Look upon your Hands!—They are stained with the Blood of your Relations!—You and I were long Friends:—You are now my Enemy,—and

I am,

Yours,

B Franklin

*To his English friend
—a letter never sent*

To William Temple Franklin in New Jersey

Philadelphia, September 19, 1776

Dear Billy:

I received yours of the 16th, in which you propose going to your father, if I have no objection. I have considered the matter, and cannot approve of your taking such a journey at this time, especially alone, for many reasons, which I have not time to write. I am persuaded, that if your mother [stepmother] should write a sealed letter to her husband, and enclose it under cover to Governor Trumbull of Connecticut, acquainting him that it contains nothing but what relates to her private family concerns, and requesting him to forward or deliver it (opening it first if he should think fit), he would cause it to be delivered safe without opening. I hope you do not feel any reluctance in returning to your studies. This is the time of life in which you are to lay the foundations of your future improvements, and of your importance among men. There seems to be a kind of fatality attending

At the signing of the Declaration of Independence Franklin is supposed to have said: "We must indeed all hang together, or most assuredly we shall all hang separately."

the conveyance of your things between Amboy and Philadelphia. Benny [Bache] had written as I told you, but his letter it seems was not sent. It was thought to be too full of pothooks & hangers, and so unintelligible by the dividing words in the middle and joining ends of some to beginnings of others, that if it had fallen

into the hands of some committee, it might have given them too much trouble to decipher it, on a suspicion of its containing treason, especially as directed to a Tory house. He is now diligent in learning to write better, that he may arrive at the honor of corresponding with his aunt after you leave her.

Philadelphia, September 22, 1776

Dear Grandson:

You are mistaken in imagining that I am apprehensive of your carrying dangerous intelligence to your father; for while he remains where he is, he could make no use of it were you to know & acquaint him with all that passes. You would have been more in the right if you could have suspected me of a little concern for your welfare, on account of the length of the journey, your youth and inexperience, the number of sick returning on that road with the infectious camp distemper, which makes the beds unsafe, together with the loss of time in your studies, of which I fear you begin to grow tired. To send you on such a journey merely to avoid the being obliged to Governor Trumbull for so small a favor as the forwarding a letter, seems to me inconsistent with your mother's usual prudence. I rather think the project takes its rise from your own inclination to a ramble, & disinclination for returning to college, joined with a desire I do not blame of seeing a father you have so much reason to love—I shall by next post if desired send several franked covers directed to Governor Trumbull, for Mrs. F. to use as she has occasion. I write to him in the first now sent, to introduce her request. She may desire her husband to send his letters under cover to me. It will make but 2 days odds. The family is well & join in love to her & you. . . .

Philadelphia, September 28, 1776

Dear Tempe:

I hope you will return hither immediately, and that your mother will make no objection to it, something offering here that will be much to your advantage if you are not out of the way. I am so hurried that I can only add

Ever your affectionate Grandfather

My love to her.

four

American
Minister

Paris

1776: Mission to France

In late September, Franklin was chosen in strictest secrecy
to be one of three commissioners to the court of France, the
others being Jefferson and Silas Deane, who was already in
Paris. In late October, Franklin embarked quietly on the
armed sloop, *Reprisal,* this being the "something offering,"
for which he summoned his grandson from Amboy. Franklin
was accompanied on this voyage by two grandsons, William
Temple, now almost seventeen, and Benjamin Franklin
Bache, aged seven. Now seventy, the indomitable Franklin
would certainly have been hanged for high treason if he
had fallen into the hands of the British. On the journey
across, however, he continued to measure the temperature
of the Gulf Stream. Thomas Jefferson declined the appointment and was replaced by Arthur Lee.

To Mrs. Mary Stevenson Hewson in London

Paris, January 12, 1777

My dear, dear Polly:

Figure to yourself an old man, with gray hair appearing under
a marten fur cap, among the powdered heads of Paris. It is this
odd figure that salutes you, with handfuls of blessings on you
and your dear little ones.

I have with me here my young grandson, Benjamin Franklin
Bache, a special good boy. I shall give him a little French language
and address, and then send him over to pay his respects to Miss
Hewson. My love to all that love you. . . .

P.S. Temple, who attends me here, presents his respects. I must
contrive to get you to America. I want all my friends out of that
wicked country. I have just seen in the papers seven paragraphs
about me, of which six were lies.

*Franklin in his fur hat, hailed
as rustic American philosopher*

*The French king receives the
American minister.*

1778: Alliance with France

For a year Franklin waited patiently in Paris, appearing in his fur cap and spectacles, the humble philosopher and scientist from the New World, the ideal and idol of the Age of Reason in French eyes. On October 7, 1777, an English army, under General Burgoyne, surrendered to the Americans at Saratoga, and the French, who had been helping the Americans secretly with money, ships and volunteers, were ready to sign treaties with the struggling new country and to exchange ambassadors. Franklin was soon named sole minister plenipotentiary to the court of Louis XVI. For the ceremony of signing the Treaty of Alliance with France, Franklin, for the only time since he had stood in the Cockpit and been showered with English abuse, donned his simple blue coat.

To Thomas Cushing in Boston

February 27, 1778

Sir:

I received your favor with your most agreeable congratulations on the success of the American arms in the northern department [Burgoyne's defeat]. In return, give me leave to congratulate you on the success of our negotiations here, in the completion of the two treaties with his most Christian Majesty; the one of amity and commerce, on the plan of that projected in Congress, with some good additions; the other of alliance for mutual defense, in which the most Christian King agrees to make a common cause with the United States, if England attempts to obstruct the commerce of his subjects with them; and guarantees to the United States their liberties, sovereignty, and independence, absolute and unlimited, with the possessions they now have, or may have, at the conclusion of the war; and the States in return guarantees to him his possessions in the West Indies. The great principle in both treaties is a perfect equality and reciprocity; no advantages being demanded by France, or privileges in commerce, which the States may not grant to any and every other nation.

English view of Saratoga: "The generals in America doing nothing . . ."

In short, the King has treated with us generously and magnanimously; taking no advantage of our present difficulties, to exact terms which we would not willingly grant, when established in prosperity and power. I may add that he has acted wisely, in wishing the friendship contracted by these treaties may be durable, which probably it might not be, if a contrary conduct had been observed.

Several of our American ships, with stores for the Congress, are now about sailing, under the protection of a French squadron. England is in great consternation, and the minister, on the 17th instant, confessing in a long speech that all his measures had been wrong, and that peace was necessary, proposed two bills for quieting America; but they are full of artifice and deceit, and will, I am confident, be treated accordingly by our country.

P.S. The treaties were signed by the plenipotentiaries on both sides, February 6th, but are still for some reason kept secret, though soon to be published. It is understood that Spain will soon accede to the same. The treaties are forwarded to Congress by this conveyance.

To Mr. and Mrs. Richard Bache in Philadelphia

Passy, March 31, 1778

Dear Son & Daughter,

His Excellency, M. Gerard who does me the honor to take charge of this letter, goes minister from this Court to Congress.

He is a friend to your country and to your father, which gives him a double claim to your civilities. It is so long since I have heard from you, and there have been such burnings & devastations made by the enemy, that I know not whether, even if Philadelphia is recovered, you have a house left to entertain him in. Benny continues well, and minds his learning. Temple presents his duty. I hope soon to hear from you, and that you and yours are all as well and as hearty as

Your affectionate Father

✒ 1778: New Friends

Franklin was now seventy-two. He had settled down in a suburb of Paris, called Passy. Life was not unpleasant, as he described it in a letter to his old landlady in London. In Passy, he had found a charming new neighbor, Madame Brillon, forty years his junior, married to a French Treasury official and the mother of several daughters, one of whom Franklin hoped to match with his grandson, Temple. But the pattern of the Franklin family was repeated: William Temple fathered a short-lived illegitimate son, and the French family refused the match with the young American. For years, however, Franklin and Madame Brillon maintained an open and gallant relationship. In nearby Auteuil lived another new friend, the widowed Madame Helvétius, whose husband, a respected and rich philosopher, had died seven years before.

To Mrs. Margaret Stevenson of Craven Street

January 25, 1779

It is always a great pleasure, when I think of our long continued friendship, which had not the least interruption in the course of twenty years (some of the happiest of my life) that I spent under your roof and in your company. If I do not write to you as often as I used to do, when I happened to be absent from you, it is owing partly to the present difficulty of sure communication, and partly to an apprehension of some possible inconvenience, that my correspondence might occasion you. Be assured, my dear friend, that my regard, esteem and affection for you, are not in the least impaired or diminished; and that, if circumstances would permit, nothing would afford me so much satisfaction, as to be with you in the same house, and to experience again your faithful, tender care, and attention to my interests, health and comfortable living, which so long and steadily attached me to you and which I shall ever remember with gratitude.

I rejoice to learn that your health is established and that you live pleasantly in a country town, with agreeable neighbors, and have your dear children about you. My love to every one of them. I long to see them and you; but the times do not permit me the hope of it. Why do you never write to me? I used to love to read your letters, and I regret your long silence.

You wish to know how I live. It is in a fine house, situated in a neat village, on a high ground, half a mile from Paris, with a large garden to walk in. I have abundance of acquaintance, dine

Franklin's house at Passy, drawn by the French novelist Victor Hugo

French troops in America, commanded by Rochambeau; an English cartoon

abroad six days in seven. Sundays I reserve to dine at home, with such Americans as pass this way; and I then have my grandson Ben, with some other American children from his school.

To Madame Brillon

Since you have assured me that we shall meet and know each other in heaven, I have been constantly thinking about how we might arrange our affairs in that country, for I have great confidence in your assurances, and I implicitly believe what you believe.

More than 40 years will probably elapse from the time of my arrival there before you follow me. I fear in the course of such a long period you may forget me. I have thought therefore of proposing to you that you give me your word of honor not to renew there your contract with Mr. B———. I shall at the same time give you mine that I shall wait for you. But that gentleman is so good, so generous toward us—he loves you so much and we love him—that I cannot think of this proposition without certain scruples of conscience. And yet the idea of an eternity, during which I would not be more favored than being allowed to kiss your hand or your cheek sometimes, and to spend two or three hours in your sweet company on Wednesday and Saturday evenings is terrible: however, I cannot make this proposition, but as (with all who know you) I wish to see you happy in all things, we can agree not to speak any more about it at present, and leave it to you to decide when we shall meet in the other world and there to settle the matter as you may think best for your own happiness and ours. Decide in what way you will, I feel that I shall love you for all eternity—if you reject me, perhaps I may address myself to Madame d'Hardancourt [Mme. Brillon's mother], whom it may please to take up housekeeping with me; then shall I spend my domestic hours agreeably with her, and shall be nearer at hand to see you. I shall have enough time during these 40 years to practice on the harmonica, and perhaps I may be able to accompany you on the pianoforte. From time to time we shall have little concerts. And the dear good girls, accompanied by some other young angels whose portraits you have already given me, will sing alleluias with us; we shall eat together apples of paradise roasted with butter and nutmeg, and we shall pity those who are not dead.

To Madame Helvétius, following Franklin's proposal of marriage

Mortified at the barbarous resolution pronounced by you so positively yesterday evening, that you would remain single the rest of your life as a compliment due to the memory of your huband, I retired to my chamber. Throwing myself upon my bed, I dreamt that I was dead and was transported to the Elysian Fields.

I was asked whether I wished to see any persons in particular to which I replied that I wished to see the philosophers. "There are two who live here at hand in this garden; they are good neighbors, and very friendly toward one another." "Who are they?" "Socrates and Helvétius." "I esteem them both highly; but let me see Helvétius first, because I understand a little French, but not a word of Greek." I was conducted to him. He received me with much courtesy, having known me, he said, by character, some time past. He asked me a thousand questions relative to the war, the present state of religion, of liberty, of the government in France. "You do not inquire, then," said I, "after your dear friend, Madame Helvétius; yet she loves you exceedingly. I was in her company not more than an hour ago." "Ah," said he, "you make me recur to my past happiness, which ought to be forgotten in order to be happy here. For many years I could think of nothing but her, though at length I am consoled. I have taken another wife, the most like her that I could find; she is not indeed altogether so handsome, but she has a great fund of wit and good sense, and her whole study is to please me. She is at this moment gone to fetch the best nectar and ambrosia to regale me; stay here awhile and you will see her." "I perceive," said I, "that your former friend is more faithful to you than you are to her; she has had several good offers, but has refused them all. I will confess to you that I loved her extremely; but she was cruel to me, and rejected me peremptorily for your sake." "I pity you sincerely," said he, "for she is an excellent woman, handsome and amiable. But do not the Abbé de La Roche and the Abbé Morellet visit her?" "Certainly they do; not one of your friends has dropped her acquaintance." "If you had gained the Abbé Morellet with a bribe of good coffee and cream, perhaps you would have succeeded; for he is as deep a reasoner as Duns Scotus or St. Thomas; he arranges and methodizes his arguments in such a manner that they are almost irresistible. Or if by a fine edition of some old classic you had gained the Abbé de La Roche to speak *against* you, that would have been still better, as I always observed that when he recommended anything to her, she had a great inclination to do directly the contrary." As he finished these words the new Madame Helvétius entered with the nectar, and I recognized her immediately as my former American friend, Mrs. Franklin! I reclaimed her, but she answered me coldly: "I was a good wife to you for forty-nine years and four months, nearly half a century; let that content you. I have formed a new connection here, which will last to eternity."

The American Rattlesnake presenting Monsieur his Ally a Dish of Frogs.

Above, *English cartoon urges the break-up of American-French alliance;*
below, *the American rattlesnake, coiled to crush a third British army*

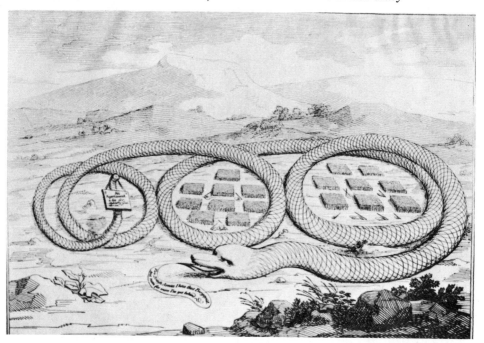

Indignant at this refusal of my Eurydice, I immediately resolved to quit those ungrateful shades, and return to this good world again, to behold the sun and you; here I am; let us *avenge ourselves.*

✒ 1779: Jealousies at Home

Franklin's personal success in Paris was so overwhelming that it led to jealousies among the American commissioners. Arthur Lee, one of the three American representatives, had already suffered in Franklin's shadow in England as his successor in the agency for Massachusetts. Lee wrote letters to his brother and to Samuel Adams which spread suspicions in the Congress in Philadelphia. Young William Temple Franklin was a vulnerable target because of his Tory father, who, still loyal to the British Crown, had taken refuge with the Loyalist community in British-occupied New York.

To Richard Bache in Philadelphia

Passy, June 2, 1779

Dear Sir:

I have received yours of June (January?) 16. You observe that you seldom hear from me. I have the same reason to complain but I do not complain of you. It is the loss of ships, and the sinking of dispatches, when chased, that cuts our correspondence to pieces.

Yours of Oct. 22 gave me a good deal of satisfaction in informing me of the adventures of your family, your return to Philadelphia, welfare, etc. . . .

Passy, June 2, 1779

I am very easy about the efforts Messrs. Lee and Izard are using, as you tell me, to injure me on that side of the water. I trust in the justice of the Congress that they will listen to no accusations against me that I have not first been acquainted with, and had an opportunity of answering. I know those gentlemen have plenty of ill will to me, though I have never done to either of them the smallest injury, or given the least just cause of offense. But my too great reputation, and the general good will this people have for me, and the respect they show me, and even the compliments they make me, all grieve those unhappy gentlemen; unhappy indeed in their tempers, and in the dark, uncomfortable passions of jealousy, anger, suspicion, envy, and malice. It is enough for good minds to be affected at other people's misfortunes; but they that are vexed at everybody's good luck can never be happy. I take no other revenge of such enemies than to let them remain in the miserable situation in which their malignant natures have placed them, by endeavoring to support an estimable character; and thus, by continuing the reputation the world has hitherto indulged me with, I shall continue them in their present state of damnation; and I am not disposed to reverse my conduct for the alleviation of their torments.

I am surprised to hear that my grandson, Temple Franklin, being with me, should be an objection against me, and that there is a cabal for removing him. Methinks it is rather some merit that I

English cartoon: "The Horse America throwing His Master" (1779)

Franklin presents his grandson to the French philosopher Voltaire.

have rescued a valuable young man from the danger of being a Tory, and fixed him in honest republican Whig principles; as I think, from the integrity of his disposition, his industry, his early sagacity, and uncommon abilities for business, he may in time become of great service to his country. It is enough that I have lost my *son;* would they add my *grandson?*

An old man of seventy, I undertook a winter voyage at the command of the Congress, and for the public service, with no other attendant to take care of me. I am continued here in a foreign country, where, if I am sick, his filial attention comforts me, and if I die, I have a child to close my eyes and take care of my remains. His dutiful behavior toward me and his diligence and fidelity in business are both pleasing and useful to me. His conduct, as my private secretary, has been unexceptionable, and I am confident the Congress will never think of separating us.

I have had a great deal of pleasure in Ben too. He is a good, honest lad, and will make, I think, a valuable man.

Thanks be to God, I continue well and hearty. Undoubtedly I grow older, but I think the last ten years have made no great difference. I have sometimes the gout, but they say that is not so much a disease as a remedy. God bless you. I am your affectionate father. . . .

1782: Peace with England

On October 19, 1781, the English under Cornwallis surrendered at Yorktown. The stage was now set for peace
negotiations between the United States and Great Britain.
For several months, Franklin, alone in Paris, awaited the
arrival of three other peace commissioners—John Adams
from Holland, John Jay from Spain, Henry Laurens, free on
parole from the Tower of London—representing the interests
of America in Paris. The French foreign minister, Count
Vergennes, tried to satisfy the conflicting interests of
America and Spain, which was also a party to the Treaty of
Alliance. Franklin kept a careful "Journal of the Negotiations for Peace with Great Britain," covering the period
from March 22 to June 28, 1782. The American commissioners carried on separate negotiations with the English, in
spite of instructions from Congress to the contrary. A pre-
liminary treaty with England was signed late in November
1782.

To Robert R. Livingston in the United States

Passy, December 5, 1782

Sir:

I am honored by your several letters dated September 5, 13, 15,
and 18. I believe that the complaints you make in them, of my not
writing, may ere now have appeared less necessary, as many of
my letters written before those complaints must have since come
to hand. I will nevertheless mention some of the difficulties
your ministers meet with, in keeping up a regular and punctual
correspondence. We are far from the seaports, and not well informed, and often misinformed, about the sailing of vessels. Frequently we are told they are to sail in a week or two, and often
they lie in the ports for months after, with our letters on board,
either waiting for convoy or for other reasons. The post office
here is an unsafe conveyance; many of the letters we receive by it
have evidently been opened, and doubtless the same happens to
those we send; and at this time particularly there is so violent
a curiosity in all kinds of people to know something relating to

the negotiations, and whether peace may be expected or a continuance of the war, that there are few private hands or travelers that we can trust with carrying our dispatches to the seacoast; and I imagine that they may sometimes be opened and destroyed, because they cannot be well sealed.

Again, the observation you make that the Congress ministers in Europe seem to form themselves into a privy council, transacting affairs without the privity or concurrence of the sovereign, may be in some respects just; but it should be considered that, if they do not write as frequently as other ministers here do to their respective courts, or if, when they write, their letters are not regularly received, the greater distance of the seat of war and the extreme irregularity of conveyances may be the causes, and not a desire of acting without the knowledge or orders of their constituents. There is no European court to which an express cannot be sent from Paris in ten or fifteen days, and from most of them answers may be obtained in that time. There is, I imagine, no minister, who would not think it safer to act by orders than from his own discretion; and yet, unless you leave more to the discretion of your ministers in Europe than courts usually do, your affairs may sometimes suffer extremely from the distance, which, in the time of war especially, may make it five or six months before the answer to a letter shall be received.

It is in vain for me to repeat again what I have so often written, and what I find taken so little notice of, that there are bounds to everything, and that the faculties of this nation are limited like those of all other nations. Some of you seem to have established as maxims the suppositions that France has money enough for all her occasions and all ours besides, and that if she does not supply us it is owing to her want of will, or to my negligence. As to the first, I am sure it is not true; and to the second, I can only say I should rejoice as much as any man in being able to obtain more; and I shall also rejoice in the greater success of those who may take my place.

The arrival of Mr. Jay, Mr. Adams, and Mr. Laurens has relieved me from much anxiety, which must have continued if I had been left to finish the treaty alone; and it has given me the more satisfaction,

English views of the
war: a family quarrel
and reconciliation

as I am sure the business has profited by their assistance.

Much of the summer has been taken up in objecting against the powers given by Great Britain, and in removing those objections. The not using any expressions that might imply an acknowledgment of our independence, seemed at first industriously to be avowed. But our refusing otherwise to treat, at length induced them to get over that difficulty, and then we came to the point of making propositions. After some weeks an undersecretary, Mr. Strachey, arrived, with whom we had much contestation about the boundaries and other articles, which he proposed and we settled; some of which he carried to London, and returned with the propositions, some adopted, others omitted or altered, and new ones added. We spent many days in disputing, and at length agreed on and signed the preliminaries, which you will see by this conveyance. The British minister struggled hard for two points: that the favors granted to the Royalists should be extended, and all our fishery contracted. We silenced them on the first by threatening to produce an account of the mischief done by those people; and as to the second, when they told us they could not possibly agree to it as we requested it, and must refer it to the ministry in London, we produced a new article to be referred at the same time, with a note of facts in support of it. Apparently, it seemed that to avoid the discussion of this they suddenly changed their minds, dropped the design of recurring to London, and agreed to allow the fishery as demanded.

Every one of the present British ministry has, while in the ministry, declared the war against us as unjust, and nothing is clearer in reason than that those who injure others by an unjust war should make full reparation. They have stipulated too, in these preliminaries, that in evacuating our towns they shall carry off no plunder, which is a kind of acknowledgment that they ought not to have done it before.

We communicated all the articles as soon as they were signed to Count de Vergennes [French Foreign Minister] (except the separate one), who thinks we have managed well, and told me that we had settled what was most apprehended as a difficulty in the work of a general peace, by obtaining the declaration of our independency.

Left to right, *John Jay, John Adams, Franklin, Henry Laurens and William Temple Franklin—the American peace commission; the English negotiators refused to sit for their portrait*

I have this day signed a common letter to you, drawn up by my colleagues, which you will receive herewith. We have kept this vessel longer for two things: a passport promised us from England, and a sum to send in her; but she is likely to depart without both, being all of us impatient that Congress should receive early intelligence of our proceedings, and for the money we may probably borrow a frigate.

I am now entering on my seventy-eighth year; public business has engrossed fifty of them; I wish now to be, for the little time I have left, my own master. If I live to see this peace concluded, I shall beg leave to remind Congress, of the promise then to dismiss me.

✒ 1783: The Treaty Letter

On September 3, 1783, the final Treaty of Peace between the new United States of America and Great Britain was signed in Paris. Sometime, perhaps during the preceding year, with treaty-making so much on his mind, Franklin composed his famed "Treaty of Peace with a Lady."

To Madame Brillon

Passy, July 27

What a difference, my dear friend, between you and me!—You find my faults so many as to be innumerable, while I can see but one in you; and perhaps that is the fault of my spectacles.—The fault I mean is that kind of covetousness, by which you would engross all my affection, and permit me none for the other amiable ladies of your country. You seem to imagine that it cannot be divided without being diminished: In which you mistake the nature of the thing and forget the situation in which you have placed and hold me. You renounce and exclude arbitrarily everything corporal from our amour, except such a merely civil embrace now and then as you would permit to a country cousin,—what is there then remaining that I may not afford to others without a diminution of what belongs to you? The operations of the mind, esteem, admiration, respect, & even affection for one object, may be multiplied as more objects that merit them present themselves, and yet remain the same to the first, which therefore has no room to complain of injury. They are in their nature as divisible as the sweet sounds of the forte piano produced by your exquisite skill: Twenty people may receive the same pleasure from them, without lessening that which you kindly intend for me; and I might as reasonably require of your friendship, that they should reach and delight no ears but mine.

You see by this time how unjust you are in your demands, and in the open war you declare against me if I do not comply with them. Indeed it is I that have the most reason to complain. My poor little boy, whom you ought methinks to have cherished,

Pencil sketch of Franklin and a friend, from an American artist's diary

instead of being fat and jolly like those in your elegant drawings, is meager and starved almost to death for want of the substantial nourishment which you his mother inhumanly deny him, and yet would now clip his little wings to prevent his seeking it elsewhere!—

I fancy we shall neither of us get anything by this war, and therefore as feeling myself the weakest, I will do what indeed ought always to be done by the wisest, be first in making the propositions for peace. That a peace may be lasting, the articles of the treaty should be regulated upon the principles of the most perfect equity & reciprocity. In this view I have drawn up & offer the following, viz.—

ARTICLE 1. There shall be eternal peace, friendship & love, between Madame B. and Mr. F.

ARTICLE 2. In order to maintain the same inviolably, Made B. on her part stipulates and agrees, that Mr. F. shall come to her whenever she sends for him.

ART. 3. That he shall stay with her as long as she pleases.

ART. 4. That when he is with her, he shall be obliged to drink tea, play chess, hear music; or do any other thing that she requires of him.

ART. 5. And that he shall love no other woman but herself.

ART. 6. And the said Mr. F. on his part stipulates and agrees, that he will go away from M. B.'s whenever he pleases.

ART. 7. That he will stay away as long as he pleases.

ART. 8. That when he is with her, he will do what he pleases.

ART. 9. And that he will love any other woman as far as he finds her amiable.

Let me know what you think of these preliminaries. To me they seem to express the true meaning and intention of each party more plainly than most treaties.—I shall insist pretty strongly on the eighth article, though without much hope of your consent to it; and on the ninth also, though I despair of ever finding any other woman that I could love with equal tenderness: being ever, my dear dear friend,

1783: Friends in England

With peace assured, Franklin, approaching eighty, renewed correspondence with London. He learned the sad news of the deaths of many friends and loved ones, including his landlady for eighteen years, Mrs. Margaret Stevenson, the Queen of Craven Street. To Bishop Shipley, at whose home Franklin began writing his *Autobiography* twelve years before, he sent his strongest hopes that the two peoples could "forgive and forget."

To Mrs. Mary Stevenson Hewson in London

Passy, January 27, 1783

. . . The departure of my dearest friend, which I learn from your last letter, greatly affects me. To meet with her once more in this life was one of the principal motives of my proposing to visit England again, before my return to America. The last year carried off my friends, Dr. Pringle, Dr. Fothergill, Lord Kames, and Lord le Despencer. This has begun to take away the rest, and strikes the hardest. Thus the ties I had to that country, and indeed to the world in general, are loosened one by one, and I shall soon have no attachment left to make me unwilling to follow.

I wrote and hope it came to hand. I therein asked your counsel about my coming to England. On reflection, I think I can, from my knowledge of your prudence, foresee what it will be, viz., not to come too soon, lest it should seem braving and insulting some who ought to be respected. I shall therefore omit that journey till I am near going to America, and then just step over to take leave of my friends, and spend a few days with you. I purpose bringing Ben with me, and perhaps may leave him under your care.

At length we are in peace, God be praised, and long, very long, may it continue! All wars are follies, very expensive, and very mischievous ones. When will mankind be convinced of this, and agree to settle their differences by arbitration? Were they to do it, even by the cast of a die, it would be better than by fighting and destroying each other.

In looking forward, twenty-five years seems a long period, but in looking back, how short! Could you imagine that it is now full a quarter of a century since we were first acquainted? It was in 1757. During the greatest part of the time, I lived in the same house with my dear deceased friend, your mother; of course you and I saw and conversed with each other much and often. It is to all our honors that in all that time we never had among us the smallest misunderstanding. Our friendship has been all clear sunshine, without the least cloud in its hemisphere. Let me conclude by saying to you, what I have had too frequent occasions to say to my other remaining old friends: "The fewer we become, the more let us love one another."

To Bishop Jonathan Shipley in England

March 17, 1783

I received with great pleasure my dear and respected friend's letter of the 5th instant, as it informed me of the welfare of a family I so much esteem and love.

The clamor against the peace in your Parliament would alarm me for its duration, if I were not of opinion with you, that the attack is rather against the minister. I am confident, none of the opposition would have made a better peace for England, if they had been in his place; at least, I am sure that Lord Stormont, who seems loudest in railing at it, is not the man that could have mended it. My reasons I will give you, when I have, what I hope to have, the great happiness of seeing you once more, and conversing with you.

They talk much of there being no *reciprocity* in our treaty. They think nothing, then, of our passing over in silence the atrocities committed by their troops, and demanding no satisfaction for their wanton burnings and devastations of our fair towns and countries. They have heretofore confessed the war to be unjust, and nothing is plainer in reasoning than that the mischiefs done in an unjust war should be repaired. Can Englishmen be so partial to themselves, as to imagine they have a right to plunder and destroy as much as they please, and then, without satisfying for the injuries they have done, to have peace on equal terms? We were favorable, and did not demand what justice entitled us to. We shall probably be blamed for it by our constituents; and I still think it would be the interest of England voluntarily to offer reparations of those injuries, and effect it as much as may be in her power. But this is an interest she will never see.

Let us now forgive and forget. Let each country seek its advancement in its own internal advantages of arts and agriculture, not in retarding or preventing the prosperity of the other. America will, with God's blessing, become a great and happy country; and

England, if she has at length gained wisdom, will have gained something more valuable, and more essential to her prosperity, than all
she has lost; and will still be a great and respectable nation.

1783: Flight Experiments

By the end of 1783, Franklin was becoming very infirm,
but still he responded to the excitement of man's first trial
flights by balloon. On December 1st, he watched the second
ascent of human passengers in a free balloon and that same
day sat down to write an account of the event. But since he
was not only a scientist, but a diplomat, statesman, and ob-
server of human affairs, Franklin looked into the future and
saw aerial warfare. Two years later the old postmaster re-
corded the beginning of air mail. Asked what was the value
of these new ventures, Franklin responded, "What is the use
of a new-born babe?"

To Sir Joseph Banks in London

Passy, December 1, 1783

Dear Sir:

In mine of yesterday I promised to give you an account of
Messrs. Charles & Robert's experiment, which was to have been
made this day, and at which I intended to be present. Being a little
indisposed, and the air cool and the ground damp, I declined going
into the garden of the Tuileries, where the balloon was placed, not
knowing how long I might be obliged to wait there before it was
ready to depart; and chose to stay in my carriage near the statue of
Louis XV, from whence I could well see it rise and have an extensive view of the region of air through which, as the wind sat,
it was likely to pass.

The morning was foggy, but about one o'clock the air became
tolerably clear, to the great satisfaction of the spectators, who

were infinite, notice having been given of the intended experiment several days before in the papers, so that all Paris was out. Never before was a philosophical experiment so magnificently attended.

Some guns were fired to give notice that the departure of the great balloon was near, and a small one was discharged, which went to an amazing height, there being but little wind to make it deviate from its perpendicular course, and at length the sight of it was lost. Means were used, I am told, to prevent the great balloon's rising so high as might endanger its bursting. Several bags of sand were taken on board before the cord that held it down was cut, and the whole weight being then too much to be lifted, such a quantity was discharged as to permit its rising slowly. Thus it would sooner arrive at that region where it would be in equilibrium with the surrounding air, and by discharging more sand afterward, it might go higher if desired. Between one and two o'clock all eyes were gratified with seeing it rise majestically from among the trees, and ascend gradually above the buildings, a most beautiful spectacle. When it was about two hundred feet high, the brave adventurers held out and waved a little white pennant, on both sides their car, to salute the spectators, who returned loud claps of applause. The wind was very little, so that the object, though moving to the northward, continued long in view; and it was a great while before the admiring people began to disperse. The persons embarked were Mr. Charles, professor of experimental philosophy and a zealous promoter of that science; and one of the Messieurs Robert, the very ingenious constructors of the machine. When it arrived at its height, which I suppose might be three hundred or four hundred toises, it appeared to have only horizontal motion. I had a pocket-glass with which I followed it, till I lost sight, first of the men, then of the car, and when I last saw the balloon it appeared no bigger than a walnut. I write this at seven in the evening. What became of them is not yet known here. I hope they descended by daylight, so as to see and avoid falling among trees or on houses, and that the experiment was completed without any mischievous accident, which the novelty of it and the want of experience might well occasion. I am the more anxious for the event, because I am not well informed of

America, like the first free balloon flight (1783), has flown away, with Washington (10) and Silas Deane in the basket. The English army is a mouse (8). Dr. F-k-n (3) holds a knife marked Sedition.

the means provided for letting themselves down, and the loss of these very ingenious men would not only be a discouragement to the progress of the art, but be a sensible loss to science and society.

Tuesday morning, December 2. I am relieved from my anxiety by hearing that the adventurers descended well near l'Isle Adam before sunset. This place is near seven leagues from Paris. Had the wind blown fresh they might have gone much farther.

To Dr. Jan Ingenhousz in Vienna

Passy, January 16, 1784

Dear Friend:

I have this day received your favor of the 2d instant. Every information in my power respecting the balloons I sent you just before Christmas, contained in copies of my letters to Sir Joseph Banks.

It appears, as you observe, to be a discovery of great importance, and what may possibly give a new turn to human affairs. Convincing sovereigns of the folly of wars may perhaps be one effect of it, since it will be impracticable for the most potent of them to guard his dominions. Five thousand balloons, capable of raising two men each, could not cost more than five ships of the line; and where is the prince who can afford so to cover his country with troops for its defense as that ten thousand men descending from the clouds might not in many places do an infinite deal of mischief before a force could be brought together to repel them?

To John Bowdoin in Boston

Philadelphia, January 1, 1786

My dear Friend:

It gave me great pleasure, my dear friend, to receive your kind letter of congratulation, as it proved that all my old friends in Boston were not estranged from me by the malevolent misrepresentations of my conduct that had been circulated there, but that one of the most esteemed still retained a regard for me. Indeed, you are now almost the only one left me by nature; death having, since we were last together, deprived me of my dear Cooper, Winthrop, and Quincy.

I sent to you some weeks since Dr. Jeffries's account of his aerial voyage from England to France. My acquaintance with Dr. Jeffries began by his bringing me a letter in France, the first through the air, from England.

✑1784-85: Briefly Reconciled

With peace between the warring parties, an overture for reconciliation between son and father came from William, who was having an unhappy time in London. Franklin sent a reply by the hand of Temple Franklin, whom his grandfather sent across the English Channel to see not only the youth's father but also many of his grandfather's old friends. Franklin's letters to his grandson in England indicate some anxiety about the boy and his new-found father. Franklin's deep feeling about his son's estrangement—"nothing has ever hurt me so much"—could only have been deepened by the disappointment that the brief reconciliation did not endure. Franklin and his son meet again in Southampton, England, where the old man was taking ship for his last voyage home. The entries in Franklin's "pocket" journal are eloquent in starkness and in what they do not say.

To William Franklin in England

Passy, August 16, 1784

Dear Son:

I received your letter of the 22d ultimo, and am glad to find that you desire to revive the affectionate intercourse that formerly existed between us. It will be very agreeable to me; indeed, nothing has ever hurt me so much, and affected me with such keen sensations, as to find myself deserted in my old age by my only son; and not only deserted, but to find him taking up arms against me in a cause wherein my good fame, fortune, and life were all at stake. You conceived, you say, that your duty to your king and regard for your country required this. I ought not to blame you for differing in sentiment with me in public affairs. We are men, all subject to errors. Our opinions are not in our own power; they are formed and governed much by circumstances that are often as inexplicable as they are irresistible. Your situation was such that few would have censured your remaining neuter, *though there are natural duties which precede political ones, and cannot be extinguished by them.*

This is a disagreeable subject. I drop it. And we will endeavor, as you propose, mutually to forget what has happened relating to it, as well as we can. I send your son over to pay his duty to you. You will find him much improved. He is greatly esteemed and beloved in this country, and will make his way anywhere. It is my desire that he should study the law, as the necessary part of knowledge for a public man, and profitable if he should have occasion to practice it.

I did intend returning this year; but the Congress, instead of giving me leave to do so, have sent me another commission which will keep me here at least a year longer; and perhaps I may then be too old and feeble to bear the voyage. I am here among a people that love and respect me, a most amiable nation to live with; and perhaps I may conclude to die among them; for my friends in America are dying off, one after another, and I have been so long abroad that I should now be almost a stranger in my own country.

First map of the new United States, engraved in America, 1783

I shall be glad to see you when convenient, but would not have you come here at present. You may confide to your son the family affairs you wished to confer upon with me, for he is discreet; and I trust that you will prudently avoid introducing him to company that it may be improper for him to be seen with. I shall hear from you by him; and any letters to me afterward will come safe under cover directed to Mr. Ferdinand Grand, banker, at Paris. Wishing you health, and more happiness than it seems you have lately experienced, I remain your affectionate father. . . .

To William Temple Franklin in England

Passy, September 13, 1784

My dear Child:

I received last night yours of the 7th & am glad to hear you are quit of your fever.

I consent to your going with your father, and to your stay in England until the middle of October. Don't omit writing to me by every post. The uncertain state of your health makes me more anxious to hear from you.

Give my love to your father.

Remember me affectionately to all inquiring friends.

I am your loving grandfather. . . .

Passy, October 2, 1784

Dear Grandson:

I have not received a line from you since that of Sept. 7, now near a month. I have waited with impatience the arrival of every post—but not a word—all your acquaintance are continually inquiring what news from you—I have none. Judge what I must feel, what they must think, and tell me what I am to think of such neglect. I must suppose it neglect: for if your fever had returned, and you were unable to write, surely your father, or somebody would have informed me of it—I shall continue however till this conduct of yours is cleared up, hoping it may be explained to my satisfaction,

Your affectionate grandfather. . . .

Franklin's "Pocket" Journal

Having stayed in France about eight and a half years, I took leave of the court and my friends, and set out on my return home, July 12, 1785, leaving Passy with my two grandsons. I found that the motion of the litter did not much incommode me. It was one of

The ailing Franklin, 1783, America's minister plenipotentiary in Paris

the Queen's, carried by two very large mules, the muleteer riding another.

July 24.—We had a fair wind all night, and this morning at seven o'clock, being off Cowes, the captain represented to me the difficulty of getting in there against the flood; and proposing that we should rather run up to Southampton, which we did, and landed there between eight and nine. Met my son, who had arrived from London the evening before. Wrote a letter to the Bishop of St. Asaph, acquainting him with my arrival, and he came with his lady and daughter, Miss Kitty, after dinner to see us; they talk of staying here as long as we do. Our meeting was very affectionate.

July 25.—The Bishop and family lodging in the same inn, the Star, we all breakfast and dine together. I went at noon to bathe in Martin's salt-water hot bath, and, floating on my back, fell asleep, and slept near an hour by my watch, without sinking or turning; a thing I never did before, and should hardly have thought possible. Water is the easiest bed that can be. Read over the writings of conveyance, etc., of my son's lands in New Jersey and New York to my grandson. Southampton a very neat, pretty place. The Bishop gives me a book in quarto, and the family dine with us. Sundry friends came to see me from London.

July 26.—Deeds signed between W. Franklin and W. T. Franklin.

July 27.—Give a power to my son to recover what may be due to me from the British government.

We all dine once more with the bishop and family, who kindly accept our invitation to go on board with us. We go down in a shallop to the ship. The captain entertains us at supper. The company stay all night.

July 28.—When I waked in the morning found the company gone and the ship under sail.

Last Will and Testament

To my son, *William Franklin*, late Governor of the Jerseys, I give and devise all the lands I hold or have a right to, in the province of Nova Scotia, to hold to him, his heirs, and assigns forever. I also give to him all my books and papers which he has in his possession, and all debts standing against him on my account books, willing that no payment for, nor restitution of, the same be required of him, by my executors. The part he acted against me in the late war, which is of public notoriety, will account for my leaving him no more of an estate he endeavored to deprive me of.

five

Citizen

United States of America

1785-87: Home Again

Franklin's last voyage, like his first almost sixty years earlier, was taken up with scientific observations. He wrote three papers: "Maritime Observations," which included detailed observations of the Gulf Stream; "On the Causes and Cure of Smoky Chimneys," and "Descriptions of a New Stove for Burning Pitcoal." He was received in Philadelphia on September 14th with a grateful people's cheers, which rang around his ears for a week. He met with his old Union Fire Company, founded fifty years before, and promised to have "his bucket, etc. in good order by the next meeting." He took the chair at a meeting of the American Philosophical Society at the University of Pennsylvania. Messages of welcome and greeting poured in from George Washington, John Jay, Thomas Paine and others. On the twenty-ninth of the month he was elected President of Pennsylvania. He was elected to the Constitutional Convention and at eighty-one, the oldest man present, on the final day of the session, September 17, 1787, had his famous "Last Speech" read to the delegates. His signature on the United States Constitution makes him the only man to sign all four major documents of the American Revolution: the three others being the Declaration of Independence, the Treaty of Alliance with France and the Treaty of Peace with England. His letters to lifelong friends hint at final farewells.

Franklin's "pocket" journal

Tuesday, September 13.—The wind springing fair last evening after a calm, we found ourselves this morning, at sun-rising, abreast of the lighthouse, and between Capes May and Henlopen. We sail into the bay very pleasantly; water smooth, air cool, day fair and fine.

We passed Newcastle about sunset, and went on to near Red Bank before the tide and wind failed; then came to an anchor.

Wednesday, September 14.—With the flood in the morning came a light breeze, which brought us above Gloucester Point, in full view of dear Philadelphia! when we again cast anchor to wait for the health officer, who, having made his visit and finding no sickness, gave us leave to land. My son-in-law came with a boat for us; we landed at Market Street wharf, where we were received by a crowd of people with huzzas, and accompanied with acclamations quite to my door. Found my family well.

God be praised and thanked for all his mercies!

Philadelphia: the Arch Street Ferry, c. 1800

Closing Speech to the Constitutional Convention, September 17, 1787

Mr. President:

I confess that I do not entirely approve of this Constitution at present; but, sir, I am not sure I shall never approve it; for, having lived long, I have experienced many instances of being obliged, by better information or fuller consideration, to change my opinions even on important subjects, which I once thought right, but found to be otherwise. It is therefore that, the older I grow, the more apt I am to doubt my own judgment of others. Most men, indeed, as well as most sects in religion, think themselves in possession of all truth, and that wherever others differ from them, it is so far error. Steele, a Protestant, in a dedication, tells the Pope that the only difference between our two churches in their opinions of the certainty of their doctrine is, the Romish Church is *infallible*, and the Church of England is *never in the wrong*. But though many private persons think almost as highly of their own infallibility as of that of their sect few express it so naturally as a certain French lady who, in a little dispute with her sister, said, "But I meet with nobody but myself that is *always* in the right." "*Je ne trouve que moi qui aie toujours raison.*"

In these sentiments, sir, I agree to this Constitution, with all its faults—if they are such; because I think a general government necessary for us, and there is no *form* of government but what may be a blessing to the people if well administered; and I believe, farther, that this is likely to be well administered for a course of years, and can only end in despotism, as other forms have done before it, when the people shall become so corrupted as to need despotic government, being incapable of any other. I doubt, too, whether any other Convention we can obtain may be able to make a better constitution; for when you assemble a number of men to have the advantage of their joint wisdom, you inevitably assemble with those men all their prejudices, their passions, their errors of opinion, their local interests, and their selfish views. From such an assembly, can a *perfect* production be expected? It therefore astonishes me, sir, to find this system approaching so near to perfection as it does; and I think it will astonish our enemies, who are waiting with confidence to hear that our councils are confounded like those of the builders of Babel, and that our States are on the point of separation, only to meet hereafter for the purpose of cutting one another's throats. Thus I consent, sir, to this Constitution, because I expect no better, and because I am not sure that it is not the best. The opinions I have had of its *errors* I sacrifice to the public good. I have never whispered a syllable of them abroad. Within these walls they were born, and here they shall die. If every one of us, in returning to our constituents, were to report the objections he has had to it, and endeavor to gain partisans in support of them, we might prevent its being generally received, and thereby lose all the salutary effects and great advantages resulting naturally in our favor among foreign nations, as well as among ourselves, from our real or apparent unanimity. Much of the strength and efficiency of any government, in procuring and securing happiness to the people, depends on *opinion,* on the general opinion of the goodness of that government, as well as of the wisdom and integrity of its governors. I hope, therefore, for our own sakes, as a part of the people, and for the sake of our posterity, that we shall act heartily and unanimously in recommending this Constitution, wherever our influence may extend, and turn our future thoughts and endeavors to the means of having it *well administered.*

On the whole, sir, I cannot help expressing a wish that every member of the Convention who may still have objections to it, would with me on this occasion doubt a little of his own infallibility, and, to make *manifest* our *unanimity,* put his name to this instrument.

Franklin's speech helped make the adoption of the Constitution unanimous.

To Bishop Jonathan Shipley in England

February 24, 1786

Dear Friend:

I received lately your kind letter of Nov. 27th. My reception here was, as you have heard, very honorable indeed; but I was betrayed by it, and by some remains of ambition, from which I had imagined myself free, to accept of the chair of government for the state of Pennsylvania, when the proper thing for me was repose and a private life. I hope, however, to be able to bear the fatigue for one year, and then to retire.

As to my domestic circumstances, of which you kindly desire to hear something, they are at present as happy as I could wish them. I am surrounded by my offspring, a dutiful and affectionate daughter in my house, with six grandchildren, the eldest of which you have seen, who is now at a college in the next street, finishing the learned part of his education; the others promising, both for parts and good dispositions. What their conduct may be, when they grow up and enter the important scenes of life, I shall not live to *see*, and I cannot *foresee*. I therefore enjoy among them the present hour, and leave the future to Providence.

My son's son, Temple Franklin, whom you have seen, having had a fine farm of 600 acres conveyed to him by his father when we were at Southampton, has dropped for the present his views of acting in the political line, and applies himself ardently to the study and practice of agriculture. This is much more agreeable to me, who esteem it the most useful, the most independent, and therefore the noblest of employments. His lands are on navigable water, communicating with the Delaware, and but about 16 miles from this city.

You will kindly expect a word or two concerning myself. My health and spirits continue, thanks to God, as when you saw me. The only complaint I then had, does not grow worse, and is tolerable. I still have enjoyment in the company of my friends; and, being easy in my circumstances, have many reasons to like living. But the course of nature must soon put a period to my present mode of existence. This I shall submit to with less regret, as, having seen during a long life a good deal of this world, I feel a growing curiosity to be acquainted with some other; and can cheerfully, with filial confidence, resign my spirit to the conduct of that great and good Parent of Mankind, who created it, and who has so graciously protected and prospered me from my birth to the present hour. Wherever I am, I hope always to retain the pleasing remembrance of your friendship. . . .

P. S. We all join in respects to Mrs. Shipley, and best wishes for the whole amiable family.

To Mrs. Mary Stevenson Hewson in England

Philadelphia, May 6, 1786

My dear Friend:

A long winter has passed, and I have not had the pleasure of a line from you, acquainting me with you and your children's welfare since I left England. I suppose you have been in Yorkshire, out of the way and knowledge of opportunities; for I will not think that you have forgotten me.

To make me some amends, I received a few days past a large packet from Mr. Williams, dated September 1776, near ten years since, containing three letters from you, one of December 12, 1775. This packet had been received by Mr. Bache, after my departure for France, lay dormant among his papers during all my absence, and has just now broke out upon me, *like words* that had been, as somebody says, *congealed in northern air*. Therein I find all the pleasing little family history of your children: how William had begun to spell, overcoming, by strength of memory all the difficulty occasioned by the common wretched alphabet, while you were convinced of the utility of our new one; how Tom, geniuslike, struck out new paths, and, relinquishing the old names of the letters, called U *bell*, and P *bottle*; how Eliza began to grow jolly, that is, fat and handsome, resembling Aunt Rooke, whom I used to call *my lovely*.

I have found my family here in health, good circumstances, and well respected by their fellow citizens. The companions of my youth are indeed almost all departed, but I find an agreeable society among their children and grandchildren. I have public business enough to preserve me from *ennui*, and private amusement besides in conversation, books, my garden, and *cribbage*. Considering our well-furnished, plentiful market as the best of gardens, I am turning mine, in the midst of which my house stands, into grass plots and gravel walks, with trees and flowering shrubs. Cards we sometimes play here, in long winter evenings; but it is as they play at chess, not for money, but for honor, or the pleasure of beating one another. This will not be quite a novelty to you, as you may remember we played together in that manner during the winter at Passy. I have indeed now and then a little compunction in reflecting that I spend time so idly; but another reflection comes to relieve me, whispering: "You know that the soul is immortal; why then should you be such a niggard of a little time, when you have a whole eternity before you?" So, being easily convinced, and, like other reasonable creatures, satisfied with a small reason when it is in favor of doing what I have a mind to, I shuffle the cards again, and begin another game.

As to public amusements, we have neither plays nor operas, but we had yesterday a kind of oratorio, as you will see by the enclosed paper; and we have assemblies, balls, and concerts, besides little parties at one another's houses, in which there is sometimes dancing, and frequently good music; so that we jog on in life as pleasantly as you do in England; anywhere but in London, for there you have plays performed by good actors. That however is, I think, the only advantage London has over Philadelphia.

To Mrs. Catherine Ray Greene in New England

Philadelphia, March 2, 1789

Dear Friend:

Having now done with public affairs, which have hitherto taken up so much of my time, I shall endeavor to enjoy, during the small

remainder of life that is left to me, some of the pleasures of conversing with my old friends by writing, since their distance prevents
my hope of seeing them again.

I am too old to follow printing again myself, but, loving the
business, I have brought up my grandson Benjamin to it, and have
built and furnished a printing house for him, which he now man-
ages under my eye. I have great pleasure in the rest of my grandchildren, who are now in number eight, and all promising, the
youngest only six months old, but shows signs of great good nature.
My friends here are numerous, and I enjoy as much of their conversation as I can reasonably wish; and I have as much health and
cheerfulness as can well be expected at my age, now eighty-three.
Hitherto this long life has been tolerably happy; so that, if I were
allowed to live it over again, I should make no objection, only
wishing for leave to do what authors do in a second edition of their
works, correct some of my errata. Among the felicities of my life
I reckon your friendship, which I shall remember with pleasure as
long as that life lasts.

✒ 1788: Hint of Ingratitude

Franklin, at the urging of his friends in London and Paris,
was working on completing his *Autobiography*. He is believed to have reedited some of his first draft, working with
his two grandsons, Benjamin Bache and William Temple
Franklin, who was to be his literary heir and executor. Re-
viewing his life led Franklin to recall that there was still
owing to him some large sums on unsettled accounts with
Congress. In an effort to straighten the matter out, he wrote
to his old correspondent, Charles Thomson. Congress did not
settle these accounts during Franklin's lifetime, nor did it
send him either any official acknowledgment or thanks.

To Charles Thomson, Secretary of Congress

Philadelphia, December 29, 1788

Dear old Friend:

Enclosed I send a letter to the President of Congress for the time being, which, if you find nothing improper in it, or that in regard to me you could wish changed or amended, I would request you to present. I rely much on your friendly counsel, as you must be better acquainted with persons and circumstances than I am; and I suppose there will be time enough before the new Congress is formed to make any alterations you may advise, though, if presented at all, it should be to the old one.

In the copy of my letter to Mr. Barclay you may observe that mention is made of some "considerable articles which I have not charged in my accounts with Congress, but on which I should expect from their equity some consideration." That you may have some information what those articles are, I enclose also a *Sketch of My Services to the United States*, wherein you will find mention of the *extra services* I performed, that do not appertain to the office of plenipotentiary, viz.: as judge of admiralty, as consul before the arrival of Mr. Barclay, as banker in examining and accepting the multitude of bills of exchange, and as secretary for several years, none being sent to me though other ministers were allowed such assistance.

I must own, I did hope that, as it is customary in Europe to make some liberal provision for ministers when they return home from foreign service during which their absence is necessarily injurious to their private affairs, the Congress would at least have been kind enough to have shown their approbation of my conduct by a grant of some small tract of land in their western country, which might have been of use and some honor to my posterity. And I cannot but still think they will do something of the kind for me, whenever they shall be pleased to take my services into consideration, as I see by their minutes that they have allowed Mr. Lee handsomely for his services in England, before his appointment to France, in which services I and Mr. Bollan cooperated with him, and have had no such allowance; and since his return he has been very properly rewarded with a good place, as well as my friend Mr. Jay; though these are trifling compensations in comparison with what was granted by the King to Mr. Gérard on his return from America.

But how different is what has happened to me! On my return from England [in 1775], the Congress bestowed on me the office of postmaster general, for which I was very thankful. It was indeed an office I had some kind of right to, as having previously greatly enlarged the revenue of the post by the regulations I had contrived and established, while I possessed it under the Crown. When I was sent to France, I left it in the hands of my son-in-law, who was to act as my deputy. But soon after my departure it was taken from me and given to Mr. Hazard. When the English ministry formerly thought fit to deprive me of the office, they left me, however, the privilege of receiving and sending my letters free of postage, which is the usage when a postmaster is not displaced for malfeasance in the office; but in America I have ever since had the postage demanded of me, which, since my return from France, has amounted to above fifty pounds, much of it occasioned by my having acted as minister there.

When I took my grandson, William Temple Franklin, with me to France, I proposed, after giving him the French language, to educate him in the study and practice of the law. But, by the repeated expectations given me of a secretary, and constant disappointments, I was induced, and indeed obliged, to retain him with me to assist in the secretary's office, which disappointments continued till my return, by which time so many years of the opportunity of his studying the law were lost, and his habits of life become so different, that it appeared no longer advisable; and I then, considering him as brought up in the diplomatic line, and well qualified by his knowledge in that branch for the employ of a secretary at least (in which opinion I was not alone, for three of my colleagues, without the smallest solicitation from me, chose him secretary of the commission for Treaties, which they had been empowered to do), I took the liberty of recommending him to the Congress for their protection. This was the only favor I ever asked of them; and the only answer I received was a resolution super-seding him, and appointing Colonel Humphreys in his place, a gentleman who, though he might have indeed a good deal of military merit, certainly had none in the diplomatic line, and had neither the French language, nor the experience, nor the address proper to qualify him for such an employment.

This is all to yourself only as a private friend; for I have not, nor ever shall, make any public complaint; and even if I could have foreseen such unkind treatment from Congress, their refusing me thanks would not in the least have abated my zeal for the cause and ardor in support of it. For I know something of the nature of such changeable assemblies, and how little successors are informed of the services that have been rendered to the corps before their admission, or feel themselves obliged by such services; and what effect in obliterating a sense of them, during the absence of the servant in a distant country, the artful and reiterated malevolent insinuations of one or two envious and malicious persons may have on the minds of members, even of the most equitable, candid, and honorable dispositions. Therefore I would pass these reflections into oblivion.

My good friend, excuse, if you can, the trouble of this letter; and if the reproach thrown on republics, that *they are apt to be ungrateful,* should ever unfortunately be verified with respect to *your* services, remember that you have a right to unbosom yourself in communicating your griefs to your ancient friend and most obedient humble servant. . . .

SKETCH OF THE SERVICES OF B. FRANKLIN TO THE UNITED STATES OF AMERICA

In England he combated the Stamp Act, and his writings in the papers against it, with his examination in Parliament, were thought to have contributed much to its repeal.

He opposed the Duty Act; and though he could not prevent its passing, he obtained of Mr. Townshend an omission of several articles, particularly salt.

In the subsequent difference he wrote and published many papers refuting the claim of Parliament to tax the colonies.

He opposed all the oppressive acts.

He had two secret negotiations with the ministers for their repeal, of which he has written a narrative. In this he offered payment for the destroyed tea, at his own risk, in case they were repealed.

He was joined with Messrs. Bollan and Lee in all the applications to government for that purpose. Printed several pamphlets at his own considerable expense against the then measures of government, whereby he rendered himself obnoxious, was disgraced before the privy council, deprived of a place in the post office of £300 sterling a year, and obliged to resign his agencies, viz.:

of Pennsylvania, £500; of Massachusetts, 400; of New Jersey, 100; of Georgia, 200; [total] £1200. In the whole £1500 sterling per annum.

Orders were sent to the King's governors not to sign any warrants on the treasury for the orders of his salaries; and though he was not actually dismissed by the colonies that employed him, yet, thinking the known malice of the court against him rendered him less likely than others to manage their affairs to their advantage, he judged it to be his duty to withdraw from their service, and leave it open for less exceptionable persons, which saved them the necessity of removing him.

Returning to America, he encouraged the Revolution. Was appointed chairman of the Committee of Safety, where he projected the *chevaux de frise* for securing Philadelphia, then the residence of Congress.

Was sent by Congress to headquarters near Boston with Messrs. Harrison and Lynch, in 1775, to settle some affairs with the northern governments and General Washington.

In the spring of 1776 was sent to Canada with Messrs. Chase and Carroll, passing the Lakes while they were not yet free from ice. In Canada was, with his colleagues, instrumental in redressing sundry grievances, and thereby reconciling the people more to our cause. He there advanced to General Arnold and other servants of Congress, then in extreme necessity, £353 in gold, out of his own pocket, on the credit of Congress, which was of great service at that juncture, in procuring provisions for our army.

Being at the time he was ordered on this service upward of seventy years of age, he suffered in his health by the hardships of this journey; lodging in the woods, etc., in so inclement a season; but being recovered, the Congress in the same year ordered him to France. Before his departure he put all the money he could raise, between three and four thousand pounds, into their hands; which, demonstrating his confidence, encouraged others to lend their money in support of the cause.

He made no bargain for appointments, but was promised by a vote the *net* salary of £500 sterling per annum, his expense paid, and to be assisted by a secretary, who was to have £1,000 per annum, to include all contingencies.

When the Pennsylvania Assembly sent him to England in 1764, on the same salary, they allowed him one year's advance for his passage, and in consideration of the prejudice to his private affairs that must be occasioned by his sudden departure and absence. He has had no such allowance from Congress, was badly accommodated in a miserable vessel, improper for those northern seas (and which actually foundered in her return), was badly fed, so that on his arrival he had scarce strength to stand.

His services to the States as commissioner, and afterward as minister plenipotentiary, are known to Congress, as may appear in his correspondence. His *extra services* may not be so well known, and therefore may be here mentioned. No secretary ever arriving, the business was in part before, and entirely when the other commissioners left him, executed by himself, with the help of his grandson, who at first was only allowed clothes, board, and lodging, and afterward a salary, never exceeding £300 a year (except while he served as secretary to the Commissioners for peace), by which difference in salary, continued many years, the Congress saved, *if they accept it, £700 sterling a year.*

He served as *consul* entirely several years, till the arrival of Mr. Barclay, and even after, as that gentleman was obliged to be much and long absent in Holland, Flanders, and England; during which absence, what business of the kind occurred, still came to Mr. Franklin.

He served though without any special commission for the purpose, as a *judge of admiralty;* for, the Congress having sent him a quantity of blank commissions for privateers, he granted them to cruisers fitted out in the ports of France, some of them manned by old smugglers, who knew every creek on the coast of England, and running all round the island, distressed the British coasting trade exceedingly, and raised their general insurance. One of those privateers alone, the *Black Prince,* took in the course of a year seventy-five sail! All the papers, taken in each prize brought in, were in virtue of an order of council sent up to Mr. Franklin, who was to examine them, judge of the legality of the capture, and write to the admiralty of the port, that he found the prize good, and that the sale might be permitted. These papers, which are very voluminous, he has to produce.

He served also as *merchant,* to make purchases, and direct the shipping of stores to a very great value, for which he has charged no commission.

But the part of his service which was the most fatiguing and confining, was that of receiving and accepting, after a due and necessary examination, the bills of exchange drawn by Congress for interest money, to the amount of *two millions and a half of livres annually;* multitudes of the bills very small, each of which, the smallest, gave as much trouble in examining, as the largest. And this careful examination was found absolutely necessary, from the constant frauds attempted by presenting *seconds* and *thirds* for payment after the *firsts* had been discharged. As these bills were arriving more or less by every ship and every post, they required constant attendance. Mr. Franklin could make no journey for exercise, as had been annually his custom, and the confinement brought on a malady that is likely to afflict him while he lives.

In short, though he has always been an active man, he never

went through so much business during eight years, in any part of his life, as during those of his residence in France; which, however, he did not decline till he saw peace happily made, and found himself in the eightieth year of his age; when, if ever, a man has some right to expect repose.

✐ 1789-90: To the Very End

Retired at eighty-three, idle "with dignity" at last, Franklin continued to write with a serene clarity even though the pain of kidney stones was intense. He never stopped experimenting: testing even his own diminishing hearing and describing his results in an exchange of letters with one of the few surviving old friends in Great Britain. His last public statement was a characteristic thrust for human liberty. It was one of his greatest hoaxes, a satirical jab at slavery in the new United States. In his lifetime he had owned and sold slaves, but in 1787 Franklin became the first president of the first society for the abolition of slavery in the New World. In late March 1790, less than four weeks before he died, he wrote a barbed letter to the editor of the *Federal Gazette*. With a straight face, he comments about the Barbary Coast pirates, who were then raiding the seas and enslaving captives. The parallel was devastating. Bedridden for a year, Franklin remained always available to his new country. Thomas Jefferson, much like Franklin in spirit, sought the old man's advice and received it in his last letter, written "perfectly clear in remembrance" nine days before Franklin died in Philadelphia, on April 17, 1790, aged eighty-four years and three months.

To Alexander Small in Scotland

Philadelphia, February 17, 1789

Dear Friend:

Having served my time of three years as President, I have now renounced all public business, and enjoy the *otium cum dignitate*. My friends indulge me with their frequent visits, which I have now leisure to receive and enjoy. The Philosophical Society, and the Society for Political Inquiries, meet at my house, which I have enlarged by additional building, that affords me a large room for those meetings, another over it for my library, now very considerable, and over all some lodging rooms. I have seven promising grandchildren by my daughter who play with and amuse me, and she is a kind, attentive nurse to me when I am at any time indisposed; so that I pass my time as agreeably as at my age [83] a man may well expect, and have little to wish for except a more easy exit than my malady seems to threaten.

The deafness you complain of gives me concern, as if great it must diminish considerably your pleasure in conversation. If moderate, you may remedy it easily and readily by putting your thumb and fingers behind your ear, pressing it outward and enlarging it, as it were, with the hollow of your hand. By an exact experiment I found that I could hear the tick of a watch at forty-five feet distance by this means, which was barely audible at twenty feet without it. The experiment was made at midnight when the house was still.

P.S. You never mention the receipt of any letters from me. I wish to know if they come to hand, particularly my last, enclosing the *Apologue*. You mention some of my friends being dead, but not their names.

To the Editor of the Federal Gazette

March 23, 1790

Sir:

Reading last night in your excellent paper the speech of Mr. Jackson [of Georgia] in Congress, against their meddling with the affair of slavery, or attempting to mend the condition of slaves, it put me in mind of a similar one made about one hundred years since, by Side Mehemed Ibrahim, a member of the Divan [council of state] of Algiers, which may be seen in Martin's account of his consulship, Anno, 1687. It was against granting the petition of the sect called *Erika* or *Purists,* who prayed for the abolition of piracy and slavery as being unjust. Mr. Jackson does not quote it, perhaps he has not seen it. If therefore some of its reasoning are to be found in his eloquent speech, it may only show that men's interests and intellects operate and are operated on with surprising similarity in all countries and climates, whenever they are under similar circumstances. The African's speech, as translated, is as follows:

"Allah Bismillah, God is great, and Mahomet is his prophet.

"Have these *Erika* considered the consequence of granting their petition? If we cease our cruises against the Christians, how shall we be furnished with the commodities their countries produce; and which are so necessary for us? If we forbear to make slaves of their people, who in this hot climate are to cultivate our lands? Who are to perform the common labors of our city, and in our families? Must we not then be our own slaves? And is there not more compassion and more favor due to us as Musselmen than to these Christian dogs? We have now above fifty thousand slaves in and near Algiers; this number, if not kept up by fresh supplies, will soon diminish and be gradually annihilated. If we then cease taking and plundering the infidel ships and making slaves of the seamen and passengers, our lands will become of no value for want of cultivation; the rents of houses in the city will sink one half; and the revenue of government arising from its share of prizes be totally destroyed? And for what? To gratify the whims of a whimsical sect, who would have us not only forbear making more slaves, but even to manumit those we have! And if we set our slaves free, what is to be done with them? Few of them will return to their countries, they know too well the greater hardships they must there be subject to: they will not embrace our holy religion; they will not adopt our manners; our people will not pollute ourselves by intermarrying with them; must we maintain them as beggars in our streets; or suffer our properties to be the prey of their pillage? For men long accustomed to slavery will not work for a livelihood when not compelled. And what is so pitiable in their present condition? Were they not slaves in their own countries? Even England treats its sailors as slaves, for they are, whenever the government pleases, seized and confined in ships of war, condemned not only to work but to fight, for small wages, or a mere subsistence, not better than our slaves are allowed by us. No, they have only exchanged one slavery for another, and I may say a better: for here they are brought into a land, where the sun of Islamism gives forth its light and shines in full splendor, and they have an opportunity of making themselves acquainted with the true doctrine, and thereby saving their immortal souls. What is to be done with them? I have heard it suggested that they may be planted in the wilderness, where there is plenty of land for them to subsist on, and where they may flourish as a free state, but they are, I doubt, too little disposed to labor without compulsion as well as too ignorant to establish a good government, and the wild Arabs would soon molest and destroy or again enslave them. While serving us, we take care to provide them with everything, and they are treated with humanity. Here their lives are in safety. They are not liable to be impressed for soldiers and forced to cut one another's Christian throats, as in the wars of their own countries. How grossly mistaken to suppose slavery to be disallowed by the Koran! Are not the two precepts, to quote no more—'Masters treat your slaves with kindness; slaves serve your masters with cheerfulness and fidelity,' clear proofs to the contrary? Nor can the plundering of infidels be in that sacred book forbidden, since it is well known from it, that God has given the world, and all that it contains, to his faithful Musselmen, who are to enjoy it of right as fast as they conquer it. Let us then hear no more of this detestable proposition. . . ."

The result was that the Divan came to this resolution: "The doctrine that plundering and enslaving the Christians is unjust, is at best problematical; but that it is the interest of this state to continue the practice, is clear; therefore let the petition be rejected."

And it was rejected accordingly.

To Thomas Jefferson, Secretary of State

Philadelphia, April 8, 1790

Sir:

I received your letter of the 31st of last past, relating to encroachments made on the eastern limits of the United States by settlers under the British Government, pretending that it is the *western* and not the *eastern* river of the Bay of Passamaquoddy which was designated by the name of St. Croix in the treaty of peace with that nation; and requesting of me to communicate any facts which my memory or papers may enable me to recollect, and which may indicate the true river which the commissioners on both sides had in their view, to establish as the boundary between the two nations.

Your letter found me under a severe fit of my malady, which prevented my answering it sooner, or attending, indeed, to any kind of business. I now can assure you that I am perfectly clear in the remembrance that the map we used in tracing the boundary was brought to the treaty by the commissioners from England, and that it was the same that was published by Mitchell above twenty years before. Having a copy of that map by me in loose sheets, I send you that sheet which contains the Bay of Passamaquoddy, where you will see that part of the boundary traced. I remember, too, that in that part of the boundary we relied much on the opinion of Mr. Adams, who had been concerned in some former disputes concerning those territories. I think, therefore, that you may obtain still further light from him.

That the map we used was Mitchell's map, Congress were acquainted at the time by a letter to their Secretary for Foreign Affairs, which I suppose may be found upon their files. I have the honor to be, etc. . . .

1706-1790: Benjamin Franklin

Two years before he died, Franklin drew up his last will and testament. He began, "I, Benjamin Franklin, Printer," and then listed himself as minister plenipotentiary to France and president of Pennsylvania. He made charitable bequests to the hospital and gave books to the library and to the Philosophical Society. His grandson, William Temple, was named his literary heir. The codicil to the will was added in 1789, almost a year later. Franklin's accumulated wealth of a lifetime was adequate without being princely. But he knew the value of time and patience. For two hundred years, gifts of £2000 (about $5000) each to Boston and Philadelphia could provide handsomely for young men needing a start in business. In Philadelphia, Franklin's bequest grew to $172,350 by 1907, when $133,076 was transferred to the Franklin Institute in that city. The balance, less than $40,000, had swelled to $470,000 by December 1968. In Boston, Franklin's gift had multiplied ninety times to $431,735 after a hundred years. Part was used to help build and equip the Franklin Institute there, and the balance had grown to almost $2,500,000 in 1968. The two bequests expire in 1991, when they will be divided between each city and its respective state.

Codicil to the Last Will and Testament

I, Benjamin Franklin, in the foregoing or annexed last will and testament named, having further considered the same, do think proper to make and publish the following codicil or addition thereto.

It having long been a fixed political opinion of mine, that in a democratic state there ought to be no offices of profit, for the reasons I had given in an article of my drawing in our Constitution, it was my intention when I accepted the office of president, to devote the appointed salary to some public uses. Accordingly, I had already, before I made my will in July last, given large sums of it to colleges, schools, building of churches, etc.

It has been an opinion, that he who receives an estate from his ancestors is under some kind of obligation to transmit the same to their posterity. This obligation does not lie on me, who never inherited a shilling from any ancestor or relation. I shall, however, if it is not diminished by some accident before my death, leave a considerable estate among my descendants and relations. The above observation is made merely as some apology to my family for making bequests that do not appear to have any immediate relation to their advantage.

I was born in Boston, New England, and owe my first instructions in literature to the free grammar schools established there. I have, therefore, already considered these schools in my will. But I am also under obligations to the State of Massachusetts for having, unasked, appointed me formerly their agent in England, with a handsome salary, which continued some years; and although I accidentally lost in their service, by transmitting Governor Hutchinson's letters, much more than the amount of what they gave me, I do not think that ought in the least to diminish my gratitude.

I have considered that, among artisans, good apprentices are most likely to make good citizens, and, having myself been bred to a manual art, printing, in my native town, and afterward assisted to set up my business in Philadelphia by kind loans of money from two friends there, which was the foundation of my fortune, and of all the utility in life that may be ascribed to me, I wish to be useful even after my death, if possible, in forming and advancing other young men that may be serviceable to their country in both those towns. To this end, I devote two thousand pounds sterling, of which I give one thousand thereof to the inhabitants of the town of Boston, in Massachusetts, and the other thousand to the inhabitants of the city of Philadelphia, in trust, to and for the uses, intents, and purposes hereinafter mentioned and declared.

The said sum of one thousand pounds sterling, if accepted by the inhabitants of the town of Boston, shall be managed under the direction of the selectmen, united with the ministers of the oldest Episcopalian, Congregational, and Presbyterian churches in that town, who are to let out the sum upon interest at five percent per

Benjamin Franklin: the "thumb portrait," by David Martin

annum, to such young married artificers, under the age of twenty-five years, as have served an apprenticeship in the said town, and faithfully fulfilled the duties required in their indentures, so as to obtain a good moral character from at least two respectable citizens, who are willing to become their sureties, in a bond with the applicants, for the repayment of the moneys so lent, with interest. These aids may therefore be small at first, but, as the capital increases by the accumulated interest, they will be more ample. And in order to serve as many as possible in their turn, as well as to make the repayment of the principal borrowed more easy, each borrower shall be obliged to pay, with the yearly interest, one tenth part of the principal, which sums of principal and interest, so paid in, shall be again let out to fresh borrowers.

If this plan is executed, and succeeds as projected without interruption for one hundred years, the sum will then be one hundred and thirty-one thousand pounds; of which I would have the managers of the donation to the town of Boston then lay out, at their discretion, one hundred thousand pounds in public works, which may be judged of most general utility to the inhabitants, such as fortifications, bridges, aqueducts, public buildings, baths, pavements, or whatever may make living in the town more convenient to its people, and render it more agreeable to strangers resorting thither for health or a temporary residence. The remaining thirty-one thousand pounds I would have continued to be let out on interest, in the manner above directed, for another hundred years, as I hope it will have been found that the institution has had a good effect on the conduct of youth, and been of service to many worthy characters and useful citizens. At the end of this second term, if no unfortunate accident has prevented the operation, the sum will be four millions and sixty-one thousand pounds sterling, of which I leave one million sixty-one thousand pounds to the disposition of the inhabitants of the town of Boston, and three millions to the disposition of the government of the State, not presuming to carry my views farther.

All the directions herein given, respecting the disposition and management of the donation to the inhabitants of Boston, I would have observed respecting that to the inhabitants of Philadelphia. At the end of the second hundred years, I would have the disposition of the four million and sixty-one thousand pounds divided between the inhabitants of the city of Philadelphia and the government of Pennsylvania, in the same manner as herein directed with respect to that of the inhabitants of Boston and the government of Massachusetts.

I wish to be buried by the side of my wife, if it may be, and that a marble stone, to be made by Chambers, six feet long, four feet wide, plain, with only a small moulding around the upper edge, and this inscription:

> BENJAMIN
> AND } FRANKLIN
> DEBORAH 178–

to be placed over us both.

My fine crab-tree walking stick, with a gold head curiously wrought in the form of the cap of liberty, I give to my friend, and the friend of mankind, *General Washington*. If it were a scepter, he has merited it, and would become it.

My picture, drawn by Martin in 1767, I give to the *Supreme Executive Council of Pennsylvania*, if they shall be pleased to do me the honor of accepting it and placing it in their chamber.

And lastly, it is my desire that this, my present codicil, be annexed to, and considered as part of, my last will and testament to all intents and purposes.

In witness whereof, I have hereunto set my hand and [SEAL] seal this twenty-third day of June, Anno Domini one thousand seven hundred and eighty-nine.

B. Franklin

✐ Sources

Text

Most of the correspondence in this book is from *The Writings of Benjamin Franklin*, edited by Albert Henry Smyth (New York and London, 1905). The exceptions are listed below by the page number in this edition.

American Philosophical Society, 162–63, 172–73, 197, 197–98, 210 (bottom)

Thomas Balch, ed., *Letters and Papers relating chiefly to the Provincial History of Pennsylvania* (Philadelphia, 1855), 124

John Bigelow, ed., *The Complete Works of Benjamin Franklin* (New York, 1888), 244, 267–71

The British Museum, 196

William L. Clements Library, University of Michigan, Ann Arbor, 164–67

Memoirs of the Life and Writings of Benjamin Franklin, written by Himself to a Late Period, and continued to the Time of His Death, by his Grandson William Temple Franklin (London, 1818), 131–33, 242–44, 246–47, 263–66.

The Historical Society of Pennsylvania, 61–62

Joseph Priestley, *The History and Present State of Electricity*, 1st edn. (London, 1767), 110–12

Putnam's Monthly (November 1906), 218–19

A. S. W. Rosenbach, *A Book Hunter's Holiday* (Boston, 1936); courtesy of the Philip H. and A. S. W. Rosenbach Foundation and The Houghton Mifflin Company, 230–32

Jared Sparks, ed., *The Works of Benjamin Franklin*, rev. edn. (Philadelphia, 1840), 4, 89–91, 219–22

Yale University Library, New Haven, 169–72, 201–06

Pictures

American Philosophical Society, 79, 87, 174, 231
The British Museum, 237

Fogg Art Museum, Harvard University: Bequest of Dr. John C. Warren
     (1856), 87

Memoirs of the Life and Writings of Benjamin Franklin, William
     Temple Franklin, ed. (see above), 176, 207

Free Library of Philadelphia: Lewis Portrait Collection, 143

The Historical Society of Pennsylvania, 146

Insurance Company of North America, 110–11

Library Company of Philadelphia, 18–19, 106

Library of Congress, Frontispiece, 92, 118–19, 152–53, 183, 188–89, 213
     (both), 215, 218, 223, 247

The Metropolitan Museum of Art, New York:
     The Edward W. C. Arnold Collection of New York Prints, Maps
          and Pictures. Bequest of Edward C. Arnold (1954), 75
     Harris Brisbane Dick Fund (1933), 6, 49, 59
     Bequest of William H. Huntington, 221 (bottom), 224, 227 (both)
     Bequest of Charles Allen Munn (1924), 202, 205, 221 (top)

Courtesy, Museum of Fine Arts, Boston: Gift of Dr. Franklin Greene
     Balch, 121

The New-York Historical Society, 70

New York Public Library, xii, 30, 217
     I. N. Phelps Stokes Collection of American Historical Prints, 241

Courtesy, Pennsylvania Academy of Fine Arts, 269

Courtesy of the Abby Aldrich Rockefeller Folk Art Collection, Wil-
     liamsburg, Va., 126–27, 208–09

United States House of Representatives, 251

Walters Art Gallery, Baltimore, 243

The White House Collection, 131

Courtesy Henry Francis du Pont Winterthur Museum, 15, 164–65, 229

Yale University Library, New Haven, 42

Index

Italics refer to illustrations.